In Tuneful Accord

In Tuneful Accord

The Church Musicians

Trevor Beeson

scm press

Published in 2009 by SCM Press
Editorial office
13–17 Long Lane,
London, EC1A 9PN, UK

SCM Press is an imprint of Hymns Ancient and Modern Ltd
(a registered charity)
St Mary's Works, St Mary's Plain,
Norwich, NR3 3BH, UK
www.scm-canterburypress.co.uk

British Library Cataloguing in Publication data

A catalogue record for this book is available
from the British Library

978 0 334 04193 1

Typeset by Regent Typesetting, London
Printed and bound by
CPI Antony Rowe, Chippenham SN14 6LH

Contents

Preface

Of the many books for which I have been responsible over the last fifty years, the writing of *In Tuneful Accord* has given me the greatest pleasure. I entered upon the task with some hesitation but, now completed, I hand it over to my publisher with the sadness that attends parting from a valued friend.

It might be argued, and I am ready to concede the point, that a survey of the development of church music during the nineteenth and twentieth centuries should have preceded a trilogy on bishops, deans and canons. After all, the musicians have a deeper, wider, and usually longer-lasting influence than all but a handful of church leaders. Music is more attractive to most churchgoers than even the most eloquent of sermons, though both have their place. The personalities of musicians can also be interesting and I have included something about the most important of them in my period.

During these early years of a new millennium music is everywhere. Never before has so much music, and in such a variety of forms of music, been created, performed and heard by so many people. The development of broadcasting and sound recording is largely responsible for this, and it is difficult to withhold sympathy from the man who sought to have a quiet drink in his local pub and offered to pay for a short period of relief from the rowdy jukebox. But of course the music explosion of the last half-century has also given joy, inspiration, illumination and consolation to millions.

Music is the most spiritual of the arts. When words fail, music often speaks. When men and women seek closer communion with the Divine, music is most likely to open the door to transcendence. For those in the depths of sadness and despair, music may, more than anything else, offer rays of light and hope.

This is true of all music wherever it is performed and heard. But the church is bound to have, and indeed has always had from its earliest days, a special concern to link music to its primary task of offering worship to God. It is no accident therefore that some of the greatest advances in the music of the West, and some of the most sublime compositions, have emerged from within the life of Christian communities.

The Church of England – I have not dared to look far beyond its boundaries – has played a significant part in this great human endeavour, not least in the nurturing and conserving of a distinctive choral tradition. Hence the responsibility of every generation to ensure that this tradition is not broken or compromised.

It is always hazardous to suggest that a turning point has been reached in any enterprise, but at the conclusion of this survey I have felt drawn to highlight three particular challenges, the response to which could well determine, for better or for worse, the future of something fundamental to the life of the church.

In doing this, as in the writing of the book itself, I have been deeply conscious of my amateur status in the field of church music and also of my aim to engage with other amateurs and general readers. There is nothing here about 'E minor triads' or 'fourths' or even 'pentatonic scales'. But, over the course of a long ministry in the Church of England, I have experienced church music in a considerable variety of settings – a Durham coal-mining village, a Teesside new housing area, St Martin-in-the-Fields in Trafalgar Square, a Hertfordshire market town, Westminster Abbey, Winchester Cathedral, and now Romsey Abbey and five small Hampshire villages.

During this time I have been fortunate enough to accumulate a large number of friends and former colleagues who are among the leading practitioners in the field and on another page I express my indebtedness to them for their most generous assistance and encouragement. They must of course be exonerated from any responsibility for the use I have made of their guidance.

Once again Kathleen James has worked wonders with a much-amended, often barely decipherable, handwritten script, and Fiona Mather has lent an invaluable hand with the research. My best thanks to them for their contributions.

Romsey   *TB*
Trinity Sunday 2009

Acknowledgements

I acknowledge with much gratitude the assistance patiently and enthusiastically given to me by many friends and former colleagues whose knowledge of church music is infinitely greater than my own. Their contribution has been invaluable.

Canon Roger Job, sometime Academical Clerk, Magdalen College, Oxford; Precentor, Manchester Cathedral; Westminster Abbey; Winchester Cathedral.

Martin Neary, sometime Organist, St Margaret's, Westminster; Organist and Master of the Music, Winchester Cathedral; Organist and Master of the Choristers, Westminster Abbey.

Malcolm Archer, sometime Organist and Master of the Choristers at Bristol, Wells and St Paul's Cathedrals; now Director of the Chapel Choir, Winchester College.

James Bowman, Counter-tenor; sometime Academical Clerk, New College, Oxford; Lay Vicar, Westminster Abbey; now Gentleman of the Chapel Royal.

Dr Francis Jackson, sometime Organist, York Minster.

Gordon Appleton, sometime Master of the Music, Perth Cathedral, Australia; since 1993 on the staff of the Royal School of Church Music, working mainly in the North of England; Director of the Northern Cathedral Singers.

Sir David Lumsden, sometime Rector Chori, Southwell Minster; Organist, New College, Oxford; Principal of the Royal Scottish Academy of Music and Drama; Principal of the Royal Academy of Music.

David Hill, sometime Organ Scholar, St John's College, Cambridge; Master of the Music, Westminster Cathedral; Organist and Master of the Music, Winchester Cathedral; Director of Music, St John's College, Cambridge; now Conductor of the BBC Singers; Musical Director of the Bach Choir; Associate Guest Conductor, Bournemouth Symphony Orchestra.

Katharine Edmonds, Organist at St John's Church, Farley Chamberlayne, and St Mary's Church, Michelmersh, Hampshire.

Andrew Lumsden, sometime Organ Scholar of St John's College, Cambridge; Sub-Organist, Westminster Abbey; Organist and Director of

Music, Lichfield Cathedral; now Organist and Director of Music, Winchester Cathedral.

Canon Charles Stewart, sometime Choral Scholar, St John's College, Cambridge; Precentor, Bath Abbey; Precentor, Winchester Cathedral; now Vicar of Walton on Thames; conductor of Southern Voices.

The Very Revd Charles Taylor, sometime Organ Scholar of Selwyn College, Cambridge; Chaplain, Westminster Abbey, Precentor, Lichfield Cathedral; now Dean of Peterborough.

The Very Revd Paul Burbridge, sometime Precentor of York Minster; Archdeacon of Richmond; Dean of Norwich.

William Kendall, sometime Choral Scholar of St John's College, Cambridge; now Tenor, Winchester Cathedral.

Irvine Watson, whose experience of the music of York Minster extends from the time of Sir Edward Bairstow to the present day.

Readers will share my gratitude to them all.

The Changing Pattern of Anglican Worship

Music, in common with the spoken word, silence, ceremonial, furnishings and architecture, is always a servant of the liturgy. That is to say, it is an aid to a community seeking to respond to God in worship and adoration. It follows therefore that changes in liturgical understanding and application will always influence the use, and often the content, of the music.

Until about 1840 there had been no significant change in the Church of England's use of the Book of Common Prayer since its introduction in 1662. Music played little part in the worship of the parish churches and in the cathedrals its performance had declined in quality to a point where it was more of a hindrance than a help. As the nineteenth century progressed, however, this changed, partly as a consequence of a deepening of understanding, particularly of the place of the Eucharist, and partly because of the Victorian zest for 'improvement' in all things.

A serious attempt to revise the Book of Common Prayer failed in 1928, though some changes in the content of some services were permitted. But it was not until the 1950s that the constraining floodgate was breached and during the next 50 years the Church of England experienced more changes in its forms of worship, as indeed in many other aspects of its life, than it had during the whole of the previous 400 years.

The music of the church was inevitably affected by this New Reformation, as it has been called, and any study of the development of this music during the nineteenth and twentieth centuries requires awareness of the development of the liturgy itself.

The state of the Church of England during the early decades of the nineteenth century continues to divide historians. In some respects the evidence is, as might be expected, varied and furthermore not always entirely reliable, having been transmitted by partisan messengers. Certain facts are nonetheless reasonably clear. The bishops were scandalously negligent in the performance of their episcopal ministries and had more in common with the aristocracy of their time than with their apostolic ancestors. Inasmuch as the Church of England was, and remains, essentially a parochial church this lamentable state of affairs was much less significant than it would have been in a more centralized institution. The parishes relied on their bishops only for the ordination of a sufficient supply of clergymen and possibly for an occasional Confirmation, though even this was often regarded as an optional extra.

The congregations attending church were still large. Attendance at worship was no longer enforced legally, but the social pressure to conform remained strong and the parish church had the central place in a closely knit community life. It was 'natural' to share in the worship on Sundays and the church's teaching was regarded as an infallible guide to daily living. The clergy were, as always, of mixed ability and conscientiousness. There were far too many absentees from parishes, as many as three-fifths were said to be elsewhere. Pluralism, caused sometimes by sheer avarice, but more often by the need to combine several parishes in order to produce a reasonable income for one priest, was a serious problem. But by and large the clergy, many of them poorly paid curates, were diligent in carrying out their duties – in the conducting of worship, albeit it often slovenly, careful preparation of sermons, teaching of children, pastoral care of every soul in the parish and administering a mini-welfare state for the benefit of the poor and needy.

There was, however, a major deficiency almost everywhere, the existence of which can hardly be denied. The parish churches and cathedrals were places of formal conformity to a prescribed religion rather than centres of corporate holiness in which the mystery of the divine could be frequently experienced by the individual believer. Much of this was due to the prevailing theology which for the previous 100 years had been predominantly rationalist and ethical. But even more was due to lack of awareness of the true nature of the church as a worshipping community caused by slavish conformity to the Book of Common Prayer which had been demanded by Act of Parliament in 1662, and become a lifeless routine in which congregations had only a passive part with little to excite the religious imagination.

In 1843 Joseph Leech, the owner and editor of the *Bristol Times* began a series of weekly visits to the parish churches of the city and its surrounding districts, and later extended this to the villages of South Gloucestershire and North Somerset. Candid reports of what he found in these churches appeared week by week under the pseudonym 'The Churchgoer' and for some time he went undetected at the Sunday morning services. Eventually however he was identified in many places and, although some of the clergy welcomed a visit, many lived in dread of his appearances and what might be published the following week.

Unsurprisingly, he encountered some variations in the style of the worship and its setting, but these were quite limited. Most of the churches were crowded with box pews and galleries and, as a visitor, he normally sat in one of the four free benches allocated to the poor. At the east end of the nave, sometimes forming a barrier to the chancel, was a three-deck pulpit – the lower desk of which was allocated to the parish clerk, the next desk to the minister responsible for conducting the service and, above both, the pulpit for the preacher. A simple, unadorned table served as the altar but was given no prominence and sometimes used for mundane non-sacramental purposes such as a place for hats and coats. In a gallery at the west end there was, by this time, often a small organ, which had replaced an earlier band, and also a group of singers of varied accomplishments.

The service itself was Morning Prayer followed by the Litany, the Ante-Communion, and a sermon lasting at least 30 minutes and often much longer. Holy Communion was celebrated only infrequently and after due notice had been given the previous Sunday. The congregation played little vocal part in the worship – many of its members were unable to read – and were content to leave everything, except perhaps a metrical psalm, to the minister and the parish clerk, and, if there was one, the choir. In those parishes where the priest was negligent, or possibly depressed, the worship was a long way from edifying – as it can be today. At Bleadon, a small village not far from Weston-super-Mare, Leech found:

The worshippers were few, and the worship was cold. The priest delivered his part in a tone of apathy, and the replies of the people were faint and languid; the reading of the clergyman was not good, that of the poor clerk barbarous; the pews were dusty and yellow damp-stains disfigured the walls of the chancel; there was no altar screen or reredos of any kind, and a rude railing enclosed a ruder communion table; some windows in the chancel had been roughly stopped up and in fact nothing was wanting to make an originally good parish Church, a poor, wretched desolate structure. It has a fair tower and a very fair specimen of a stone pulpit; the former was struck, some twelve or fourteen years ago, by lightning, but I question if the stroke of neglect has not since proved more ruinous to the edifice at large.

On the other hand he was much more impressed by what he discovered at Lympsham, another village near Weston:

I do not know when I have been in a country church with so large a congregation: it was not merely the pews that were filled, but the forms placed in the aisles were closely occupied also. I could not help thinking it was some special occasion. Indeed, several, I could see, were strangers like myself, for they looked about, uncertain where to go, and more than that, when they got a place they seemed uncertain what to do. The Rector is one of the most active men I have ever seen in the reading-desk or pulpit, and, from what I learn, out of it too: he not only read the service and preached, but he led the singing and chanting, both of which they did, and did well, without an organ: indeed, I never before heard such hearty general congregational singing – everyone took their share, and a man with a bass voice somewhat more than his share.

Most churches fell somewhere between these extremes and this was as true of the city churches as of those in rural areas. Leech, himself a well-informed churchman, did not hesitate to suggest improvements. There were nevertheless signs of a new spirit showing here and there. Methodists, who often attended their parish church, might well leave before the end of the service to share in more lively worship, with loud hymn singing, in a nearby room. There were rumours of suspicious forms of doctrine and a special emphasis on the Eucharist being promoted by a Dr Pusey and a Dr Newman in Oxford.

John Keble's Assize Sermon in the University Church on 14 July 1833 marked the beginning of what became known as the Oxford Movement. This would transform the Church of England's life. It sought to get behind the arid, rationalist, Erastian religious thought that, in spite of the small-scale Evangelical revival, was still in vogue, to the High Church theology and worship of the early seventeenth century when Archbishop Laud was at Canterbury. This involved the revival of the doctrines concerning the nature of the church and of the sacraments that characterized Laud's Primacy and went back to the earliest Christian centuries. The Oxford reformers did not however require a revision of the Book of Common Prayer. On the contrary they emphasized the importance of retaining it, and recovering the use of some neglected parts of it as a defence against those who were pressing for modifications in what today would be described as a liberal direction.

John Henry Newman, one of the Movement's founding fathers, who later caused a national sensation by becoming a Roman Catholic and eventually a cardinal, urged the clergy to petition their bishops to resist any moves in the direction of Prayer Book revision. After a decade of influential preaching and writing it soon became apparent, however, that the new emphasis of the Tractarians, particularly their high doctrine of the Eucharist, would require some changes in the way in which this central sacrament of the church was celebrated. What this might involve was demonstrated at St Paul's, Knightsbridge, in 1846 where the vicar had introduced a weekly celebration of Holy Communion, following Sunday Morning Prayer, with a surpliced choir, two lit candles on the Holy Table, separated readings of the Epistle and Gospel and a few small parts of the service sung – all conducted with precise dignity, and with the entire congregation receiving communion. At the end of the following year a visitor to the Margaret Street Chapel, later replaced by All Saints' Church, Margaret Street, in London's West End, reported what he described as 'a complete musical Mass' in which substantial parts of the service were sung. He added, 'I venture to assert that there has been nothing so solemn since the Reformation.' The reporter was a founder member of the Cambridge Camden Society, which had been established to complement the Oxford Movement by research into the traditional furnishings and vestments prescribed by the Prayer Book in a rubric that referred to those in use 'in the second year of the reign of King Edward VI', that is, 1549. These were essentially those of the late medieval church, though the detail is often disputed.

By this time the aims of the Movement were becoming more widely accepted, but following the conversion of Newman and some others among its leadership to Roman Catholicism the old High Church ideals were replaced in some parts of the Church of England by Roman Catholic understandings of the Eucharist and the accompanying liturgical practices, largely imported from the continent. Ritualism, as it came to be called, formed a sub-group within the Oxford Movement and was to be found mainly in the poorest parishes of the inner cities. There devout and gifted priests were often exercising heroic ministries among people long alienated from the life of the church. The forms of worship adopted in these parishes were based on high doctrines of the church and sacraments but they were also a response to the belief that the services and ceremonial of the BCP were now quite unsuited to the missionary situations in which they were ministering. Movement, drama, colour, symbols and scent all had a part to play in the Eucharist.

This development caused considerable alarm in still sensitive Protestant circles where the establishment of a Roman Catholic hierarchy of bishops in 1851 had already aroused fears of a return to papal jurisdiction. They complained that the new forms of worship were not only doctrinally unsound but also illegal inasmuch as they contravened the provisions of the Prayer Book, which had behind it the authority of Parliament. Having failed to secure disciplinary action by the bishops, who were in any case severely limited in what they could impose upon a clergy who enjoyed the security of a freehold office, they had recourse to law. Much unedifying public controversy ensued and, incredible and shameful as it now seems, a small number of priests were sent to prison for refusing to comply with the judgement of the courts.

The bishops were themselves not exempt from the law's demands and in 1888 the saintly Edward King of Lincoln was arraigned before the Judicial Committee of the Privy Council to answer a series of charges – allowing lighted candles on the altar, mixing wine and water in the chalice at the Eucharist and ceremonially washing the vessels afterwards, permitting the

Agnus Dei to be sung after the consecration, and absolving and blessing with the sign of the cross. The Council eventually remitted the matter to the Archbishop of Canterbury who found largely in King's favour.

By the end of the century there was no sign of agreement on what forms of worship might or might not be permissible in the Church of England. There were in fact four separate traditions operating in the parish churches. The Evangelicals, untouched by the Oxford Movement or much else in the liturgical field apart from the revival of hymn singing, still worshipped in austere churches in which Bible reading and preaching dominated the Prayer Book services, and Holy Communion was celebrated infrequently. At the other extreme the churches influenced by Ritualism offered worship that hardly differed from that of the Roman Catholics, apart from the use of English rather than Latin. They were now known as Anglo-Catholics. Another, rapidly growing, section of the church accepted the doctrines of the Oxford Movement, rejected Ritualist developments and, instead, remained faithful to the Prayer Book, accompanying it with dignified ceremonial as well as the vesture and furnishings believed to be prescribed by the ornaments rubric. A guild of craftsmen was created to produce appropriate items and during the twentieth century the dignified, colourful ceremonial of Westminster Abbey became the leading example of this worship, which there owed as much to good taste as it did to doctrine.

These three groups represented, however, only a quite small part of the Church of England's life. The overwhelming majority of parishes continued largely unchanged. Morning and Evening Prayer remained the mainstay of Sunday worship, albeit with a robed choir in chancel and some dignity of movement, more music and shorter sermons. Holy Communion was celebrated more frequently, usually at 8 a.m. and, perhaps, once a month after Morning Prayer. Inclusive Protestantism was still alive and well, 'C of E' was a badge of national as well as religious identity. Many new church buildings, almost all in Gothic style, had been erected in urban areas since 1850, and on the whole congregations were large, peaking in about 1900, though the buildings were, contrary to later mythology, rarely filled to capacity and in the large towns and cities most people did not attend church, except for baptisms, marriages and funerals.

It was because religion retained an important place in the national consciousness that so much concern was expressed at the unlawful deviation from the provisions of the Book of Common Prayer. Thus in 1904 the government decided to set up a Royal Commission on Ecclesiastical Discipline to investigate the situation, especially the alleged breaches of the law. During the next two years the Commission received evidence from 164 witnesses and the Archbishop of Canterbury, Randall Davidson, occupied three days of its time. A good deal of useful information was gathered and the Commission's report offers an interesting picture of worship in the

Church of England at the end of the nineteenth century, but the number of serious complaints lodged with the Commission was comparatively small and it stated that 'in most parishes the work of the Church is being quietly and diligently performed by clergy who are entirely loyal to the principles of the English Reformation as expressed in the Book of Common Prayer'. Nonetheless it concluded, in words that became the official basis for liturgical reform for much of the remainder of the century, 'the law of public worship in the Church of England is too narrow for the religious life of the present generation'.

That they should have continued to be quoted for so long is the clearest evidence that the Church of England's response to the Commission's labours was not hasty. The Convocations of Canterbury and York discussed the matter from time to time without deciding anything significant, until the 1914–18 war intervened. An advisory committee of liturgical scholars appointed in 1911 lacked the wholehearted support of the Northern Convocation and was also frustrated by the outbreak of war.

The war did, however, stimulate the demand for reform. Chaplains ministering in the horrific circumstances of the trenches found the BCP virtually unusable for soldiers' services and the burial of the fallen. Even as traditional and fastidious a liturgist as Eric Milner White, who had gone to France from King's College, Cambridge, and returned to the college for another 13 years before becoming Dean of York, confessed in characteristically elegant language, not frequently heard in the trenches:

> Suddenly it became apparent to all that the 1662 Book was out of date. It was plain, especially to chaplains in the field, that the country had no semblance of a popular familiar devotion ... The Prayer Book did not seem able to reflect the lineaments of the Lord Jesus Christ, therefore failing to minister the love of God to souls desperately wistful.

Furthermore, the close encounters with soldiers, especially the other ranks, confirmed what the best of the chaplains already knew, namely, that most expressions of Christian faith and worship were more or less meaningless to the overwhelming majority of Britain's working-class population. The chaplains returned to their parishes therefore firmly determined to demand substantial revision of the church's services and to work for the restoration of the Holy Communion to that central place in the church's life which it had held from the earliest Christian centuries until the early seventeenth century. There could be no prevarication, no delaying tactics. There proved to be many.

During the immediate post-war years many suggestions for revision were made by groups of liturgical scholars and other interested parties, and between the autumn of 1925 and the beginning of 1927 the House of Bishops held 45 day-long meetings to devise a revised prayer book. This was intended to be an alternative to the 1662 book, not a substitution for it. The proposed changes were nothing if not conservative, but although the new book was accepted by the Church Assembly later that year, this was in spite of strong opposition from some Evangelicals and Anglo-Catholics. When it was presented to the House of Commons on 15 December it was rejected by 238 votes to 205, and, in spite of some intensive lobbying, the margin of defeat was slightly larger when it was re-presented in 1928.

The opposition in the church was, as is often the case in controversial matters, united by opposing convictions. The Evangelicals believed that some aspects of the proposed book would take the Church of England in a Rome-ward direction, whereas the extreme Anglo-Catholics believed it would inhibit the liturgical freedom they had already seized and now enjoyed, and would be used by the bishops as an instrument of discipline. The proposals were, in any case, nowhere near to solving the acute problem delineated by the wartime chaplains. Had the church been more united in its enthusiasm for the new book it seems likely that the House of Commons would have voted differently. But there was another division of which many MPs were aware: there was no enthusiasm for liturgical change among ordinary churchgoers (there rarely is) and it seemed that the professionals, including the laity in the Church Assembly, were seeking to impose new ways of worship on reluctant congregations.

Whatever the explanation, however, the leadership of the Church of England was left in some disarray. There were calls for disestablishment. These were not pursued, though the implications for church–state relations of what had happened would never be forgotten. The bishops restored calm, rather cleverly and, it turned out, very helpfully, by consulting their diocesan conferences, then announcing that 'during the present emergency and until further order be taken' they would 'not regard as inconsistent with loyalty to the principles of the Church of England the use of such additions or deviations as fall within the limits of the "Deposited Book"'.

Thus what became known as the 1928 Prayer Book went into widespread use. Or at least, parts of it did. The minor changes proposed for Morning and Evening Prayer, and for the Baptism, Marriage and Burial services, were generally welcomed but a more substantial change to the Prayer of Thanksgiving at the Eucharist did not win much support and was firmly rejected by Evangelicals. Among the war-veteran reformers there was deep disappointment that the new book did nothing to bridge the gap between the church and its absentee artisan members and offered no encouragement to those who wished to make the Holy Communion the central focus of parish life.

The 'emergency' lasted for 27 years and embraced another catastrophic world war. During this time the bishops made no serious attempt to impose liturgical discipline, except in a few extreme instances, and the clergy were left free to order the worship of their churches as they thought best. Lacking liturgical skill and much imagination, most of them were happy to accept the limitations of the new, alternative book, and, although members of the travelling public sometimes complained that no two churches had the same forms of worship, everything on offer was clearly derived from the Book of Common Prayer, which was still regarded as the distinctive, unifying expression of the Church of England's doctrine and devotion.

There emerged, however, during the 1920s and 30s a small number of priests who were determined that the Holy Communion should become the chief act of Sunday worship in their churches, and this without turning to an 11 a.m. High Mass with no communicants – the standard practice of the extreme Anglo-Catholics. In several industrial parishes, often where the clergy were Christian Socialists, a celebration of Holy Communion was held at about 9.30 a.m., usually with the Prayer Book rite. Hymns were sung, Merbecke or the Martin Shaw Folk Mass was used as the setting, a sermon was preached, all the confirmed received communion, and families and young people were encouraged to attend. There was a strong corporate emphasis and in some places the congregations remained after the service to share breakfast in the church hall. 'The Lord's people, gather on the Lord's day, for the Lord's own service', became a descriptive slogan.

In 1935 Father Gabriel Hebert, a priest of the Society of the Sacred Mission, published *Liturgy and Society*, a seminal work which emphasized the vital importance of relating the Eucharist to the life of the secular world. At the same time, he advocated 'The Parish Eucharist with the communion of the people as the central act of worship every Sunday'. The book was widely read and its liturgical emphasis proved to be influential. Two years later Hebert edited a volume of essays, *The Parish Communion*, in which several clergy explained how such a service might be introduced in town and country parishes. Essays demonstrating the links with the practice of the early church were also included, and in the dioceses of Chichester and Newcastle the number of parishes moving in this direction became significant.

The 1939–45 war produced another generation of ex-service chaplains and ordination candidates who regarded the reformation of the church as an integral part of the creation of a better world and saw the Parish Communion as the key to the reform of worship. At a conference held in Birmingham in January 1948, an organization, 'Parish and People', was launched to promote the Parish Communion, along with the parish breakfast and the parish meeting. Its membership (mainly clergy) grew rapidly and during the next two decades the Parish Communion replaced Morning Prayer and High Mass as the chief Sunday service in most parishes.

The speed of this development became a matter of concern to the leaders of Parish and People, who were in touch with a parallel liturgical movement in the Roman Catholic Church on the continent. The theological foundation of the change and its social implications were being ignored and the Parish Communion was being adopted as 'a nice service at a convenient time'. This greatly worried Michael Ramsey who was at the time Bishop of Durham. Nevertheless the movement was powerful enough to stimulate a period of intense liturgical experiment and revision that began with the appointment by the archbishops in 1955 of a Liturgical Commission. During the next 25 years many different versions of all the services were produced in booklet form and tried out, and in 1980 what were deemed to be the best, or at least the most widely acceptable, forms of these were published in a 1,293-page Alternative Service Book. Some were in modern English, though the gain in intelligibility was offset for many lay users by the complexity of the range of choice on offer to those conducting the services. Again, the emphasis was on the experimental and it was explained that another 20 years would be needed for the creation of texts that could be regarded as fixed for a reasonably settled period of time.

Change was, however, by no means confined to the structure and words of the liturgy; it extended to its ceremonial presentation. The insight that in the Eucharist priest and laity are engaged in a shared action, each with a distinctive role, required all to be in reasonably close proximity to the altar; preferably gathered around it. The same insight required the laity to have a more active role in the liturgy itself, expressed in the reading of the Bible, the leading of intercessions, the presentation of the bread and the wine at the Offertory, and the administration of communion. It led also to a reconsideration of the place of music and the function of a choir, with emphasis on congregational participation and sometimes the introduction of instruments to augment or even replace the organ. Back to the church band.

Such a liturgical reformation could not easily be arranged in medieval buildings designed for eucharistic worship in which the priest alone had a significant part to play and the laity were banished to a nave distant from the altar, even screened from it. The 1960s therefore saw the beginning of what would become a widespread reordering of church interiors, including the many Victorian buildings erected on Gothic principles. Nave altars were installed and fixed pews replaced by mobile chairs. In order to create a more corporate atmosphere the priest faced the congregation across the altar and a number of laypeople were located close by in the sanctuary.

Even with the most imaginative use of space and furnishings, however, this proved to be quite a long way from ideal, especially in large churches where many members of the congregation were, of necessity, still disposed in formal ranks and far from the focus of the eucharistic action. The need for a considerable number of new church buildings went some way to solving the problem in new housing developments where buildings of circular, octagonal and trapezoid shape began to appear.

The establishing of an Institute for the Study of Worship and Religious Architecture at Birmingham University offered the church an opportunity to match its buildings with its worshipping needs. But unlike France, Germany and other continental European countries, Britain was lacking in first-class, innovative architects, as well as wealthy churches, and by the end of the century most of the new buildings seemed sad, shabby even. Nonetheless the worship offered in the overwhelming majority of parishes at about ten o'clock on Sunday mornings was significantly different from anything previously experienced in Britain and closer in pattern to that of the earliest Christian communities of the Mediterranean world.

Meanwhile steps had been taken to ensure that there could be no repeat of the 1927/28 debacle. In 1970 Parliament accepted a Worship and Doctrine Measure which allowed the Church of England to make its own decisions in these areas without political approval. A change of outlook in liturgical studies also led to the abandonment of uniformity as an ideal and to the acceptance of a considerable degree of variety. Thus, in the sensitive area of eucharistic doctrine and its expression, both Evangelicals and Anglo-Catholics were offered liturgies they could use. They were themselves also more open to change than ever before.

The long period of experiment ended in 2000 with the publication and authorization of Common Worship, which included eight different eucharistic rites. This was followed by several more volumes which covered the remainder of the services – all attractively printed and costing in total about £75. The Rector of St Michael's, Cornhill, in the City of London complained that a wheelbarrow was needed to carry them all to church. The policy enunciated in the 1662 Book of Common Prayer, 'And whereas heretofore there hath been great diversity in saying and singing in Churches within this Realm ... now from henceforth all the whole Realm shall have but one use', had been turned on its head.

The revival of Evangelicalism, particularly in its charismatic form, had by this time, moreover, raised new and difficult issues. A Pentecostal movement, sweeping like fire through many parts of Latin America and Africa, eventually reached Britain, and immigrants from the Caribbean and Africa added their own spontaneous forms of worship – all far removed from the traditions of the long-established churches. Their style was not dissimilar to that of the nineteenth-century revivalist movements, with a strong emphasis on worship – hymns, songs and choruses – as a tool of evangelism and the saving of souls.

The number of Anglican churches embracing the charismatic tradition in its fullness was, and remains, relatively small. But elements of it exist in a large number of fairly typical Evangelical congregations and the effect on their worship has often been sharply divisive. The introduction of songs and choruses of an exuberant sort, accompanied by guitars and percussion instruments, represents a radical change, both of form and underlying spirituality, for traditional churchgoers. Those attending only at the great festivals have often been surprised, and sometimes distressed, to find the much-loved Christmas hymns and carols replaced by unknown revivalist hymns and choruses. The end of the century therefore found the Church of England with the widest possible variety of forms of worship and, although the virtues of diversity, rather than those of uniformity, were now extolled, serious issues relating to underlying unity remained unresolved.

2

The Victorian Musical Inheritance

Very little is known about music in England prior to the eleventh century, though there is some evidence from the late seventh century that boys, some as young as seven, were recruited to monastic communities to assist in the chanting of the services and to prepare for the day when they would themselves take religious vows. Gregorian chant, once thought to have been imported from Rome by St Augustine and his fellow missionaries, is now believed to be a fusion of Roman and Northern European chants which took place in the late eighth or early ninth century. The Viking invasions of these centuries put paid to the monasteries, but the mission of the church in Saxon England continued in some places from minster churches. There communities of clergy, sometimes led by a bishop, sang Mass, Mattins and Vespers daily and some of their number undertook missionary and pastoral work in the district, often over a fairly wide area.

During the tenth century monasticism was reintroduced from the continent and once more boys were admitted as singers and oblates. But two centuries later this practice ceased, as it came to be regarded as undesirable that they should be drawn into the religious life so early. The collegiate cathedrals, differentiated from those served by religious (mainly Benedictine) communities, recruited boys to share in their worship and made alternative arrangements for their education in what became the first choir schools. The education provided was, however, often poor and sometimes virtually non-existent.

By this time significant developments were taking place in the composition of music. The earliest surviving evidence of this is to be found in the *Winchester Troper*, dating from 1050, in which the single lines of plainsong, using only about half a dozen notes and about the same number of rhythmic patterns, were augmented by the additional notes to create a richer texture and to provide the basis for harmonious polyphony.

Once this breakthrough, pioneered at Notre Dame Cathedral in Paris, had been achieved its method spread quickly and led during the fourteenth and fifteenth centuries to a marvellously rich output of polyphonic settings of the Mass and the divine offices. The Lady Chapels of the major monasteries were opened for public worship – consisting of the offering of a choral 'Lady Mass' – and large numbers of laypeople often assembled in naves when choirs sang an evening hymn before a statue of the Virgin.

In the rest of the church, the minster-church pattern of organization did not survive the Norman Conquest, except at the collegiate cathedrals and some collegiate churches. The development of the parochial system, which became and remains a distinctive feature of the Church of England's life, led to the building of churches, served by one priest, for clearly defined geographical areas. Services – Mass, Mattins and Vespers – were conducted in Latin by the parish priest, assisted by a layman known as the parish clerk. They were mainly spoken but sometimes chanted. The laity, if present, had no vocal part in the worship.

Between 1450 and 1550, however, the larger parish churches incorporated one or more chantry chapels, endowed by wealthy laymen to ensure that Masses for the repose of their souls would be frequently offered. A priest was provided with a small stipend in return for this duty, and in order to augment their stipends some of the musically competent clergy travelled to the best-endowed churches to join the local clergy in the formation of a choir. This enabled some at least of the parish churches to share in the development of polyphonic music in worship, by the recruiting of boys for Lady Chapel choirs and the installation of choir stalls in their chancels. During this relatively brief period there was in fact more music in English parish churches than there would be again until the mid-nineteenth century, though in many village churches there was little or no music and even where volunteer choirs were formed the Latin services permitted no vocal congregational participation.

The sixteenth-century Reformation did not, initially, change this situation fundamentally. King Henry VIII confiscated most of the considerable wealth of the cathedrals but left them with sufficient funds to maintain their regular round of worship and to embark on a new programme of education. Lay clerks and choristers were included in the reformed capitular bodies, and grammar schools took care of the boys' education. For a time the worship continued to be offered in Latin, but in 1544 Archbishop Thomas Cranmer produced a version of the Litany in English, intended to be sung in procession by trained musicians, without congregational involvement. Five years later came the first Book of Common Prayer which was intended for congregational use, and the English of which did not fit the existing plainchant and polyphony.

John Merbecke, who was both a theologian and a musician, filled the gap with an adaptation of plainsong to the new liturgy (further adaptation was needed for the 1662 Prayer Book), which proved easy for congregations to learn, became popular and continued widely in use until the liturgical reforms of the late twentieth century. Where the Nicene Creed is still sung it remains serviceable. Other composers, principally Thomas Tallis and his pupil William Byrd, also responded to the challenge with settings for Mattins and Evensong of the highest quality which are now regarded as classics of sixteenth-century music. All demanded professional skill but the versicles and responses from one of Tallis's services went into common use following the nineteenth-century revival of church music and remain his best-known work.

What had become a glorious era of Tudor church music, and included many anthems and settings that found a permanent place in the repertory of the best choirs, came to an end with the rise of Puritanism. The Puritans were themselves divided over an issue which, four centuries later, remains a bone of contention among Anglicans: is music intended to assist the church to offer to God in worship the highest and best of which it is capable or should it be designed to help the individual members of congregations to lift up their hearts in acts of corporate praise and thanksgiving that are both edifying and challenging?

During the reign of Queen Elizabeth I, when Calvinism was dominant, the second of these emphases eventually prevailed. The organs in the parish churches were dismantled and where there were choirs these were disbanded. Instead, the services were spoken, except for the Psalms, which, in a metrical version, were often sung, unaccompanied, to simple tunes adapted from folk and theatre songs – a method copied from the continental reformers. In some places the canticles were given similar treatment, all sung slowly. The overall style of worship could hardly have been more different from that which is expressed in parish churches today. There were exceptions however, not least in Westminster where, at the Chapel Royal and the Abbey, the organist Orlando Gibbons composed some of the finest ever service settings and anthems. But during the Commonwealth the cathedral choirs and organs also disappeared and the worship, when offered, was austere in the extreme.

The Restoration of the Monarchy in 1660 brought little change initially to the musical content of the worship but gradually significant developments took place in town churches. Organs were recovered or replaced and attracted some gifted organists who also composed new church music. Choirs came back and included children who were carefully rehearsed. Henry Purcell, arguably the greatest of English composers, became organist of Westminster Abbey and the Chapel Royal in 1680 and composed service settings and anthems which broke new ground in church music and thereafter became high points in the offering of worship everywhere. He died when he was only 36 and the epitaph on his gravestone in Westminster Abbey reads, 'Here lyes Henry Purcell Esq., who left this life and is gone to that blessed place where only his harmony can be exceeded.' Another composer who achieved greatness at this time, despite his Puritan background, was John Blow.

In country churches, too, there were signs of new musical life. Voluntary choirs, usually of young men, were formed to improve the quality of the psalm singing. Some of these aspired to sing other music – canticles and anthems by Purcell and later, Bach, Handel and Pergolesi, and this offered scope for the introduction of musical instruments. By the end of the eighteenth century many village churches had bands consisting of bassoons, flutes, serpents and various stringed instruments. The quality of these varied considerably and it must not be supposed that this century featured a feast of glorious church music enhancing inspiring worship. On the contrary, as the century advanced, the quality of both went into serious decline. The clergy and educated laity lost interest in church music, while the embracing of Latitudinarianism and new scientific thinking led to a devaluing of the mysterious, supernatural element in religion in favour of a more rational, moralistic approach. All of which, allied to scandalous misuse of endowments and neglect of some of the basics of church life, resulted in acts of worship, in both parish churches and cathedrals, that were formal, dreary and cold. The services, recited by the priest and the parish clerk, left little opportunity for congregational participation, except perhaps for the singing of metrical psalms.

In some places, however, the High Church tradition, associated with the reforms initiated by Archbishop Laud in the early part of the previous century, survived and retained dignified liturgical worship. From the mid-eighteenth century onwards, and as a reaction against the Church of England's neglectfulness, Methodism also provided a warmer alternative, albeit outside the walls of parish churches. And by the end of the century an evangelical revival within the Church of England was beginning to change its worship for the better in some places, not least by the introduction of hymns. The replacement of the bands by organs or harmoniums proved, however, to be highly controversial in most villages, and in his preface to *Under the Greenwood Tree,* based on such a controversy, Thomas Hardy alleged that a direct result of this change had been 'to curtail and extinguish the interest of parishioners in such doings'.

Whether or not this be true, it is indisputable that by 1830, on the eve of the great reform movement that was to galvanize and change virtually every aspect of life in Victorian England, the worship offered in most parish churches and cathedrals remained at a shockingly low ebb.

3

The Last of the Old Wine – John Goss

When John Goss became organist of St Paul's in 1838 he found the music of the great cathedral, as well as almost every other aspect of its life, appalling. This could hardly have surprised him, since he had been involved in the capital's musical life from an early age. What is more, only a slight acquaintance with other English cathedrals would have made him aware that the situation at St Paul's was commonplace. There it was more deplorable than most, however, inasmuch as it had huge resources of money and manpower that a corrupt capitular regime had directed from the furtherance of the cathedral's worship and witness to the pockets of a number of privileged clergymen.

Goss found a community that consisted of a dean, three residentiary canons, 30 prebendaries, 12 minor canons, six vicars choral, eight singing boys and a large complement of vergers and other minor functionaries. The deans of St Paul's, who received a stipend of £5,000 per annum, had for many years also been diocesan bishops. The residential canons, who had £2,000 per annum, also held one or more other appointments in the church, while the 30 prebendaries, all appointed by the Bishop of London from among his relations and friends, received an income of varying amounts from the land allocated to their stalls; these also held one or more other appointments.

The minor canons, who were responsible for the ordering and conducting of worship on Sundays and weekdays, formed a college with its own legal identity, and its own endowments. They, too, held other appointments, usually livings in the City of London, and whenever vacancies occurred in the college, they recruited the replacements, nearly always from clergymen who were professional musicians. The vicars choral were laymen and professional musicians who also sang at Westminster Abbey and the Chapel Royal. One of their number was the organist, who employed a permanent deputy to sing in his place, another was the master of the choristers. All the appointments at St Paul's were to freehold offices, tenable until death, and as at other cathedrals they continued to be held even when their occupants were incapable of performing their duties.

What should have been an impressive great church was, moreover, fatally flawed by persistent absenteeism. The dean put in an appearance only infrequently, he being preoccupied with his bishopric. The canons residentiary were required by the statutes to occupy houses in Amen Court for four months of the year and during this time to attend the daily services. Since they were answerable only to their apparently untutored consciences, they were often absent. One of their number, who held with his canonry the sinecure office of precentor, appeared so infrequently that on one occasion when he did turn up for a service the dean's verger failed to recognize him and refused him admission to his stall. Sydney Smith, a fellow canon, referred to him as 'the Absenter'. The minor canons were not much better than their superiors. In theory they should have been present and involved in the daily services, augmenting the choir, but they were frequently absent and there was rarely anyone in authority to hold them to account. They were a law unto themselves.

Morning Prayer was said on weekdays at 7 a.m. (8 a.m. in the winter), sung at 9.45 a.m., and Evening Prayer was sung at 3.15 p.m. The same pattern was observed on Sundays, except that Holy Communion was cele-brated after 9.45 a.m. Morning Prayer, as it was also on saints' days falling in the week. The east end of the building, which housed the choir stalls, was separated from the nave by the huge organ screen, and the mostly un-rehearsed performance of the eight singing boys and as many of the vicars choral and minor canons as chose to turn up was poor – very much worse than that achieved in the best of the nearby City churches. The choice of anthems was determined, and generally limited, by the number of vicars choral likely to be available and sometimes had to be changed at the last minute. They tended therefore to be kept short and simple, though on one occasion Handel's Hallelujah Chorus was attempted with only two men present.

Yet, in spite of this, the congregations at the daily services were often fairly large – as many as 150 at Evening Prayer – and on a Sunday, after the organ screen had been removed, the nave could be crowded with, it was reputed, 'not a seat to be had except in the gallery and that by slipping half a crown to the verger'. Part of the explanation of this was that the canons were all distinguished scholars and, whatever their other shortcomings, they were fine preachers whom thoughtful people wanted to hear. It is also the case that sometimes, and especially on great occa-sions when everyone reported for duty, the worship could be of a very high quality and win praise.

By 1838 it was evident that the situation of the English cathedrals could not be tolerated for much longer. Reform was in the air and eleven years earlier there had been a faint, very faint, indication of change at St Paul's when Dean Copleston, who stayed until 1849, chose to neglect the bishop-ric of Llandaff, to which he had also been appointed, and instead resided in the Deanery for most of the year. In response to the badgering of Miss Maria Hackett, 'the choristers' friend', he appointed a master to teach and generally care for the singing boys. At the national level the Prime Minister, Sir Robert Peel, appointed a Commission of Enquiry in 1834 to investigate the substantial finances of the Church of England's bishoprics and cathedrals. This led in 1836 to a permanent Ecclesiastical Commission, which was given responsibility, with increasing power, for the administration of the church's financial assets.

An Act of Parliament in 1840 required the dean and canons residential of cathedrals to be full-time appointments. Prebendaries were to be honorary rather than stipendiary posts. At St Paul's, the college of minor canons was reduced from twelve to six, those remaining being required to undertake pastoral and educational work in the City and to live in the cathedral's precincts rather than hold City livings. But the effects of these reforms on the music was for many years minimal, mainly because the freeholders remained in their offices, normally until death. When H. H. Milman, a poet as well as a church historian (he was the author of the hymn 'Ride on, Ride on in majesty'), succeeded Copleston in 1849 and became the first full-time dean for more than 100 years, he and the chapter resolved to increase the choir to a size appropriate to the huge building. By this time, however, the capitular revenues had been so depleted by the 1840 reforms that expansion could not be afforded It was not until 1871, when the saintly R. W. Church became dean and acquired an outstandingly able chapter, that significant progress became possible. By this time Goss was within 12 months of retirement, his health having declined.

John Goss was born in 1800 at Fareham, Hampshire, where his father was the highly regarded organist of the parish church. By the age of eleven he was a chorister at the Chapel Royal in London, joining his uncle, an alto, who also sang at Westminster Abbey and St Paul's. Young John boarded with the other choristers in a house near Westminster Abbey where the regime was strict and general education confined to one and a half hours on Wednesdays and Saturdays when a 'writing master' taught reading, writing and arithmetic and a little English grammar. If a boy wished to learn an instrument, he had to teach himself and this was not encouraged. Goss recalled:

Walking across the schoolroom one day with Handel's Organ Concertos under my arm, Mr. Stafford Smith (the Choir Master and a son-in-law of William Boyce) met me and asked me what I had there. 'If you please, Sir, it's only Handel's Organ Concertos; I thought I should like to learn to play them.' 'Oh! Only Handel's Concertos' replied my Master; 'and pray, Sir, did you come here to learn to learn to *play* or to sing?' Mr. Stafford Smith then seized the book and crowned the argument by hitting me on the head with it. I had bought it out of my hardly saved pocket money, and never saw it again.

Sometime later Stafford Smith advised Goss:

Remember, my child, that melody is the one power of music which all men can delight in. If you wish to make those for whom you write love you, if you wish to make what you write amiable, turn your heart to melody; your thoughts will follow the inclinations of your heart.

This precept was followed by a mild beating, designed to ensure that it would always be remembered. He left the choir when his voice broke and studied composition, with special attention to Mozart's symphonies, under Thomas Attwood, the then organist of St Paul's who had been a pupil of Mozart. He financed this by singing in the chorus at the opera – he was a fine tenor – and published a few secular part-songs.

In 1821 he was appointed organist of Stockwell Chapel, which became St Andrew's Church in Lambeth, and three years later moved to a more prestigious and better paid post at the newly built St Luke's Church, Chelsea, where he remained until 1838. Shortly before his twenty-seventh birthday he became Professor of Harmony at the Royal Academy of Music – a chair he occupied for the next 47 years, retiring on health grounds in 1874. He proved to be a gifted teacher as well as a virtuoso organist, though he was unwilling to use a pedalboard, then starting to be added to English organs, and once advised a young organist, 'Charm with your fingers, not with your feet.' This excluded from his repertory the great works of J. S. Bach, which were just becoming known in Britain, so eventually he came to be regarded as an organist from another era. In 1833 he won a prize for an anthem, 'Have mercy upon me, O Lord', and in the secular field he continued to compose part-songs that were popular with the Glee Clubs of that time.

Not long after the death of Thomas Attwood in 1838 Goss wondered whether he might apply to succeed him at St Paul's, and sought a meeting with Sydney Smith the legendary wit, who had become a canon in 1831 and, contrary to all expectations, proved to be an industrious administrator.

'I suppose Mr Goss, you are aware what the statutory salary is?' 'Not exactly.' 'Well, it is about £34 per annum.' 'Oh indeed, is that all? Well, as I am receiving about £100 at Chelsea, I think I will, if you will allow me, consider the matter a little further before I leave my name.' As he was about to leave, Smith said, 'Perhaps Mr Goss, before you go, you would like to know whether any other appointment or any other perquisite appertain to the office of Organist.' He then gave details of these, which were not inconsiderable, and Goss immediately made his application. A long delay followed and Goss, anxious to know whether or not he had been successful, chanced to meet Smith at a large dinner party. He felt unable to enquire about the situation but Smith, who had been entrusted with carving a fine salmon, said on handing to Goss a generous slice, 'I trust Sydney Smith will always be ready to assist Mr Goss through thick and thin.' On his return home Goss found a letter offering him the post.

Appointment to St Paul's was an honour, but was in many ways a poisoned chalice. For one thing, he was contracted only to play the organ. The choice of music for the services was in the hands of the succentor, and the training of the choristers, who often stayed long after their voices had broken, was delegated to one of the vicars choral – a tradition that remained throughout Goss's time in office. A major reconstruction of the entire choral foundation was urgently needed but, in the circumstances of the time, this was impossible. Sydney Smith, being a Whig, favoured reform – at least up to the point where it might adversely affect his own income – and he was joined in 1840 by the appointment of Archdeacon Hale to an additional canonry, and he, too, was a reformer. The problems were, however, too deeply rooted for them to be solved overnight.

In any case, Smith was no lover of cathedral music and although he had promised to assist Goss 'though thick and thin', his help proved to be severely limited. Not long after he became organist, Goss drew his attention one day after Evensong to the organ's limitations. Smith responded, 'Mr. Goss, what a strange set of creatures you organists are. First you want the bull stop, then you want the tom tit stop; in fact you are like a jaded cab-horse, always longing for another stop. However, I will ascertain what may be done in this matter.' Goss got his new stop. But he was not so lucky when he asked for an increase in the number of boys in the choir. Smith declared, 'It is a matter of perfect indifference to me whether Westminster bawls louder than St Paul's. We are there to pray and the singing is a very subordinate consideration.'

Had the circumstances been favourable, it is by no means certain that Goss would have been a strong enough character to carry through a major reform of the cathedral's music. But he soldiered on for 34 years within the constraints imposed upon him and, until the final phase of his career, raised the standard to a level well above that of most other cathedrals.

He was a prolific composer, in spite of a lean period in the 1840s following the cool reception given by St Paul's choir to an anthem 'Blessed is the man' (1842). Based on Psalm 1, this was intended to begin an ambitious series of anthems relating to all 150 psalms, but he was so discouraged by the choir's verdict that he composed no more anthems until 1850. He then produced two short works, 'God so loved the world' and 'Let the wicked forsake his way', which were widely acclaimed. These were followed in 1852 by his masterpiece, 'If ye believe that Jesus died and rose from the dead', a work of great beauty composed for the funeral in St Paul's of the Duke of Wellington, attended by an astonishing 17,000 people. There was a choir of 150.

After his appointment as composer to the Chapel Royal in 1856 Goss composed many anthems and service settings which were at the time highly regarded (the competition was weak), but few proved to have enduring attraction. Most were too difficult for the non-professional parish church choirs for which they were primarily intended. Yet two of his hymn tunes – for 'Praise, my soul, the King of Heaven' and 'See amid the winter's snow' – remain deservedly popular. So also about a dozen of his psalm chants, which still seem just right for Mattins and Evensong in any parish church or cathedral. He edited *Chants Ancient and Modern* (1843), which contained 257 chants, and, with James Turle of Westminster Abbey, who had been a fellow pupil of Thomas Attwood, three volumes of *Cathedral Services Ancient and Modern* (1848). All these had some influence on the development of church music during the nineteenth century.

Goss was a devout composer – many of the compositions in his sketchbooks are prefixed INDA (*In Nomine Domini Amen*) – kind, generous and modest. It was only under pressure from his friends that he exerted his right, as Composer to the Chapel Royal, to provide the Te Deum and anthem 'The Lord is my strength' for a Thanksgiving Service held at St Paul's for the restoration to health of the Prince of Wales, the future King Edward VII, in 1872. This involved the painful refusal of an offer of music from the great French composer, Charles Gounod, who often attended St Paul's when in London, but Gounod took this in good part and dedicated one of his new anthems to Goss.

Soon after the thanksgiving service he was knighted and received the personal thanks of Queen Victoria. He then retired, but continued to worship at St Paul's, rejoicing in the improvements wrought by his successor John Stainer, until his death in 1880.

During the second half of the twentieth century, Goss's music became much less popular in cathedral and other choral foundations. In 1958 the anthem 'If we believe that Jesus died and rose again' was sung in 69 per cent of these, but in 1998 this was reduced to 15 per cent. 'O Saviour of the World' declined from 67 per cent to 21 per cent, and 'O Praise the Lord' from 24 per cent to 1 per cent. 'The Wilderness' still has its admirers, though it is not a patch on S. S. Wesley's masterpiece. Of his canticles, only those in E remained in use and these were reduced from 61 per cent (82 per cent in 1938) to 12 per cent. It is possible, however, that some good parish church choirs view his work more favourably.

4

The Beginnings of Reform – Samuel Sebastian Wesley

Samuel Sebastian Wesley (1810–76) was the foremost church musician of the nineteenth century. A brilliant organist – generally considered the best of his time in Britain – he was also an unusually innovative composer, who initiated a breakthrough in church music, and a visionary who had firm ideas as to how the music of cathedrals might be rescued from the abyss into which it had descended during the previous 100 years. He was a long way ahead of his time and, given his combination of gifts and artistic temperament, it was unsurprising that he was a prickly character, quick to take offence, and found it virtually impossible to collaborate with others, especially those who chanced to be his capitular employers. In fairness, however, it must be recognized that his experience of negligent cathedral authorities would have tested the patience of a saint.

Wesley was the organist of four cathedrals – Hereford, Exeter, Winchester and Gloucester – as well as of the cathedral-like Leeds Parish Church. He composed about 30 anthems, a few service settings and some hymn tunes and psalm chants, but only a small amount of this is in current use. Part of the explanation is that his anthems and chief service settings are of considerable musical complexity and demand cathedral, rather than parish church, choirs for their performance. Fashion is another factor. Although Wesley was a pioneer, most of his music bears the clear stamp of the Victorian era, sometimes exhibiting an element of sentimentality, and many of the twenty-first century's church musicians do not find this attractive. Dr Arthur Hutchings, who was Professor of Music at Durham in the 1960s, and who denied the existence of any significant church music between Purcell and Stanford, described Wesley's work as 'feeble', but this probably tells us more about the limited taste of the professor than it does about the skill of the musician. Eric Routley, who appreciated him more, described him as

easily the most cultivated musician of his day ... and the most adventurously unreliable musician. He could write every cliché in the book; but he could also induce a sense of spaciousness and authority which none of his contemporaries could approach.

Wesley's style was in fact a reversion to that of the sixteenth- and seventeenth-century composers, but with the addition of the new harmonic concepts of his own time. Of his hymn tunes 'Aurelia' is still without serious competition for 'The Church's one foundation', 'Hereford' seems just right for 'O Thou who camest from above' and 'Harewood' appropriately upbeat for 'Christ is our Corner-stone'. 'Alleluia' has just about retained its claim on 'Alleluia! Sing to Jesus', but few of his many other fine tunes survived for long and today they are unknown to congregations.

In 1844 Wesley's personal experience and accumulated knowledge of many English cathedrals led him to pen *A Few Words on Cathedral Music and the Musical System of the Church, with a Plan of Reform*. The 'few words' were a 90-page monograph which sold for 2s. 6d. and was not designed to win him friends among the deans and chapters. He began with a stark warning to aspiring cathedral organists:

> Painful and dangerous is the position of a young musician who, after acquiring great knowledge of his art in the Metropolis, joins a county Cathedral. At first he can scarcely believe that the mass of error and inferiority in which he has to participate is habitual and irremediable. He thinks he will reform matters gently, and without giving offence; but he soon discovers that it is his approbation and not his advice that is needed.
>
> The painter and the sculptor can choose their tools and the material on which they work, and great is the care they devote to the selection: but the musician of the Church has no power of this kind; nay worse, he is compelled to work with tools which he knows to be inefficient and unworthy – incompetent singers and a wretched organ. He must learn to tolerate error, to sacrifice principle, and yet to indicate by his outward demeanour the most perfect satisfaction in his office. His position, in fact, is that of a clergyman compelled by a dominant power to preach the principles of the Koran instead of the Bible. This censure may not apply to *all* Cathedrals, it is allowed; to *some* it assuredly may and does.

He then went on to make constructive proposals for reform.

1 Every cathedral foundation should employ at least twelve Lay Clerks, each to be paid a minimum of £85 p.a. If possible this should be raised to £100–£150 p.a. which would be sufficient to remove the necessity for the men to find additional employment.

2 Lay Clerks should be chosen by a panel consisting of the cathedral

organist, the organists of two neighbouring cathedrals, to 'judge' their musical competence, and one or more members of the Chapter to 'judge the religious fitness of the candidate'.

3 Besides the twelve Lay Clerks, another three deputies or supernumeraries should be appointed on a retainer of £52 p.a. to take the place of those who might be absent because of illness or for other good reasons. In large towns competent amateur singers should be recruited to augment the contribution of the professionals on special occasions or when the music demands larger forces.

4 The cathedral organist should be 'a professor of the highest ability', competent not only as an organist, but also as a choir-trainer and a composer. He should be chosen by the organists of seven other cathedrals and rewarded with a salary of £500–£800 p.a. (more at St Paul's and Westminster Abbey) for 'such men are the bishops of their calling – men consecrated by their genius, and set apart for duties which only the best talent of the kind can adequately fulfil.' They would, however, be required to take no outside engagements.

5 A College of Music should be founded for training of all organists, choirmasters, composers and lay clerks – this to serve and be funded by several cathedral or other choral foundations.

6 A national 'Musical Commission' should be founded to advise, and where necessary exercise authority over, the church's music. It should also administer a common fund to assist with the training of choristers, the purchase of printed music and the repair or rebuilding of organs wherever local resources were limited.

A few years later (1854) Wesley sent these proposals, accompanied by a number of characteristically pungent comments, in a published *Reply to the Inquiries of the Cathedral Commissioners relative to the Improvement in the Music of Divine Worship in Cathedrals*.

Admirable though Wesley's ideas might, in principle, seem to those responsible for cathedral music in the twenty-first century, it was unrealistic to believe that they would be enthusiastically welcomed in his own time. He probably recognized this and offered them as a challenge that might provoke some positive response. But, although he lived and worked for almost another 30 years, he was destined to be disappointed. It was not until well into the twentieth century that most deans and chapters began to increase significantly the financial resources necessary for the production of high-quality music, and although cathedral music has now reached a standard never previously attained, except possibly in the High Middle Ages, this is due at least as much to the selfless dedication of the musicians as it is to the priorities of those who employ them.

Samuel Sebastian Wesley was born in London's West End in 1810. His father Samuel was a son of Charles Wesley, the great hymn writer and brother of John, the founder of the Methodist movement. Samuel was one of the finest organists of his time, a notable composer and an early student and performer in Britain of the works of J. S. Bach, hence the choice of Sebastian for the second Christian name of his son. Samuel Sebastian was, in fact, the first of seven illegitimate children born after the failure of his father's first marriage and when he had established a new relationship with his housekeeper. This irregularity undoubtedly stood in the way of a cathedral appointment for the gifted father; he also had a depressive personality that quite soon limited both the quality and quantity of his compositions.

Young Samuel Sebastian displayed unusual musical talent from his earliest years and in 1818 was sent to the Chapel Royal where the choir was under the direction of a notable musician, William Hawes, who combined this with responsibility for the music at the English Opera House and the training of the choristers at St Paul's Cathedral. The musical education provided by Hawes could not have been bettered and he later described his prodigy as the best pupil he ever had. But the level of general education offered to the boys was poor and the boarding conditions harsh. Nevertheless, Samuel Sebastian flourished and in 1823 went to Brighton to sing before King George IV. In December of the same year he performed a piano duet with Rossini which so pleased the King that he presented him with a gold watch.

Aged 15 he was appointed organist of St John's proprietary chapel in Hampstead and was capable enough to join his father in organ duets performed for audiences in London and Bristol. Four years later he moved to become organist of St Giles Parish Church, Camberwell, in South London, and quickly added to this responsibility for the music at what was then the new church of St John, Waterloo Road. He also found time and energy to play for the evening services at Hampton in West London, and, to keep himself occupied on weekdays, he conducted the band at performances of comic opera at the Opera House in the Strand. He once regretted that he had never managed to compose a comic opera.

In 1831, aged 21, he composed his first anthem, 'O God, whose nature and property is always to have mercy', and in the following year was appointed organist of Hereford Cathedral. The dean, John Merewether, was one of the earliest cathedral reformers and there was much to claim his attention, not least in the music department. The eight adult members of the choir were all clergymen, whose ages ranged from 49 to 78. Five of these were in poor health, two were deemed to be sub-standard, and the eighth, the 78-year-old, exempt from attending. In order to meet this situation, the previous organist, himself in an advanced state of infirmity, had composed three Communion service settings for boys and a single bass voice.

Wesley's appointment was designed to deal with this situation, but, since the organ was due to be enlarged, his arrival in Hereford was delayed by just over a year. This left him with time for a lengthy holiday in the Black Mountains of Wales, the experience of which inspired his landmark verse-anthem 'The wilderness and the solitary place'. This was performed for the first time (with what choral resources is unknown) at the re-opening of the organ in November 1832, and was widely acclaimed, though when he submitted it for the national Gresham Medal the adjudicators did not like it. One of them complained: 'It is a clever thing, but it is not cathedral music.' This did not prevent it from being performed subsequently in many cathedrals, some at the present time. Its length – a full 12 minutes – is now a major problem, and even Wesley admirers concede that it has some weaknesses, but it is a very remarkable work and would be welcomed by many cathedral congregations as an occasional substitute for the Sunday Evensong sermon. More accessible and still deservedly popular was the anthem 'Blessed be the God and Father', which he composed, at the request of the dean, for Easter Day the following year. This became his best-known anthem, and, after an inauspicious start – its first performance was by a row of trebles and a single bass (the dean's butler) – it was sung in Westminster Abbey at the wedding of the present Queen and is part of the standard repertory of every cathedral choir and of many parish church choirs.

Wesley was at Hereford for a mere three years, which was just long enough for him to be the conductor of the Three Choirs Festival, which included an eclectic mixture of fine music – sacred and secular – and also in 1835 to marry the dean's sister, Mary Anne. Evidently the dean did not approve of the union and the wedding took place quietly in Ewyas Harold Church, some miles from Hereford.

A few weeks later he moved to Exeter and in 1836, believing that he might one day secure an academic appointment, he applied for BMus and DMus degrees at Oxford. These required him to submit and perform one of his own compositions, and the anthem he chose for this purpose required a choir. The examination was therefore held in Magdalen College Chapel and the quality of the college choir at that time was candidly expressed in a local newspaper account of the event. Having congratulated Wesley on a fine composition and his introduction on the organ, it added, 'but of the vocal line we could not fairly judge, the singers, in many parts, being both out of time and out of tune'.

Wesley's early years at Exeter were without serious incident, though he was always short of money, and in a revealing letter to Vincent Novello, the music publisher, he explained his late delivery of a promised composition:

I hope to be able to comply with your desire respecting the Voluntary. I now have several engagements to fulfil with Publishers in London, but the dreadful nature of an organist's, I mean a county cathedral organist's, occupation, that of giving lessons all over the county from morning to night makes composing a pleasure hardly to be indulged in. How much should musicians strive that the offices connected with the art in Cathedrals are not of a nature to make them independent respecting money so that they might give their attention to the improvement of the decaying, much degraded musical state of the Church ... the clergy will never move in the matter. They know nothing of their real interests, and consequently the Establishment is going to ruin.

In 1839, however, the cathedral's precentor – an office for which Wesley had not the slightest respect – was elevated to the deanery and things began to go badly wrong. He always resented the fact that the precentor chose the music and that his own contribution was limited to attending a Saturday morning chapter meeting at which the forthcoming week's settings, anthems and hymns were discussed and authorized. But something more serious arose in 1840 when two choristers, with the dean's permission, went to perform one evening in a local Glee Club. On hearing of this Wesley accosted the boys, one of whom he struck hard blows with his fist on the back, then kicked him on the point of his chin, leaving a mark for several days. The other boy was struck on the side of his face and knocked down with another blow. When he was on the floor Wesley kicked him.

When the dean and chapter heard of this they summoned him to their presence in the Chapter House where he admitted the truth of the boys' evidence but argued that he was, as organist, entitled to punish them. The dean and chapter disagreed, said that he was unjustified in inflicting any punishment, deplored his uncontrollable temper and inability to apologize, and decided to suspend him from his duties, without pay, until the chapter's Christmas audit meeting several weeks hence.

He was in trouble again the following year when he was reprimanded for taking leave of absence without permission and leaving an 18-year-old pupil to play at the services. The Devon rivers were too strong a temptation for so addicted an angler. Yet, in spite of all his difficulties, the standard of music at Exeter was raised to an unusually high level for the time. The choir was greatly improved. Better service settings and anthems were introduced and Wesley's own organ playing was by now nationally famous. Large congregations were attracted. But Wesley was not happy and, after he had made a deep impression on the citizens of Leeds with his inaugural organ recital in their newly built parish church, he accepted the invitation of the vicar, Walter Farquhar Hook, to move there as organist. One person who was not sorry to see him leave Exeter was the cathedral's chapter clerk who had dealt with most of the Wesley problems and described him as 'the most to be avoided man I ever met with'.

Hook had gone to Leeds in 1837 and found there a medieval parish church which, although it provided for 1,500 worshippers, soon became too small to accommodate those who wished to attend the Sunday services. He rejected the suggestion that the decaying structure should be restored and enlarged – 'I loathe it', he declared, 'I cannot preach comfortably in it, I cannot make myself heard. The dirt and indecorum distress me.' So £28,000 was raised and the new cathedral-like church was completed and consecrated in 1841. It was intended that there should be daily choral services; there had, unusually, been a surpliced choir of men and boys in the old church since 1818.

Wesley was attracted by the enthusiasm for good music he had found in Leeds and also by a salary of £200 p.a. guaranteed for ten years by one of the city's wealthy residents. The vicar, though not himself a musician, believed that only the best was good enough for the parish church's worship and he was ready to find the money to make this possible. He and his new organist shared a dislike of plainsong and a determination to use only the new Anglican chants for the psalms. Wesley was soon admired throughout Yorkshire and the parish church became one of the county's chief centres of music-making.

His lengthy Morning, Communion and Evening Cathedral Services in E were published in 1845 and demonstrated refreshingly that canticles could provide fitting material for great music. The influence of this proved to be considerable and is now experienced in cathedrals daily in the settings of composers such as Stanford, Wood, Britten and Howells. It also included a preface in which he began what was to become a prolonged onslaught on the lamentable state of cathedral music and the urgency of reform. Later he published an admired book of psalm chants.

Once again, however, he became restless, quarrelled with his employer, and, having given the opening recital on a new organ in Tavistock Parish Church, toyed with the idea of moving there, tempted again no doubt by the fishing prospects. This proved to be only a brief flirtation and Yorkshire after all was not without attractive rivers. It was while alone on a day's fishing in the North Riding in December 1847 that he had a serious accident in which he sustained a compound fracture of his left leg. The combination of shock and infection endangered his life for a time and he had to be nursed in The Black Swan at Helmsley for almost six months. During this time he composed his masterpiece miniature anthem 'Cast me not away', which included the Psalmist's plea 'That the bones which thou hast broken may rejoice', and started to write his *A Few Words* ... He was left permanently lame, although his organ pedal work was not hampered.

It was about this time that he applied for the professorship of music at Oxford but, as with some other attempts to obtain a university chair, was passed over. Instead, he accepted in 1849 an invitation to become organist of Winchester Cathedral, aware that the Itchen was one of England's premier trout streams and that Winchester College would provide an education for his sons. The dean and chapter were pleased to engage him but they were somewhat wary, as his reputation had gone before him, and on his arrival he was summoned to a chapter meeting at which those parts of the Statutes which referred to the duties of the organist were read to him. More than this would be needed, however, to keep him in order and maintain the peace.

There was ample scope for the employment of Wesley's gifts and reforming zeal since the Winchester music was in a sorry state. But although he was able to negotiate a good salary (augmented by appointment also as organist of the college, then as the first Professor of Organ at the Royal Academy of Music), and although the dean and chapter found £2,500 to purchase the organ built for the 1851 Great Exhibition, his behaviour was erratic. He was not respectful and often downright discourteous to the canons. Moreover, the choir's performance was not improving and, in 1857, the chapter ordered an enquiry into the reasons for this. These were not difficult to find: of the 780 choral services held during the previous year, he had been present at only 397. He was now a prima donna who needed a national stage and, when not away from Winchester, was often to be found casting a fly on the Itchen. The organ was left in the hands of a 14-year-old pupil and, through lack of training, the choristers were well below an acceptable standard. Some of the lay clerks were drunkards, others were insolent and rude and sometimes deliberately sang wrong notes. Wesley was admonished for neglect of duty, but this made little difference and further censure was required two years later.

More constructively, his 16-year-long stay at Winchester was marked by the composition of some good anthems. 'Ascribe unto the Lord' (1853), 'Praise the Lord my soul' (1861), 'Give the King Thy judgement, O God' (for the wedding of the future King Edward VII in 1863) and most notably by the publication of his *Twelve Anthems* (1853) dedicated to the dean, Thomas Garnier, and considered by many to be the outstanding collection of nineteenth-century church music. 'Thou wilt keep him in perfect peace' and 'Wash me throughly' are still in constant use – and deservedly, since they have deep spiritual power. Always suspicious of music publishers, whom he believed to cheat him of his dues, Wesley recruited a long list of subscribers. This included most of the eminent names in church music at that time and more or less covered the cost of the many plates required for the printing. Thereafter his creative power declined.

In 1865 Wesley was asked to serve as an assessor for the appointment of a new organist for Gloucester Cathedral and, at the end of the interviews, startled the dean and chapter with the announcement, 'Gentlemen,

I have decided to accept the post myself.' The dean explained to a former lay clerk afterwards: 'Dr. Wesley is fond of fishing and he hears that there is some good fishing to be had about here.' Another attraction was the Three Choirs Festival and, since this was due to be held at Gloucester that year, he was immediately appointed conductor. This involved responsibility for the organizing of the programme (which he did for another two Festivals held at Gloucester), but he lacked the flair of an impresario and his choice of anthems and oratorios was sometimes too ambitious for the resources at his disposal. Moreover, his conducting was not always at an acceptable standard, but there were occasions when his own organ playing was a Festival highlight, and the performance for the first time in 1871 of Bach's *St Matthew Passion* was considered a triumph, even though the audience for it was disappointingly poor. At this Festival Wesley displayed his versatility and the catholicity of his taste by conducting at an evening concert music from Mozart's *Marriage of Figaro*. The publication in 1872 of *The European Psalmist,* a compilation of 615 hymn tunes, including 143 of his own, was a remarkable achievement though it proved to be a quarry of material from which other church musicians could mine, rather than a working hymn book.

Wesley's final years, spent at Gloucester, were comparatively tranquil. As he grew older his proposals for cathedral reform became ever more radical and he proposed to a distinguished music critic of the time, Joseph Bennett, the possibility of conducting a campaign to abolish all cathedral chapters and precentors and replace them with a small staff of what he pointedly called 'working clergymen'. organists should be given sole responsibility for the music, and the capitular funds should be directed to a central fund to be allocated to cathedrals according to need. In common with many of his musician colleagues, he had evidently heard too many poor sermons because he also proposed the setting up of a London-based College of Preachers, from which every cathedral would be supplied with a monthly preacher in residence who would have something worthwhile to say and the skill to communicate it. The campaign never got beyond the ideas stage and would have been quickly rejected if it had. He seems to have given up hope of raising the standard of his own choir.

With advancing years Wesley's health gradually deteriorated and he became increasingly eccentric, not least in an obsessive concern about his diet. But he continued to derive great pleasure from angling and shooting. He was distraught when his adored bull terrier Rob died, and he conducted a solemn funeral for the animal in his garden, which many called Dr Wesley's Wilderness. On Christmas Day 1875 he played the Hallelujah Chorus from Handel's *Messiah* after the blessing at Evensong – a departure from his usual practice of playing or extemporizing one of Bach's organ fugues – and this proved to be the last time he played the cathedral organ. He died in April of the following year and, after a simple funeral service in Gloucester Cathedral, was buried in the old cemetery at Exeter, next to the grave of his only daughter Mary, who had died when only nine weeks old.

5

Nineteenth-Century Hymn Writers and Composers

There was little hymn singing in the Church of England before about 1820. An edition of Tate and Brady's late seventeenth-century versification of the psalms included some to secular folk tunes but this was not sufficient to relieve the general austerity of Sunday worship. The explanation of this lack of hymnody lies in the fact that at the Reformation the Church of England was influenced by the theology of John Calvin, rather than that of Martin Luther. This was so tied to the Bible that it became possible to use only biblical material for worship purposes. Thus Bible readings, psalms, biblical canticles and prayers echoing the biblical themes formed the staple provided by the Book of Common Prayer. Anthems, when used, consisted of aspirations or affirmations drawn from the Bible. This was in marked contrast to the situation in those parts of Europe, most notably Germany, where the embracing of Lutheranism, whose handling of the Bible was less rigid, allowed the flowering of what became a great tradition of mighty hymns, including some written by Luther himself. These would eventually enrich the worship and devotion of Christians everywhere. Bach's Passions and his *Christmas Oratorio* have many Arias with non-scriptural words.

The breakthrough in England was created by the Methodists who abandoned Calvinist theology and came to regard music as well as preaching as a major weapon in their campaign to evangelize the English people and to rescue the Church of England from the pit of formality and complacency into which it had descended. Hymns, in common with worship as a whole, were seen as 'a converting ordinance' and the sight of huge congregations, mainly of working people, united in their enthusiastic singing of them, provided clear evidence of their effectiveness. When the preface to the first edition of the 1933 *Methodist Hymn Book* began, as all subsequent editions have done, 'Methodism was born in song', this was a plain statement of the truth.

The fact that during the early years of the nineteenth century Methodist congregations, meeting in halls and the open air, were attracting increasing numbers from parish churches was an important incentive to Anglican clergy to make hymn singing an integral part of their own services. A late eighteenth-century hymn-singing Evangelical movement within the Church of England was also influential and, as the century advanced, a widespread belief arose that the church's worship needed to be renewed and enhanced by greater congregational participation. All these factors combined to open the doors to a degree of spontaneous change that transformed the experience of worship in England's parish churches. The rise of the Anglo-Catholic Oxford Movement later contributed a rich supply of ancient hymns drawn from medieval sources and brought alive by fine translations from the Latin.

The Methodists were prolific hymn writers and one of their number, Charles Wesley, who never left the ministry of the Church of England, held a high doctrine of the Eucharist. He combined the essential gifts of the hymn writer – deep religious insight, confirmed by personal experience and expressed through the gifts of the poet – to the level of genius and wrote no fewer than 4,000 hymns. These, together with those of Isaac Watts, another genius of Independent church allegiance, and many others, became immediately available to enterprising Anglican parsons. Initially, they were not welcome everywhere: the gentry tended to regard them as vulgar and some bishops declared hymns to be illegal inasmuch as no provision for them was made by the rubrics of the Prayer Book.

Nonetheless, once started, the use of hymns became unstoppable. By 1840 about 40 different hymn books, mainly local productions, were in use and one of these, consisting of 146 hymns, edited by a Sheffield vicar and, after a struggle, authorized by the Archbishop of York, ran to 29 editions, circulating among many parishes in the north of England.

Reginald Heber

Often described as 'the father of the modern hymn book', Heber was a child of the eighteenth century, born into a Yorkshire family of landed gentry, though his father was also a Fellow of Brasenose College, Oxford. Reginald had a brilliant career at the same college, winning a number of poetry prizes and election to a fellowship of All Souls' College. After two years of travelling in Europe, he was ordained in 1804 and immediately appointed Rector of Hodnet, a family living in Shropshire, which had been kept vacant for two years until his return to England. He was also squire of the parish and his father-in-law, who was Dean of St Asaph, secured for him a prebend of that cathedral. His scholarship was recognized by appointment as Bampton Lecturer at Oxford, and his income further augmented by the preachership of Lincolns Inn, in London.

In 1822 he was offered the bishopric of Calcutta, which at first he declined, but later was persuaded to accept. For the next four years he was an exemplary missionary bishop. His diocese covered the whole of British India and he travelled extensively, preaching, confirming and generally encouraging the small, scattered expatriate communities. But in 1826, after conducting a Confirmation and visiting a school, he sought to cool down in a swimming pool and died from drowning.

In the following year, Heber's widow managed at last to obtain permission from the Archbishop of Canterbury for the publication of a hymn book compiled by her husband during his years at Hodnet. Soon after his arrival in the parish he perceived that hymns might be useful for illustrating the Bible readings in the Sunday services and at the same time involve the congregation more closely in the worship. Until then the only collection of hymns known to him was *Olney Hymns* – a product of the Evangelical movement in 1779 – which included items by important poets such as John Newton, William Cowper and Augustus Toplady.

Heber, although a High Churchman, wrote about his experience of using hymns in this way in an evangelical magazine, the *Christian Observer*, and decided that hymns were also needed to illustrate the Christian year – possibly some appropriate to every Sunday. He therefore made a collection of 98 hymns, including 57 composed by himself and another 13 by his friend H. H. Milman, a distinguished church historian who eventually became Dean of St Paul's and is best remembered for his Palm Sunday hymn 'Ride on, ride on, in majesty'. The remainder included the work of some of the greatest English poets, but neither the Bishop of London nor the Archbishop of Canterbury was willing to authorize the book's use and its editor never saw it in print. Of his own hymns, it is hard to imagine any hymn book lacking 'Holy, holy, holy' or 'Brightest and best of the sons of the morning' or 'From Greenland's icy mountains', though the use of this last hymn is now problematical.

A decisive factor in the overcoming of episcopal opposition was the work of a number of Oxford Movement scholars who demonstrated that hymns, far from being a recent Methodist invention, went back to some of the church's earliest liturgies and played an important part in the worship and devotion of the medieval church.

John Mason Neale

Chief among these scholars and an adornment of the Victorian church was John Mason Neale, whose translations from Greek and Latin and own compositions contributed 72 items – one-tenth of the whole – to *The English Hymnal* and brought enrichment to Anglican worship everywhere.

He was born in 1818, his father, an evangelical clergyman, being also a brilliant mathematician and a Fellow of St John's College, Cambridge. John, having lost his father when he was only five, went as a scholar of Trinity College, Cambridge, and became the best Classic of his year. Following ordination, he stayed on as chaplain and assistant tutor of Downing College and won many prizes for poetry. He also came under the influence of a High Church movement, parallel to the developing Oxford Movement, and in 1839, in company with two undergraduates, founded the Cambridge Camden Society (later renamed the Ecclesiological Society), to be concerned with Tractarian worship. In 1841 a periodical, *The Ecclesiologist,* began publication in order to demonstrate the implications of the new movement for church architecture. For better or (almost certainly) worse this had immense influence, leading among other things to the placing of choirs in chancels. The aim was to restore the ceremonial and vesture of medieval times, together with early Gregorian chant and Renaissance polyphony.

In 1842 Neale began work as a curate in Guildford (then in Winchester Diocese) but Bishop Charles Sumner, an evangelical, refused to license him because of his high church views, and it was left to the Bishop of Chichester to present him to the small living of Crawley in Sussex. Ill health, however, precluded his taking this up and during the next three years he divided his time between Penzance and Madeira. On his return to Sussex in 1846 he became Warden of Sackville College, East Grinstead – a charity home for 30 people. The buildings were badly dilapidated and he took the opportunity to rebuild the chapel, furnishing it according to Camden Society principle. The bishop denounced this as 'frippery' and 'spiritual haberdashery', but, since the chapel was outside his jurisdiction, he could do no more than inhibit Neale from ministering in the diocese. This inhibition remained in force for the next 16 years until Bishop Samuel Wilberforce persuaded his episcopal colleague to revoke it. Thereafter bishop and warden got on rather well.

In any case, Neale had many other interests to occupy his time. He founded a religious order for women, the Society of St Margaret, which began as a nursing order but quickly extended to include an orphanage, a girls' boarding school and a home 'for the reformation of fallen women'. Its work continues in a modified form today, with outposts in London, Sri Lanka and Boston, USA. With a wife and five children to support, his income of £30 p.a. needed considerable augmentation and from 1851–53 he employed his literary skill and encyclopaedic knowledge in the writing of three leading articles a week for the *Morning Chronicle*. He spoke 20 languages and an extraordinary number of books came from his pen on church history, liturgy, patristics, the Eastern Church, and children's interests.

But his chief life's work – he died when only 48 – was the recovery and translation of hymns from the past for which his scholarship, linguistic skill and poetic gift perfectly equipped him. A steady stream of work, including hymns of his own composition, became available – hymns chiefly medieval on the *Joys and Glories of Paradise* (1865), *Hymns for Use during the Cattle Plague* (1866), *The Invalid's Hymn Book* (1866) and, most notably, *Hymns Noted*, which appeared in two parts in 1851 and 1854 and was a joint enterprise for which Neale translated 94 items from Greek and medieval Latin, while Thomas Helmore adapted their original Sarum plainsong melodies. One-eighth of the contents of the first edition of *Hymns Ancient and Modern* were provided by Neale, from either translations or his own writing, and he edited two volumes of carols for Christmas (1853) and Eastertide (1854). *Hymns of the Eastern Church* appeared in 1862.

Among the best known of Neale's hymns (from translation) are 'Ye Choirs of new Jerusalem', 'The Day of Resurrection', 'Christ is made the sure Foundation', 'All glory, laud and honour', and 'O what their joy and their glory must be'; while among his own work 'O happy band of pilgrims' remains the most widely used.

H. F. Lyte

It would be a foolhardy editor who left out H. F. Lyte's 'Abide with me' from a new hymn book in any part of the English-speaking world. Although written nearly 200 years ago in a pre-modern world, it retains its power to cross every sort of social and cultural frontier and if not at the top of the favourite hymn charts, which it usually is, it is never far below.

In 1927 the organizers of the FA Cup Final decided, with the strong approval of King George V, that 'Abide with me' would provide a fitting climax to the community singing that preceded the kick-off. This decision was, obviously, not based on any theological ground but informed by an awareness that this particular hymn had in a unique way entered deeply into the emotional, if not the overtly religious, consciousness of the nation.

This was probably caused by the comforting reassurance offered by its words, and these were perfectly complemented and reinforced by William Henry Monk's tune 'Eventide'. Long before the 1927 Cup Final, 'Abide with me' had been sung at countless bedsides of the dying and at even more funerals. And in a world frequently devastated by war it was the one hymn known and valued by those serving at the front line or on a sinking ship, or held in a prisoner-of-war camp. The heroine nurse Edith Cavell and an army chaplain sang 'Abide with me' together in her cell before she was shot by the Germans in 1915.

The words were inspired by Luke 24.29, where during the evening of the first Easter Day the disciples, accompanied by the incognito Jesus on a journey to Emmaus, invited him to spend the night in their home: 'Abide with us; for it is toward evening and the day is far spent.' Its author was only 27 when as a young curate he heard a dying friend repeat the phrase 'Abide with me'. This led him to compose some verses on this theme which he kept to himself until shortly before his own death in 1847 when he gave the manuscript to a relative who got them published soon afterwards. The original version had three additional verses, 3–5, which were subsequently omitted from most hymn books, not because there was anything amiss with them but, presumably, because they lifted the emphasis from the deathbed to continuing daily life.

Lyte, the son of a naval captain, was born in Scotland in 1793 but soon moved with his family to Ireland. At Trinity College, Dublin, he won poetry prizes in three successive years. He intended to become a doctor, but changed his mind and, following ordination, became curate of a parish near Wexford. Ill-health caused him to resign and he lived for a time in the more hospitable climate of Marazion in Cornwall, where he married the heiress of a rich Irish clergyman.

On recovery of his health he became a curate at Lymington in Hampshire, then at Charlton in Devon, before becoming vicar of the new parish of Lower Brixham, also in Devon, where he remained for 25 years. He was, however, frequently beset by ill-health, requiring many foreign tours, and only two months after his resignation from Brixham he died of tuberculosis in Nice. Aided doubtless by the wealth of his wife, he accumulated a considerable library of theology and Old English poetry which occupied a London auction house for 17 days in the year following his death.

Lyte wrote some secular music – 'On a naval officer' was set to music by Arthur Sullivan – but most of his work, including some hymns, was first published in *Poems Chiefly Religious* (1833). *The Spirit of the Psalms* (1834) provided metrical versions of the psalms for use every Sunday of the year and one of these, 'Praise, my soul, the King of Heaven' (Psalm 103), is now hardly less dispensable than 'Abide with me'. Two others, 'Pleasant are thy courts above' (Psalm 84) and 'God of mercy, God of grace' (Palms 67), remain popular and indicate that Lyte was not always in a funereal mood.

J. B. Dykes

John Bacchus Dykes, the most prolific, as well as the most heavily criticized, of the Oxford Movement's hymn composers, was Precentor of Durham Cathedral from 1849 to 1862. When he resigned this office in order to become, on the nomination of the dean and chapter, vicar of the ancient parish of St Oswald he retained his minor canonry until the end of his relatively short life in 1876. The Durham choir was better than most, though its ceremonial was slack.

The bishop at the time was Charles Baring, a wealthy scion of the banking family and a notable church builder, who set himself the formidable task of repairing the Church of England's scandalous neglect of the rapidly developing North East. In this he was very successful, but, more than any of his episcopal colleagues, he was intolerant of clergy who had been influenced by the Oxford Movement. So, although St Oswald's embraced most of the city, Baring steadfastly refused to licence any curates to Dykes. Thus, in the context of a bitter conflict with his bishop, which included an unsuccessful appeal to the courts, Dykes struggled to minister to his parish single-handed for 12 years. In the end he was driven to resignation by a serious physical and psychological breakdown.

Most of his 300 hymns were composed before his pastoral responsibilities had become so demanding. Having heard by chance of the plans for what became *Hymns Ancient and Modern*, he sent some of his tunes to Dr W. H. Monk the music editor and had seven of them accepted for the first edition (1861). Another 24 were taken into the 1868 supplement and the edition published in 1875 included 56 of his items. His special usefulness to the editor lay in his ability to compose tunes to suit particular words, often on request. But, while this had some advantages, it meant that the music was too closely tied to inferior hymns of cloying sentimentality, narrow subjectivity or gloomy fatalism. One of the specialisms was a hymn with a short final line which he continued to drag out excruciatingly. The overall effect of many of his tunes was to reduce the atmosphere of worship.

Ralph Vaughan Williams was ruthless in his treatment of Dykes when given responsibility for the music of *The English Hymnal* (1906). He accepted only six of his tunes into the main book and was driven, only by their popularity, to place another five into an appendix which he called his 'chamber of horrors'. As late as its 1950 revision, however, *Hymns Ancient and Modern* retained as many as 30 of his tunes and Erik Routley, probably the severest critic of Victorian hymnody, surprisingly described 20 of these as 'indispensable to congregations'. Others might restrict this accolade to his generally acknowledged fine tunes to John Henry Newman's great hymns 'Lead kindly light' and 'Praise to the holiest in the height' and to the ever popular 'Holy, holy, holy, Lord God Almighty', 'Eternal Father strong to save' and 'The King of Love my shepherd is' (which Vaughan Williams regretted that copyright restrictions prevented him from using in *The English Hymnal*).

John Bacchus Dykes was born in Hull in 1823. His grandfather, an enterprising church builder in the town, was Vicar of St John's Hull, and young

John learned from the age of ten to play the organ in his church. While at St Catherine's College, Cambridge, he founded the university Musical Society and was a popular performer of comic songs. He also came under the influence of the Oxford Movement, abandoning his family's Evangelical tradition and, having sought Holy Orders, became curate of Malton, near York, in 1847. Two years later he went to Durham Cathedral, but he always said that, even though he had a great love of music, the work of a priest was more important to him. Durham University honoured him with a doctorate of music.

Hymns Ancient and Modern

In his valuable *Abide with Me: The World of Victorian Hymns* (1997), Ian Bradley quotes from an article by Bertram Barnaby in the *Guardian* (9 April 1977) in which he estimates that between 1873 and 1901 around 400,000 hymns were written. How many of these were Anglican is impossible to tell, but the contributions of Heber, Neale, Lyte and Dykes were substantially augmented by Mrs C. F. Alexander, Sabine Baring-Gould, John Ellerton, F. W. Faber, William Walsham How and John Keble (from his *Christian Year* poems). A multitude of others, mainly clergymen, added hymns of varying quality, not all of which have remained in use and some of which only briefly saw the light of day.

By the 1850s it was apparent that the plethora of collections of hymns then circulating needed to be replaced by a single volume in which the dross had been eliminated and hymns of quality provided for the entire Christian year – this last requirement indicating the growing influence of the Oxford Movement. In 1858 two London parish clergymen, William Denton and Francis Murray, both hymn-book compilers, decided while travelling together on the Great Western Railway that the time was right for such a volume. A meeting was convened at St Barnabas, Pimlico, in London, a committee of High Church parish priests formed and over the next two years a huge number of hymns were scrutinized, of which 273 were chosen. Nearly 50 per cent of these were translations from ancient Greek and Latin sources, just over one-third were nineteenth-century creations, and the remainder originated in pre-nineteenth-century England or Germany. Hence the inspired title *Hymns Ancient and Modern* (1861), which quickly established itself as an essential ingredient of Anglican worship not only in Britain but throughout the English-speaking world.

No less inspired was the choice of editors. The Revd Sir Henry Williams Baker, Bart., who was entrusted with the words, was for 27 years Vicar of Monkland, near Leominster, and himself a notable hymn writer responsible for 'The King of Love my Shepherd is' (Psalm 23), 'Lord, Thy

Word abideth' and 'O praise ye the Lord'. William Henry Monk, organist of St Matthias Church, Stoke Newington, and Professor of Vocal Music at King's College, London, applied the skills employed in the creation of a tune for 'Abide with me' to the choice of singable tunes for the other 272. His choices – which involved the commissioning of new tunes where none was already available – were probably more critical than those of the words editor in determining whether or not particular hymns would become popular. It is the measure of his success that so many of the tunes originally attached to the hymns have remained in use for 150 years and in many instances are now inseparable from them.

The immediate popularity of the book led to the production of a 113-hymn supplement (more than half being published for the first time) in 1868, and further supplements were added in 1889 and 1916. But this led to an overall decline in quality and drastic revisions were needed. This process has continued and the Proprietors (now the Council) of Hymns Ancient and Modern have remained an independent profit-making enterprise.

It is not easy now to appreciate the extent to which hymn singing entered into the culture of Victorian England. Starting as a novelty, it spread like wildfire not only to the churches but also to schools, public houses and wherever people gathered socially – more significantly to private houses where families and friends gathered round a piano or some other instrument to sing what soon became regarded as 'old favourites'. Ian Bradley, both an authority on and a stout defender of the Victorian hymn, has described hymns as the folk music of the Victorian age and even gone as far as likening them, perhaps with less justification, to modern soap operas.

They still stand in need of their defenders since, from the time of *The English Hymnal* (1906) onwards, they have been subjected to the severest of criticism from professional church musicians – subjectivity, emotionalism, banal verse and unbelievably bad music being the chief charges. That this is true of a significant proportion of the huge output can hardly be denied, but more recently there has been a growing recognition that among the Victorian material that has nurtured the devotional life of several generations of Christian believers, there is pure gold. In any event, churchgoers continue to love the best of them and complain strongly whenever they are neglected.

6

Frederick Ouseley and St Michael's College, Tenbury

The name of the Revd Sir Frederick Ouseley, Bart., means nothing to the overwhelming majority of churchgoers, though some may perhaps recall that from time to time their choir has sung his short and simple anthems 'From the rising of the sun' and 'How goodly are thy tents'. His masterpiece, the short unaccompanied eight-part 'O Saviour of the world', retains a prominent place in the cathedral repertoire. Members of some choirs will be aware that he composed a few single chants for psalms which are still in use. Of his hymn tunes only 'Contemplation', set to Joseph Addison's great hymn 'When all thy mercies O my God', is still widely used, though even this has been excluded from many modern hymn books. This is a meagre legacy from a man who composed about 75 anthems and 13 service settings and was considered to be one of the leading church musicians of the mid-Victorian era, but this was a point at which the standard of church music was, with notable exceptions, very low.

Ouseley is, however, to be remembered for the pioneering choir school he founded at Tenbury in Worcestershire and for a remarkable music library which included many important manuscripts. The choir school survived, often against formidable odds, until 1985 when financial problems caused closure. The library was then transferred to the Bodleian in Oxford and the chapel remains the parish church. The existence of the school and the library owed everything to his considerable personal wealth and to his lifelong commitment to raising the standard of music in parish churches and cathedrals.

Frederick Arthur Gore Ouseley was born in Grosvenor Square, London, in 1825. His father, the first baronet, was a distinguished Oriental scholar and served as ambassador successively to Russia and Persia. The Duke of York, the Duke of Wellington and the Marchioness of Salisbury were godparents at the baptism.

From the age of three he displayed extraordinary musical gifts and it was said that he could play before he could talk. By the age of five he was composing waltzes and marches and once cried, 'Only think, papa blows his nose in G'. At six he played a duet with Mendelssohn and, although he had no formal training, composed an opera when only eight. He was privately educated by the Vicar of Dorking and went in 1843 to Christ Church, Oxford. In his final year there the cathedral organist resigned and he offered his services as honorary organist until a replacement could be found. This took several months and during this time Ouseley was solely responsible for all the cathedral's music.

He had inherited the baronetcy in 1843 and, although it was at the time unusual for anyone of his social standing to seek Holy Orders, he nonetheless prepared for ordination in order 'to do something to revive the music of the sanctuary'. In 1849 he became a curate at St Paul's, Knightsbridge in London – a church markedly influenced by the Oxford Movement. He arrived in the parish when a new St Barnabas district church was about to be consecrated in Pimlico and lived in the nearby clergy house with three other curates. This enterprise in a slum area was seen as providing an opportunity for initiating the most advanced form of Catholic-style worship and, almost immediately, it attracted an extreme Protestant faction which, under the banner 'No Popery', began demonstrations that led to riots and the desecration of the new building.

After about 18 months of this, and with no support being offered by the Bishop of London or other senior diocesan church officials, the Vicar of St Paul's and his curates resigned. Ouseley was still in deacon's orders but during his brief time in Pimlico he had been responsible for the choir and was concerned that the crisis at St Barnabas would leave the boys stranded. He therefore purchased a large house near Windsor, took the boys into residence, engaged one of his fellow curates as master of the school, created a private chapel and started twice-daily cathedral-style services. Men of the choirs of Westminster Abbey and St Paul's who lived within reach came to lend a hand.

Having got his project under way, he went on a tour of Europe visiting cathedrals and other major churches, meeting church musicians and collecting rare church music. He had by this time taken an Oxford BMus with a cantata *The Lord is the True God*, which was deemed good enough to be performed at the Three Choirs Festival at Hereford in 1858. On his return from Europe in 1852 he began making plans for what would become St Michael's College, Tenbury. At the same time he decided that his vocation was also to be a country priest and, with the ready co-operation of the Bishop of Hereford, R. D. Hampden, the laying of the foundation stone of St Michael's College in 1854 was followed, a year later, by his ordination to the priesthood.

In the same year his achievement in publishing two volumes of anthems – the first comprising his own works and the second those of the English masters of the sixteenth, seventeenth and early eighteenth centuries – led to his appointment as Professor of Music at Oxford. The new college was erected on a large estate which Ouseley had bought some two miles from Tenbury and the bishop agreed to the creation of a new parish with a church, designed on cathedral lines with a fine Henry Willis organ; the church would also become the college chapel, a vicarage and a school – all paid for by Ouseley along with an endowment. He became the first vicar and warden when the church and college were dedicated in honour of St Michael and All Angels on 29 September 1856. The college foundation consisted of a warden and precentor, 20 honorary fellows, a headmaster, an assistant master, an organist and music master, a librarian, a sacristan, and five lay clerks. Eight choristers and eight probationers – all educated without charge – were admitted to share in the general education provided by the college, and after a few years there was a steady flow of boys to the leading public schools. After Oxford or Cambridge many of them were ordained. In term, Mattins was sung daily at 9 a.m. and Evensong at 6 p.m.

Twelve months before the dedication of the church and college the bishop appointed Ouseley to be also precentor of Hereford Cathedral. This ancient office, with a seat on the chapter, was worth £500 a year (a considerable sum at that time) but for more than 100 years none of its holders had discharged any of its duties, or even been qualified to do so. Ouseley was both eminently qualified and enthusiastic, and although the reforming Ecclesiastical Commission took the opportunity to disendow the stall, his own private income enabled him to accept the responsibilities. These were supervisory and did not require his daily attendance, though he was in Hereford frequently and towards the end of his life became a canon residentiary.

At Oxford he instituted a course of lectures in music – something un-known for 100 years or more – and revised the standard of the degrees. Candidates for the DMus were required not only to submit a substantial composition of their own, but also face a public examination on historical and critical aspects of music, and even an examination on the rudiments of the classics. In the first year of the new regime 50 per cent of the candidates failed and Ouseley was confronted in the streets of Oxford by angry, and sometimes tearful, failures. He met all the costs of the new arrangements which included additional courses of lectures.

Some of his time at Tenbury, which extended until his death while in residence at Hereford in 1889, was devoted to the accumulation of anti-quarian music books and manuscripts for his personal library. These in-cluded a copy of the *Messiah* partly in the handwriting of Handel and used by him as a conducting score for its first performance in Dublin in 1742, Thomas Tomkins's *Musica Deo Sacra* (1668), the huge organ book that bears the name of Adrian Batten (1591–1637) and much music of the Palestrina school; many manuscripts of operas from the Palais Royal Library in Paris were also acquired. The college had its own general library, which was said to equal that of many Oxford and Cambridge colleges. The most notable, and perhaps the most unlikely, alumnus of the college is Jonathan Harvey, whose late twentieth-century atonal music, employing electronic sound, would undoubtedly have astonished its founder.

7

The Parish Church Choirs

The origins of the 'traditional' parish church choir, clad in cassock and surplice and occupying stalls in the chancel, is nothing like as ancient as is commonly imagined. The first recorded instance of such a choir is dated 1818 when six men and six boy choristers led the worship at Leeds Parish Church. Not long after this St James's Church at Ryde in the Isle of Wight followed suit. The model for both was the cathedral choir.

There may have been other, unrecorded examples of this innovation but they were probably few and far between. The pioneers of the Oxford Movement were not concerned with ceremonial matters, but their successors, the so-called Ritualists, were and by about 1860 surpliced choirs were widespread and not confined to churches that had embraced the revived High Church tradition. Those that had were encouraged by J. M. Neale, the medievalist and hymn writer, who believed that, since the chancel was always intended to be the place for those leading the worship, and since choirs had this role, the chancel was the place – the only place – where they ought to be. For the most part, however, the changes were a reaction against the dull west gallery singers, in their ordinary clothes and with their often casual behaviour, and were motivated by a desire that worship should be more seemly.

It was not to be expected, however, that the removal of the singers from one end of a building to the other, combined with an investment in robes, would inevitably lead to an improvement in performance. In fact the standard of music remained low, though some brave attempts were made to remedy this. The short-lived Society for Promoting Church Music (1846–51) encouraged choirs to do better and supplied its members with well-written simple music. In 1888 a Church Choir Guild was formed, with the support of Archbishop Frederick Temple of Canterbury and Sir George Elvey, the organist of St George's Chapel, Windsor. The Victorian desire and energy for improvement had now reached this part of the church's life and in 1905 the Guild became the Incorporated Guild of Church Musicians, expanding to include organists and others involved in the making of music. Later the prefix was dropped and by this time the Guild had embarked on an ambitious educational programme, with its own certificates and diplomas related to the leadership of worship. In 1961 it took over the administration of the Archbishop's Certificate in Church Music and in 1988 it became ecumenical. The Church Music Society, started in 1906, also aimed to raise standards and Sydney Nicholson's involvement in its work was one of the factors that led to the founding of what became the Royal School of Church Music.

Another initiative, which proved to be of great importance, was the founding in 1864 of the College of Organists, which was given a Royal Charter in 1893. This was the idea of Richard Limpus, the organist of St Michael's, Cornhill, in the City of London, and had the initial aim of 'elevating and advancing our professional status'. Although membership was not confined to church organists, most of the professional organists were employed by cathedrals and churches. As the college expanded and involvement in high-quality music increased generally, this changed, but ambitious church organists and, later, choir directors have always looked to it as an institution that upholds the highest standards and awards prestigious diplomas. Few professional organists are without the ARCO, or, more commonly, the FRCO and there is also a diploma in choral directing. The college also moved into the fields of education and training and now has links with all the major music schools in Britain. It has a busy programme of lectures and recitals, as well as an important music library, and over the years has numbered some of the most distinguished musicians among its presidents. Its influence on the standard of church music has been considerable, though the number of organists and choir directors who have obtained diplomas is relatively small.

That the college was founded by a London parish church organist is a pointer to the fact that during the latter part of the nineteenth century there were here and there, in the cities and larger towns, highly competent organists who began to work wonders with their choirs. This was particularly so in the City of London, as reported by Charles Box, a well-informed and reforming church musician who published in 1884 *Church Music in the Metropolis*. He included a survey of the music performed by each of the 68 churches within the City during the previous three years, based on visits (sometimes more than once) by himself and a few collaborators.

These churches, obviously, cannot be regarded as typical of those of the Church of England as a whole. Their location, number and in most cases their financial resources make them exceptional, but not quite as exceptional as they would become during the twentieth century when wartime bombing reduced their number and huge economic and social changes decimated the size of the City's population. Today there are only 22 parishes, augmented by 12 Guild churches that do not normally have Sunday services.

The parishes of the churches surveyed all had resident populations. Most were, by modern standards, small – under 1,000 – but a significant number had 6,000 or more. A few were held in plurality, but normally each had its own rector or vicar, possibly a curate or two, and church-wardens who had civic as well as ecclesiastical responsibilities. Mattins with a sermon, followed by Ante-Communion, and Evensong and sermon, were normal every Sunday, and in a handful of churches, influenced by the Oxford Movement, there was a Sunday Eucharist. Weekday services were not uncommon.

The size of the congregations was often very small – 15 to 20 people, though there might be more on special occasions, and in a few places every seat was occupied. But virtually every church had its surpliced choir of between 12 and 20 voices – boys, men and sometimes women – who may sometimes have received a modest honorarium for their services. There were a few professional choirs and, at the other end of the scale, some churches had contingents of charity children who tried to give a lead. Every church had its organ, some of them the work of great builders, such as 'Father' Smith and Renatus Harris, and Box had a high opinion of the quality of the organists, whose number included Doctors of Music.

His verdict on the choirs was much less flattering, and their quality was on the whole not very high, though some were outstanding. He also complained about 'the great variety' of worship offered in the church, but what he describes appears today to have been remarkably uniform. The psalms and canticles were usually chanted, but professional and other competent choirs used a service setting for the canticles. Every choir, with very few exceptions, attempted an anthem (Handel was popular) with varying degrees of success. *Hymns Ancient and Modern* was most commonly used and some congregations were said to 'sing with great gusto'. The prayers tended to be intoned, rather than read, by the priest, and the use of the organ before and after services was regarded as important, requiring congregational attention.

Box also ventured beyond the confines of the City to a number of other, mainly prominent, churches in Westminster, Southwark and the West End. Most of these had large congregations drawn from parishes of 10,000 people and more, and the music of the worship was virtually the same as that to be found in the City. If the result of his research is not, at least in scale, an accurate reflection of what was taking place elsewhere, it indicates a considerable change from the situation almost a century earlier when the Bishop of London, in a charge to his clergy, complained of the low standard of music in their churches, particularly in the singing of the psalms which, in most places, was the only choral music used:

> In country parishes this is generally engrossed by a select band of singers, who have been taught by some itinerant master to sing in the worst manner a most wretched set of psalm tunes in three or four parts, so complex,

and so totally devoid of true harmony that it is altogether impossible for any of the congregation to take part with them.

In London and Westminster this business is in a great measure confined to charity children, who, though they exert their little abilities to sing their Maker's praises in the best manner they can, yet for want of right instruction to modulate their voices properly, almost constantly strain them to so high a pitch as to disgust and offend the ear and repel, instead of raising the devout attention of the hearers; and it is generally a contest between them and the organ which shall be the loudest and give most pain to the ear.

Significant improvement in church music generally had to await the wider renaissance in English music that began at the turn of the twentieth century, and even then the pace of progress varied considerably. Since there were upwards of 15,000 churches, most of these in rural areas, this is hardly surprising.

The report of an Archbishops' Committee, *Music in Worship,* published in 1922, occupied only 55 pages but was considered valuable enough to merit reprinting, with minor amendments, in 1932, 1938 and 1947. It did not comment directly on the state of the church's music at any of these times, but it emphasized the importance of high standards and warned against the 'trivial', 'tawdry', 'superficial', 'inherently poor', 'small minded' and 'cheaply sentimental'. This suggests enough of these musical vices as to require attention. The report also emphasized the importance of good congregational singing and in order to raise standards generally made a number of proposals, including the setting up of a Central Council on Church Music, diocesan music committees, and diocesan inspectors of choirs. Less ambitious perhaps was its suggestion of choral societies, day conferences, summer schools, music competitions and hymn festivals, though none of these were widely adopted – at least for several years. Interestingly, the report recommended that 'given the proper balance of harmony', the old village orchestras should be reinstated to accompany the hymns, the rest of the singing to be unaccompanied. The Committee, on which Sydney Nicholson served, did however prepare the ground for the inauguration of his Royal School of Church Music which achieved most of its aims.

The next official report, the work of another Archbishops' Committee, *Music in Church* (1951), indicated however that the notable efforts of Nicholson and the RSCM had borne only limited fruit. It spoke of the 'listlessness' of much parish worship and urged that church music should be 'noble and restrained' and never 'mawkish or sentimental or suggestive of secularity'. The 'noble language' of the Book of Common Prayer was extolled, as if its continuing use might be under threat. On a positive note, an improvement in taste and performance was recorded, though the Commission was worried about the problems of parish choir recruitment and a marked increase in the number of professional musicians leaving church posts. In spite of the RSCM's initiatives, lack of training facilities for church musicians remained a problem and the report ended by stressing the importance of maintaining voluntary church choirs, 'preferably with boys' voices'.

This proved to be much easier said than done. When the former choirmen returned from war service, few of them resumed their places in the choir stalls, and others, who were rebuilding their careers in the post-war world, found other claims on their time. The recruiting and retaining of boy choristers became even more difficult. Church schools, located in most parishes, had always been a reliable source of supply but, following a major reform of education, children moved at the age of 11 to larger state secondary schools, often several miles away from their homes. Rival attractions offered boys the choice of a range of alternative activities and school work was more demanding. Television offered greater excitement than most choir practices and after the 1950s declining congregations, combined with a wider acceptance of secular values, became a serious threat to recruitment.

In spite of all these problems, however, it was still possible in a significant number of places to retain, and even to build, a strong voluntary choir of men and boys. A local population of sufficient size to provide the requisite number of volunteers was an important factor. But even more important was the presence of a skilled, enthusiastic and imaginative organist and director of music. These could, and in many places still do, work wonders, often with no specially talented singers. The number of them, however, was also in decline and the deteriorating standard of music that resulted from the overall decline proved to be a deterrent to the recruitment of serious organists and choir members. Women and girls came increasingly to fill the vacant places and in many places to restore standards.

Meanwhile the energetic work of the Royal School of Church Music made a noticeable impact in the parishes keen enough to make use of its services. And a change of direction was required as an increasing number of parishes adopted the Eucharist as the chief act of Sunday worship. Choral Mattins disappeared very quickly and, although Evensong remained as an alternative option or a second service, it also went into decline, more slowly, yet inexorably, so that by the end of the century it was sometimes difficult to locate.

Enthusiastic choir members and those who valued tradition (usually the same people) lamented the loss of opportunity to sing the psalms and canticles, though the number of choirs that could chant them well was considerably smaller than the number of those who attempted them week by week. And the music for the Eucharist offered much less scope for a distinctive contribution by the choir, since there was a strong emphasis on simplicity and congregational participation. In some parishes questions were asked about the need for a choir at all, and there were suggestions that the presence of a robed choir might actually discourage congregations from wholehearted singing. More widely, serious questions were being raised, somewhat belatedly it might seem, about the wisdom of the church's faith in the nineteenth-century cathedral-style of worship as the pattern for the parish churches. Might not a small group of unrobed singers, placed in the middle of the congregation, be more effective?

None of which was encouraging to the musicians, and before long another unforeseen development raised even more difficult questions. The revived Evangelical movement which started in a small way in the 1960s began to grow rapidly, so that during the closing decades of the century it spread widely in the parishes and began to exert significant influence. Its approach to worship favoured the informal and the spontaneous and placed little, if any, value on the disciplined style of the traditional choir. Moreover, its new hymns and songs were designed for accompaniment by guitars, drums and other percussion instruments rather than by the organ. Before long, questions were being raised (though not in evangelical circles) about quality, appropriateness and standards, and it was not only the ultra-traditionalist and the pessimists who spoke of 'a losing battle'.

As early as 1970 Lionel Dakers, shortly to become a dynamic Director of the RSCM, lamented in an important book, *Church Music at the Crossroads*, 'That all is not well with the music of the church is evident to most of us. It is undervalued by the demise of many parish church choirs. Those responsible for the music are often discouraged and disheartened.' Almost a quarter of a century later, and in spite of the heroic efforts of Dakers and those he inspired to join him, the Archbishops of Canterbury and York prefaced the report of yet another Commission, *In Tune with Heaven* (1992), with a solemn assessment: 'The resources of the church for producing music are under pressure, and there is evidence in some circles that standards are falling and interest diminishing.' The distinguished Commission itself was equally realistic and reported, 'The maintenance of a traditional choir with a repertoire of traditional church music is becoming harder by the year.' But it also recognized, in a report that occupied 320 pages of analysis and recommendations, that 'in some respects music in the church continues to flourish', and it also acknowledged that the level of attainment in most cathedrals is 'probably higher than it has ever been'.

A series of statistics followed, based on a survey of 524 parishes, chosen scientifically to give reasonable representation of every type of parish – rural, urban, suburban; catholic, evangelical and central traditions. These indicated that 63 per cent of them had a choir and another 21 per cent a singing group; 79 per cent of the two categories wore robes of some sort. The average choir membership was 15 – 9 female and 6 male. Over two-thirds of the parishes had a director of music, ranging from the highly qualified organist to the pianist who did his or her best with an organ or an electronic keyboard. A majority (60 per cent) of those responsible for the music received payment, but this can never have been high, since the total expenditure on music was only £470 per annum in urban areas and £180 per annum in rural areas.

Underlying the Commission's recommendations was a constant emphasis on flexibility. Liturgical change, they insisted, had brought new possibilities for the use of music. The new and varied approaches to worship, involving new words, new hymns and service settings, a variety of instruments, all designed to meet differing needs and challenges, offer a great opportunity. How far the parish church choirs are ready and able to seize this opportunity is far from clear. But, whatever the outcome, the fact that in an increasingly secular age many thousands of dedicated amateur singers and instrumentalists are still ready to assist the church's worship through the gift of music is a matter for wonder and gratitude. Many of them would benefit from greater appreciation and encouragement.

8

John Stainer at St Paul's

John Stainer, the most prolific composer of late nineteenth-century church music, is generally remembered for the low quality of his anthems and service settings. Few commentators have a good word to say about his compositions. Professor Arthur Hutchings – no lover of Victorian composers – said that his work typified the shallowness of most of the music of the period and added, 'We ought to have sent most of it for pulping, and let us waste no time in delaying the pulping.' Even the more judicious Kenneth Long, in his masterly *The Music of the English Church* (1972), felt driven to conclude

> It seems all the more extraordinary that a man so cultivated and gifted should, as a composer, be so lacking in taste and discretion ... It is a tragedy that in most of his compositions he had only one idea in mind – to please. He had no burning passions or blinding visions demanding musical expression. Even self-criticism was suspended and in most of his anthems he sought no more than to gratify clerical friends and satisfy public demand by writing music which was sweetly melodious, harmonically obvious, rhythmically unadventurous and, above all, very easy and flattering to sing.

But composition was only one part of Stainer's work. He was a brilliant organist – perhaps the foremost of his day – he transformed the music and worship at St Paul's Cathedral, providing a model that every other cathedral was eventually moved to follow, and he also dragged the teaching of music at Oxford into the modern world. He was in fact an eminent musicologist and a distinguished scholar. It may also be added that he was one of the kindest and generous of men. Ruddy-faced, humble and unselfish, he was regarded with affection by his pupils, his professional colleagues, and more widely in the church.

Although the many hard words about Stainer's music cannot be ignored, it is important to remember the context in which he worked. When he began his career in the 1860s, church music was still at a low ebb. The Oxford Movement was making substantial progress in raising the standard of worship in the Church of England, but there was little music available to raise the hearts of worshippers. Stainer was among a small group of composers who sought to remedy this and, in his case, enthusiasm exceeded skill. He was not a reflective man and simply churned out whatever was in his mind at the moment. A country parson who requested something for Easter or the Harvest Festival would not be left disappointed, and would be sent something usable, even if the choice of words was no better than the music.

This raises the question, frequently asked by those responsible for the ordering of worship: is there any place for the 'sweetly melodious, rhythmically unadventurous and easy to sing'? A case in point is Stainer's own choral work *The Crucifixion*, which is widely condemned as second – or even third – rate, yet, since its composition in 1887, has never ceased to be performed in a multitude of churches and chapels during Lent and Holy Week – usually by choirs and choral societies which would not be capable of tackling one of the Bach Passions. An annual performance at St Marylebone Parish Church, which has strong associations with the Royal Academy of Music and where, under Stainer's baton, it was first heard, attracts a huge congregation. The anthem 'God so loved the world' from *The Crucifixion* is still among the most popular in parish church repertories. If those who attend claim to be spiritually enriched by their experience of the 'meditation', as he called it, what does this say about the music?

A survey carried out by John Patten and Steve Taylor in 1998 indicated that about 35 per cent of all cathedrals and choral foundations had during that year used Stainer's anthems 'God so loved the world', 'How beautiful are the mountains' and 'I saw the Lord'. In stark contrast, seven others of his anthems had been used by only one per cent. His canticles had been used in about 18 per cent, whereas in 1898 52 per cent used those in E flat, 38 per cent those in A, 33 per cent those in B flat.

Stainer's hymn tunes have suffered a marginally better fate. In 1900 he published 157 of these in one volume and in the preface anticipated the criticism that he had written too many by explaining that, almost without exception, they had been produced at the request of musical and clerical editors and personal friends. Even at the time of the book's appearance, a reviewer in the *Guardian* complained that the art of most of the tunes was elaborately bad: 'They seek the honeyed cadences and the profound phrase; they touch the surface of emotion but can never sound its depth.' It is not clear how many of the tunes went into common use, but 30 of them were included in the 1904 edition of *Hymns Ancient and Modern* and there are about 15 in modern hymnals – a fairly good survival rate for a Victorian composer. Among these are old favourites such as 'Come, thou long-expected Jesus', 'My God, I love thee not because I hope for heaven thereby', 'All for Jesus!', 'Love divine, all loves excelling' and 'Gracious Spirit, Holy Ghost'. And, since the singability as well as the appropriateness of a tune plays a large part in the popularity of hymns, it might well be thought that Stainer's contribution to Christian devotion has been not insignificant.

John Stainer, one of nine children, was born in Southwark, south London, in 1840. His father was a schoolmaster and gave him lessons on a small chamber organ installed in their home. As a result of an accident, young John lost the sight of an eye, but he was entered as a probationer at St Paul's in 1847 and admitted to the choir two years later. He proved to have an outstanding treble voice and was given much solo work in the choir, as well as being called upon to sing in the first public performance in England of Bach's *Magnificat* and his *St Matthew Passion*.

He also studied the organ under George Cooper, the sub-organist of St Paul's (his lessons being paid for by Maria Hackett, 'the choristers' friend'), and, although only 14, became organist of St Benet, Paul's Wharf, in the City of London. He was considered good enough to play for services in St Paul's whenever the organists were not available. It was on one such occasion in 1856 that Sir Frederick Ouseley heard him accompany Evensong and was so impressed that he invited him to become second organist at his newly founded St Michael's College, Tenbury – created to improve the standard of cathedral music.

He continued his organ studies there and in 1860 was appointed organist and 'informator choristarum' (choirmaster) at Magdalen College, Oxford, a year later becoming organist of the University Church, which carried the title Organist of the University of Oxford. He had taken a BMus in 1859 and now went on to complete an arts degree in 1864 and a doctorate of music in the following year. The presentation of part of his oratorio *Gideon*, which he composed for the doctorate, attracted so large an audience that it had to be transferred from Magdalen College Hall to the Sheldonian Theatre. Meanwhile the daily services in the college chapel demanded much of his time and, after a struggle, he managed to get most of the lay clerks to attend rehearsals. The result, according to a much later report in the *Manchester Guardian*, was that 'he raised the choir to a higher standard than had hitherto been known in the Anglican Church'.

Once his own academic studies were completed, Stainer played a very full part in the musical life of Oxford, conducting various musical societies and continuing his interest in madrigals and glees. He was responsible for the music at the laying of the foundation stone of Keble College, and when the Reid Professorship of Music fell vacant in 1865 it was only the casting vote of W. E. Gladstone that stood in the way of his appointment to the chair. Seven years later he returned to St Paul's as organist. Magdalen awarded him an Honorary Fellowship in 1892.

Shortly before Stainer's appointment, St Paul's had entered what turned out to be a new era following the appointment of the godly Richard Church as dean and the dynamic R. S. Gregory and H. P. Liddon as canons. They were joined later by the New Testament scholar J. B. Lightfoot and a reforming archdeacon; now the chapter was miraculously united in its determination to renew the cathedral's life. Liddon had worked with Stainer in Oxford and believed him to be exactly the right man to raise the music and worship from the deep trough of neglect in which it had long been languishing.

This called for heroic patience and diplomacy on Stainer's part. His official role was simply that of organist, with both the choice of music and the training of the choir in the hands of a minor canon who held the office of succentor. It was obvious that the choir was far too small for so huge a building, and the removal of the organ screen, separating the east end from the nave, made it virtually inaudible to congregations that now assembled under the dome and even further west. The chapter agreed to the recruitment of 12 more choristers and eight more vicars choral, bringing the size of the choir to 24 boys and 18 men, 12 of whom were required to be on duty at the weekday services. By 1875 the number of choristers, including probationers, had risen to 40 and Stainer managed not only to persuade the succentor to initiate a weekly choir rehearsal, for which he would himself be responsible, but also to insist that the choir move from their vestry to the stalls in procession, rather than simply donning their surplices while individually on the way. Most of the changes were effected by force of Stainer's personality, and the hitherto recalcitrant vicars choral were won over by his warmth and understanding of their needs. So also was the succentor, up to a point – this being when Stainer asked for a widening of the repertory to include the work of modern composers.

Progress proved to be costly to the reformer, however. After 18 months Stainer had a nervous breakdown, from which some thought he would never recover. A period of rest on the Isle of Wight, however, brought restoration of health and he resumed his transforming work. But then an injury to the eye in which he had retained his sight, sustained during a fives match with Ouseley at Tenbury, required a further six months absence. Soon after his return to duty the often uncooperative succentor retired and was succeeded in 1876 by the Revd William Sparrow-Simpson. He had been a minor canon since 1861 and before that devoted many years to recording and cataloguing the cathedral's important library. He served St Paul's from 1828 to 1897 and, proving to be a perfect partner to Stainer, made an outstanding contribution to the cathedral's life during the Victorian era.

Together, the two men, strongly supported by the dean and chapter, made St Paul's an exemplar of all that cathedral music and worship ought to be. A regular Choral Eucharist indicated the influence of the Oxford

Movement and, although not everyone who attended St Paul's welcomed the music of Mendelssohn, Gounod and other contemporary composers, the cathedral came to be regarded as one of the capital's important centres of music. Until Stainer arranged an annual Holy Week performance of Bach's *St Matthew Passion,* starting in 1873 with an orchestra of about 50 and a choir of 300, this great work was hardly known in London. At the performance of this and other oratorios he always insisted that the members of the orchestra should wear surplices to indicate that the event was an act of worship.

Stainer was one of the few professional organists of his, or any subsequent, time to recognize the importance of congregational singing. There was little scope for this at the statutory daily services, but the Sunday evening congregational service which had been instituted in 1861 was a different matter. A special choir, consisting of volunteer men and the cathedral choristers, led a service of popular hymns and chants which, together with outstanding preaching, attracted congregations of two or more thousand.

By 1888 Stainer's health was again giving cause for anxiety. His remaining good eye showed signs of failing, and the strains and stresses of ceaseless activity were taking their toll. So, although he was only 48, he resigned and was immediately knighted. His departure from St Paul's was greatly lamented – he was said to have changed for the better the entire life of the cathedral – but by this time news of his achievements was reaching many other cathedrals and inspiring their clergy and choral foundations.

Five years before his resignation Stainer had, obviously unwisely, accepted the post of Inspector of Music in the Training Colleges and Elementary Schools of the United Kingdom. He appointed two assistants, leaving himself free to concentrate on the training colleges, visiting, by train, 35 of the 43 in his first year. During the course of his annual tours he never examined fewer than 1,000 students and he carried on this work until the end of his life, exerting considerable influence on the teaching of music throughout the state educational system.

His main work, however, during the years following his departure from St Paul's, was that of Professor of Music at Oxford. Although there had in the past been many distinguished occupants of this chair, few had taken it seriously and even fewer chosen to reside in Oxford. Ouseley, Stainer's friend and predecessor, had done something to improve the teaching and the standards, but the need now was for someone to move into Oxford and devote himself to the gaining of respect for music as a valid subject of study and an integral element of the university's life. Stainer, his sight now recovered, threw himself into this task. His lectures, usually illustrated by a choir or a group of instrumentalists, were always crowded. He engaged specialists to lecture on particular subjects and widened the curriculum of the BMus and the DMus, thus encouraging more candidates. An entirely new development was the provision for practical instrument teaching. Arts undergraduates were given permission to attend these lessons in addition to their prescribed studies. Stainer's ambition to establish a university School of Music akin to the London colleges of music was, however, frustrated by opposition from the heads of houses.

He remained in Oxford following his retirement in 1899, continued as Inspector of Music and served as a sidesman, then as a churchwarden, of his parish church in Holywell. But he undertook very little public work and in March 1901 died suddenly while on holiday in Verona. Obituaries and editorials appeared in the main papers and many others, and Canon Henry Scott Holland, of St Paul's, expressed the hope that Stainer's

> great service to the cause of music in England may be neither underrated nor forgotten. He has helped to recreate and develop and elevate the general interest in music; and, as far as he has departed from the traditional type of Church music, his successful response to the demands of the changeful age in which he lived must give him a high place in that great line of which England has reason to be proud.

That proved to be far too indiscriminating and optimistic an assessment, and Stainer himself had no illusions about the quality of his work. Shortly before his death, he told E. H. Fellowes that he regretted having published so much, knowing well that most of his compositions were 'rubbish', and feared that his reputation might suffer because of their inferiority. It has, but it did not deserve to.

9

The Revival of English Music – Edward Elgar

Edward Elgar, one of the three internationally acclaimed British composers of the twentieth century – the others being Ralph Vaughan Williams and Benjamin Britten – wrote some deeply religious music, most notably *The Dream of Gerontius,* which is generally regarded as the greatest choral work of the century. Less significant, but still important, were his oratorios *The Apostles* and *The Kingdom.* There were also a number of fine anthems, but hardly any other church music.

This was almost certainly because, being a Roman Catholic by upbringing, and never going anywhere near the Oxbridge colleges or the London colleges of music, he was not in his formative years exposed to the Anglican choral tradition. The weakness of the musical resources of the Roman Catholic Church in England during his lifetime was hardly conducive to the composition of fine settings for the Mass and, in any case, his personal faith became less orthodox as he grew older. When in 1919 Sir Richard Terry, the organist of Westminster Cathedral, asked for a Mass, Elgar declined, saying that he could not undertake such a work unless in complete spiritual accord with the philosophy of the text.

His beautiful motet 'Ave verum corpus' was composed in its original form when he was still in his 20s, as was his even more beautiful 'Ecce Sacerdos Magnus'. Both had their first performances in St George's Roman Catholic Church in Worcester where his Protestant father was for many years the organist. During these early years he also composed several other motets and litanies which are of interest to Elgarian scholars but not now regarded as useable. In marked contrast, his anthem 'The Spirit of the Lord is upon me', the opening chorus of *The Apostles,* was sung in 60 per cent or more of British choral foundations in 1998, as was 'Ave verum corpus'. In the same year 'Give unto the Lord', an exuberant anthem composed for the 1914 Sons of the Clergy Festival in St Paul's Cathedral, was sung in 26 per cent of these foundations. 'O hearken thou', a deeply felt motet for the Coronation of King George V in 1911, 'Seek him that maketh the seven stars and Orion', from an oratorio first performed at the 1896 Three Choirs Festival in Worcester, and 'O salutaris hostia', another early piece, were also fairly widely used, and 15 items more here and there. A Te Deum and Benedictus in F, composed at the request of his friend G. R. Sinclair, who conducted them at the 1897 Three Choirs Festival in Hereford, were revived in several cathedrals in 1998.

If none of these works had ever been composed the world of church music would have been grievously impoverished. But Elgar's significance for music as a whole extends far beyond the strictly religious. It involves the revival and change of direction in British music that he initiated at the turn of the twentieth century. For more than 200 years, since the death of Henry Purcell in 1695, the music of this country had been virtually stagnant. No composer of international status had emerged and nearly all the great music performed was of foreign origin, mainly German and Italian. Elgar changed that and became the first British composer to write a symphony that stood alongside those of Beethoven and Brahms.

As a boy, Elgar had a very good teacher of the violin and he became an accomplished violinist, but as a composer he was entirely self-taught. During the time he worked in his father's music shop he took the opportunity to study the sheet music on sale and later acknowledged his indebtedness to the great composers of the nineteenth-century Romantic tradition. He also acquired some books on harmony and composition. But there were other influences. He used to say, 'The air is full of music and we take from it what we need', and for him the most stimulating air was what he breathed in the Worcestershire countryside where he was brought up and to which he often returned. The rushing water of the rivers, the sound of the wind in the bulrushes and the trees, the buzz of insects and the song of the birds all provided him with musical resources. The atmosphere of the Roman Catholic Church also influenced his religious music and when the Irish Protestant Stanford said of The Dream of Gerontius 'It stinks of incense', he had a point, though not one that many others would have regarded negatively.

Elgar was, it seems, particularly sensitive to the social climate of his time and was at his most creative during the vibrant Edwardian era that extended to the outbreak of war in 1914. His music has therefore always had wide popular appeal. Then there was an autobiographical influence – reflecting something of the strains and stresses, joys and sorrows within his own personality – and, overarching all, that mysterious power of visionary genius which inspires all great artists. Yet it was not until he was 40 that he made much of an impact. Born in the small village of Lower Broadheath in 1857 he was the fourth of the seven children of a piano-tuner and music dealer. When only eight he displayed unusual talent on the piano and the violin and his father gave him organ lessons. By the time he was 12 he had taught himself sufficient composition to produce the music for a local children's play, *The Wand of Youth*. (This was later revised and developed to form an orchestral work that had its first performance in the Queen's Hall, London, in 1907 under the conductorship of Sir Henry Wood.)

When he left school at 15, he was capable of playing the organ for Mass and other church services and ambitious enough to contemplate the possibility of going to Germany to study music at the Leipzig Conservatory. Lack of funds made this impossible so he went instead to work in a solicitor's office in Worcester. But he was totally unsuited to such an occupation and after six months he left to pursue a musical career, teaching violin and piano, and also lending a hand in his father's shop in Worcester. A little money was earned from performances at local concerts and other events, and he was accompanist for the local Glee Club.

In 1879 he became bandmaster of the Worcester and County Lunatic Asylum, which was hardly a prestigious appointment, but an enlightened management regarded music as an important element in the treatment of patients and some of Elgar's early compositions were in dance form for this purpose. By now the violin was his chief instrument and he played in orchestras at festivals in Worcester and Birmingham. It was a thrill to play under the direction of Antonín Dvořák who conducted some of his own works at the Worcester Three Choirs Festival in 1884, and Elgar's development as a composer was greatly influenced by him. A first visit to Germany the previous year had aroused his enthusiasm for Schumann and Wagner and he continued to compose chamber music and minor orchestral works. But none of this aroused much interest beyond the Midlands and, when attempts to break into the London scene failed, he wrote to his close friend Dr Charles Buck: 'My prospects are about as hopeless as ever. I am not wanting in energy, I think; so sometimes I conclude that 'tis want of ability and get into a mouldy despairing state which is really horrible.'

This 'mouldy, despairing state' recurred throughout his entire life. In spite of the international acclaim he eventually received and the many high honours that were heaped upon him, he remained wounded by the memory of his humble origins and the sense of rejection he experienced when his early work failed to win wide appreciation. He had periods of acute depression when he was morose and full of self-pity. Deep down he was insecure and felt inadequate. When later in life a writer described him as 'a disgruntled old man' this was probably more unkind than untrue. He was therefore exceedingly fortunate in his marriage to Alice Roberts in 1889. She was eight years older than he and went to him for piano lessons when he had extended his teaching work to Malvern. A daughter of the late Major General Sir Henry Roberts, she was used to living in some style and was known in literary circles as a poet and novelist. When engagement to Elgar was proposed, this met with strong resistance from her widowed mother and others in her family who objected to her marrying 'below her class'. Another obstacle was Elgar's lack of income, since his earnings were limited to those of a music teacher, and it took three years to overcome the opposition. His present to her when they were married quietly in Brompton Oratory was *Salut d'Amour*, which became the most popular of his short pieces. Once married, Alice never lost faith in her husband's genius and she sustained him through the many moments of despair when he was tempted to abandon his ambition to be a composer. She was also an invaluable critic of his work and, because of her background, had no difficulty in organizing the social life that attended his growing fame and entry into London society. When he hesitated over the acceptance of a knighthood in 1904, their only daughter Carice urged him on so that her mother might be restored to her former social status.

As the 1890s advanced, Elgar's reputation grew steadily, even if not sensationally. An oratorio, *The Light of Life*, was performed at the Worcester Three Choirs Festival in 1896. *Scenes from the Saga of King Olaf*, heard in London's Crystal Palace the following year, made some of the establishment critics take notice, but it was the *Imperial March* that made them really sit up. Composed for Queen Victoria's Diamond Jubilee in 1898, it was played by mass bands at the Crystal Palace, again at a Royal Garden Party, then at a state concert. *The Ballad of St George*, a ballad for chorus and orchestra, was another expression of his conservative connections and devotion to the Crown and marked the mood of the hour.

The real breakthrough came, however, in 1899 with *Variations on an Original Theme (Enigma)* – thereafter commonly known as the 'Enigma Variations'. This orchestral piece was quite unlike anything that had gone before and seemed to breathe the air of the Malvern Hills and the surrounding Worcestershire countryside. Many years after the first performance, Elgar explained that the work had begun in 'a spirit of humour'. He had evidently sat at his piano and improvised variations on a theme. These reflected something of the character of 12 friends he had seen recently; he said, 'I wrote what I think they would have written if they were asses enough to compose.' But what had begun humorously continued in 'deep seriousness', so that by the end it had become an acknowledged masterpiece and his best-loved orchestral work. It was dedicated to 'My friends pictured in them'.

The names of these friends were not disclosed but the inclusion of initials and pseudonyms offered clues and for a short time provided amusement for those who tried to work out their identities. It turned out that the first of the variations represented Alice, his wife, and the last himself. In between came George Sinclair, a close friend and the organist of Hereford Cathedral; A. J. Jaeger, the office manager of Novello, the publisher of his music; together with a country squire, an author and several local amateur musicians. Discerning the underlying 'enigma' (the word had been added to the score in pencil by the publisher and was said to refer only to the central theme, and not the variations) proved to be much less easy. It remains to be satisfactorily explained, and probably never will be; writing in *The Music Makers* (1912), Elgar confessed that the music of the theme 'symbolises the loneliness of the creative artist', but this is hardly an enigma.

Appended to the score was a setting of words adapted from Torquato Tasso, a sixteenth-century Italian poet: 'Bramo assai, poco spero, nulla chieggio' ('I long for much, I hope for little, I ask for nothing'), which may perhaps express something of the acute disappointment he had long felt at the general lack of appreciation of his work. But these depressing days were now ended – for a while. The first performance of the work, given in St James's Hall, London, under the baton of the eminent German conductor Hans Richter in 1899, was acclaimed and brought him instant fame in the musical circles of Britain, then of Germany and before long throughout the rest of Europe and in America.

This success was quickly followed by another. Ten years earlier a Roman Catholic priest gave Elgar as a wedding present a copy of Cardinal Newman's long poem *The Dream of Gerontius*, about a man who had led a worldly life and, when approaching death, became repentant. This appealed to the mystical side of Elgar and came to mean a great deal to him. It resulted in a work of deep spirituality, though its first performance at the annual Birmingham Festival in 1900 proved to be a musical disaster. The printed scores arrived late and reduced rehearsal time. The choice of soloists was wrong and some of the chorus were out of sympathy with the words. Distinguished though he was, Richter, the conductor, failed to get a grip on the work and the performance was twice on the verge of a complete breakdown – all in the presence of leading figures from the musical establishment who assembled for the occasion. The discerning members of the audience and the best of the critics recognized the importance of the new work, but Elgar was devastated by the general reaction to it and exclaimed: 'I always said that God was against art ... I have allowed my heart to open once – it is now shut against every religious feeling and every soft, gentle impulse for ever.'

Two highly acclaimed performances in Germany at the end of 1900 and in May 1902 gave him, however, the reassurance he needed, and after the second of these Richard Strauss, whose own music had influenced Elgar, proposed a toast to 'The first English progressivist, Meister Edward Elgar'. Writing about *The Dream* later, Strauss said that with it 'England for the first time became one of the modern musical states'. In September 1902 it made a deep impression when it was performed, under Elgar, at the Worcester Three Choirs Festival, as it did also a few months later at the first London performance in Westminster Cathedral. At Worcester,

Bishop Charles Gore (a notable Anglican theologian) objected to the content of Newman's poem, but the dean, using his authority over the life of the cathedral, allowed the performance to go ahead. For many Anglican and other Christians, Newman's belief in a God who dispenses cruel punishment continues to be a problem, but the beauty and wonder of the music tends to mask this and *The Dream* has a firm place in the repertory of every competent choral society.

In marked contrast to the character of these two great works, and of even wider appeal, are Elgar's *Pomp and Circumstance* marches, particularly No. 1 and No. 4, which captured perfectly the triumphalist atmosphere of the late Victorian–Edwardian era when the British Empire was at the peak of its dominating power in the world. Designed as military marches, No. 1 in D major was first performed in Liverpool, then at one of Sir Henry Wood's Queen's Hall Promenade Concerts in London in 1901. Elgar's prediction that No 1 'will knock 'em – knock 'em flat' was immediately fulfilled, as Henry Wood later recalled:

I shall never forget the scene at the close of the first of them ... The people simply rose and yelled. I had to play it again – with the same result; in fact they refused to let me get on with the programme ... I went off and fetched Harry Dearth who was to sing *Hiawatha's Vision* but they would not listen. Merely to restore order I played the march a third time.

Soon after this Elgar was commissioned to compose something for a state performance at Covent Garden on the eve of King Edward's Coronation in 1902. The King had previously suggested that the trio air from No. 1 ought to be sung and Elgar took the opportunity to adapt words from a 'Coronation ode' by A. C. Benson (one of Archbishop Edward White Benson's sons) to create the song 'Land of hope and glory'. The fact that words and music did not quite fit did not hinder its spreading like wildfire throughout the country and, in common with Parry's 'Jerusalem' and the National Anthem itself, it is one of the noble, singable items that express nationalist sentiment on a wide variety of occasions. March No. 4 is of a similar style, but more subdued, while Nos 2 and 3 are in a minor key. No. 5 in C major is different again and was composed much later in 1930. The overture *Cockaigne* (1901), with its evocation of military bands marching through the streets of London, also provides stirring music and Elgar said, 'It is intended to be honest, healthy, humorous and strong, but not vulgar.' And the Coronation of King George V in 1911 was marked by a fairly long *Coronation* march, which combines the majestic and the melancholic.

The 1914–18 war affected Elgar deeply. He joined the Special Constabulary, becoming a staff inspector and, besides a number of minor war-related works, composed a setting of Laurence Binyon's poem 'The Spirit of England'. This was performed in separate parts, as the music was completed, and the greatest impression was made by that which begins 'They shall grow not old ...'. Although 'Land of Hope and Glory' became even more widely sung during the war years, Elgar's music during this period was sombre. It expressed the pity, rather than the glory, of war. He became seriously depressed and for a long time composed nothing.

In the early part of the Edwardian era Elgar's oratorios *The Apostles* (1903) and *The Kingdom* (1906), inspired by Handel's *Messiah*, were designed as a trilogy (the third was never completed) to express more of the foundation years of the Christian church. The first dealt with Christ's call of the disciples and his teaching in Galilee and Jerusalem, while the second was based on the church's mission to the Gentiles. The libretto for each was compiled by Elgar himself and the fruit of considerable research into the New Testament and the reading of several commentaries. Although of modest education, he was probably the best-read musician of his time. He also benefited from the guidance of Canon Charles Gorton, the Vicar of Morecambe, with whom he had a close friendship, established while adjudicating a music festival in the town. The third would have dealt with the universal church.

Although the first performance of *The Apostles,* again at a Birmingham Festival, was very well done and acclaimed by the critics (the *Daily Telegraph* declared it to be 'Perhaps the most remarkable work of the present century') it did not arouse the same excitement as *The Dream of Gerontius*. Neither did *The Kingdom,* which Sir Adrian Boult, no less, described as 'a finer work than *Gerontius*', but they were enthusiastically received in New York, Chicago, Cincinnati and Pittsburgh when Elgar conducted them there. Part of the problem turned out to be that they are difficult to perform well and Michael Kennedy has pointed out that they consist of a series of separate items and lack the unifying power of Newman's poem. Nonetheless they continue to make an important contribution to Three Choirs Festivals and, along with *Messiah* and *Elijah*, are often tackled by local choral societies.

Soon after a visit to Rome in May 1908 Elgar began work on his Symphony No. 1 in A flat major. This occupied him for the next three months and its first performance in the Free Trade Hall at Manchester in December of that year proved to be another important turning point in the development of English music. At the end of the first movement the excited audience broke into such sustained applause that the conductor (Richter) felt obliged to bring Elgar on to the stage. The *Manchester Guardian*'s critic said, 'The work is the noblest ever penned for instruments by an English composer we are quite certain.' The next performance, four days later, in London's Queen's Hall, was received with no less enthusiasm.

At the rehearsal Richter, who was again conducting, said to the London Symphony Orchestra players, 'Gentlemen, let us now rehearse the greatest symphony of modern times, and not only in this country.' After the first movement Elgar was called to the platform to acknowledge the applause, several times more after the third, and after the finale the entire audience, together with the orchestra, rose to its feet in a frenzy of excitement, five times demanding the reappearance of the composer. During 1909 it was played 82 times worldwide, including 17 performances in London, besides others in America, Vienna, Berlin, Bonn, Leipzig, St Petersburg and Sydney. Everywhere it was received with a mixture of admiration and awe and the only sour note was struck by the notoriously testy English conductor, Thomas Beecham, who described it as 'neo-Gothic, the equivalent of the tower of St Pancras Station'. Many believe Symphony No. 2 in E flat major (1911) to be an even greater work, though it did not make the same initial impact, and the audience at its second performance was quite small. It was not until the end of the 1914–18 war that it came into its own.

Beecham was not alone in his outspoken criticism of his contemporaries. When Elgar unwisely accepted the chair of music at Birmingham University in 1903, his inaugural lecture complained, 'Our English composers too frequently write their works as if for an audience of musicians only.' In a later lecture he declared, 'Too many brainless singers; too many conductors (organist-conductors or composer-conductors) who if they must keep time at all would do it most successfully in a factory yard.' None of which went down well with the musical establishment and the ensuing national controversy took its toll on his health for a time so that he was unable to compose. The post eventually became too much of a burden and he gave it up in 1908. What had been a good relationship with Stanford was already broken, but this was almost certainly the result of Stanford's own fractious nature; he sooner or later fell out with everyone.

The first performance of a Violin Concerto in B minor in 1910, when Fritz Kreisler, one of the greatest ever violinists, was the soloist, had aroused enthusiasm not far short of that which had greeted the first symphony. Kreisler told Elgar, after playing it for the first time, 'You have written an immortal work.' In 1932 Elgar chose 16-year-old Yehudi Menuhin to make what became a classic recording of the work and it remains one of the great works for the violin.

A Cello Concerto in E minor, first performed in 1919, was quite different from any of his previous compositions. Subdued, and at times melancholic, bitter even, and lacking any ray of hope, Michael Kennedy, while recognizing it as one of the greatest works for the cello, described it as 'the voice of an ageing, desolate man, a valediction to an era and to the powers of music that he knew were dying with him'. It is nonetheless tremendously popular today. The death of Alice the following April left

Elgar devastated and marked the end of his own life as a leading composer. During what were to all intents and purposes his retirement years, Elgar continued in the lifestyle of an Edwardian country squire that he had adopted in middle-age. His face was adorned by a massive moustache and the garden of his fine Worcestershire house provided ample space for his dogs to roam. George Bernard Shaw, a close friend of his later years, said that Elgar's music was that of an English gentleman. Much earlier he had sometimes been mistaken for the Royal Duke of Cambridge, for many years the head of the British Army. None of which impeded the enjoyment of close friendships with a number of women, particularly Lady Stuart Wortley. These were tolerated by Alice, partly because she recognized his need, but chiefly because she realized that they posed no threat to her marriage.

He conducted a series of notable recordings of his own works and, shortly before his own death in February 1934, embarked on a third symphony which was not completed, at least not by him. In 1998, and with the permission of the Elgar Trustees who were acting contrary to his stated wishes, a performance of the symphony, completed in the Elgarian style by Anthony Payne, was given in London and considered by many to be successful.

Elgar received honorary degrees from many British and European universities and, besides the 1904 knighthood, was admitted to the Order of Merit in 1911, appointed Master of the King's Music in 1924, created a baronet in 1931, and made a Knight Grand Commander of the Victorian Order in 1933. But the peerage for which he had long angled was denied him and he harboured a constant fear that the fame that eventually came to him after many earlier disappointments would one day forsake him. It is perhaps just possible that had he lived to see the appearance of his portrait on a £20 bank note in the 1990s he would have been assured that his high place in the history of British music was secure. He is also memorialized by a stained-glass window in Worcester Cathedral, by a statue outside, and by an inscribed stone in Westminster Abbey.

10

Glad, Confident Morning

Hubert Parry

While it may be easy to exaggerate the part played by Hubert Parry in the renaissance of English music at the end of the nineteenth century, there can be no doubting his influence at that time, not least on those he taught, some of whom are numbered among the most important musicians of the twentieth century. His own prodigious output of secular music has been largely forgotten, but the small amount of church music he composed remains a source of inspiration for those who attend Choral Evensong in the Anglican cathedrals of the English speaking world.

Charles Hubert Hastings Parry was born in Bournemouth in 1848 and his mother died a few days after his birth. The family was wealthy and he was brought up by his father, a painter and art collector, at Higham Court, a country house in Gloucestershire. He attended Twyford Preparatory School, near Winchester, where he met Samuel Sebastian Wesley, at that time organist of Winchester Cathedral, and was encouraged by the headmaster to develop his evident musical gifts. At Eton, where he also earned a high reputation on the playing fields, he was taught by Sir George Elvey, the then organist of St George's Chapel, Windsor. While in the sixth form, he caused astonishment by taking the Oxford BMus with a cantata 'O Lord Thou hast cast us out', thus becoming the youngest ever successful candidate.

At Exeter College, Oxford, he read law and modern history but had no significant music training, though he was closely involved with John Stainer in the college music society. More important, however, was a visit to Stuttgart during his first long vacation, in the summer of 1867, where he studied composition under Henry Hugo Pierson, learned German and how to play the viola, and orchestrated one of his own early piano sonatas. This was subsequently given its first performance, under the baton of S. S. Wesley, at a Three Choirs Festival in Gloucester.

By the time he left Oxford he had fallen in love with Lady Maud Herbert, whose parents, when they learned of their secret engagement, strongly opposed his intention to pursue a career as a musician, as did his own father. He therefore embarked on a career in the City of London as a

Lloyds' underwriter, but continued to study music, first under the highly regarded William Sterndale Bennett, which proved to be unsatisfactory, then with a celebrated pianist, Edward Dannreuther, who became a close lifelong friend. His influence was important, for he introduced him to the work of Wagner and to Wagner himself, whom he met several times at the Bayreuth Festival in Germany and also in London.

In 1875 Parry became a part-time sub-editor of George Grove's projected *Dictionary of Music* and contributed a number of articles to its many volumes. Two years later, it now being necessary for him to earn his living from music, he embarked on a full-time musical career. Dannreuther helped by introducing him to London's musical circle, as he began to compose symphonies and other music, which aroused interest without taking the capital by storm. Combined with his scholarly articles for the *Dictionary*, they were however good enough to earn him a Cambridge DMus in 1883 and appointment as Professor of Music History at the newly founded Royal College of Music. He also began teaching at Oxford and Birmingham, where both universities honoured him with a doctorate.

He belonged clearly to the nineteenth-century Romantic tradition and some of his work up to this point was heavily criticized as being reactionary. But he was unusual in his displaying the influence not only of Wagner but also of Brahms. In retrospect it is apparent that there was sufficient originality in his work to prepare the way for the more significant twentieth-century developments led by Elgar, Vaughan Williams, Holst, Walton and Finzi.

The breakthrough with Parry's own work came in 1887, when he accepted a commission from a colleague at the Royal College of Music, Charles Villiers Stanford, for the Bach Choir's celebration of Queen Victoria's Golden Jubilee. This resulted in the composition of *Blest Pair of Sirens* – a setting of a Milton ode which created a tremendous impression and quickly entered the repertory of cathedral choirs, where it still remains. Ralph Vaughan Williams, who, in company with Gustav Holst and Herbert Howells, was a pupil of Parry, said, towards the end of his own life, 'I fully believe, and keeping in mind the achievements of Byrd, Purcell and Elgar, that *Blest Pair of Sirens* is the finest musical work that has come out of these islands.'

More commissions now flooded in and, by the time of his death in 1918, Parry had composed over 200 items, including five symphonies, three oratorios – *Judith* (1888), *Job* (1892), *King Saul* (1894) – one (unsuccessful) opera, 74 songs, published in 12 volumes of *English Lyrics*, 30 choral works and a few hymn tunes. Besides this he had been Director of the Royal College of Music (1895–1918), Professor of Music at Oxford (1900 until obliged by a period of ill health to resign in 1908), written three important books – *The Art of Music* (1893), volume 3 of *The Oxford History of Music* (1906) and *Style in Musical Art* (1911) – and been involved, usually as chairman, in most of the influential music societies and charities of his time.

It was, however, his accession, in succession to Grove, to the directorship of the Royal College of Music in 1895 that many believed to be responsible for the disappointing quality of many of his later compositions. Some said that he was hobbled by his appointment as he devoted so much time to teaching, examining and the necessary administration. He was more than generous in the time, and often the money, he gave to his pupils and one of them, Gustav Holst, said, 'At last I had met a man who did not terrify me. He gave me a vision, rather than a lecture.'

Parry had an attractive personality, and was generally charming, which made it all the more surprising, and sad, that towards the end of his life his relations with his colleague Stanford were strained to breaking point. He also had an unhappy marriage, due, it might seem, to too early a commitment to Maude who, according to his son-in-law Arthur Ponsonby, 'hampered him, rebuked him, bullied him and was a drain on him', yet he remained devoted to her. He was a prominent member of the establishment during Queen Victoria's later years and, having received a knighthood from her, was given a baronetcy immediately after Edward VII's coronation. Yet he was not conservative, socially or politically. He strongly supported Gladstone's Liberal governments and at the opening of a new organ he had presented to the Shire Hall at Gloucester during a Three Choirs Festival there he declared in a fiery speech, 'Music is too much the prerogative of the well-to-do, and I hope this organ will bring it within the experience of others.'

His religious beliefs were quite a long way from orthodox Christianity and were characterized by a mixture of agnosticism and rationalism, fused with love of the Anglican liturgy. This makes it somewhat ironic that virtually the only music of his now performed is that which the churches have recognized as being deeply religious, except perhaps 'There is an old belief'. He rarely missed a Three Choirs Festival.

No less frequently used than *Blest Pair of Sirens* as an anthem at cathedral Evensong are some of his *Songs of Farewell*, which were composed between 1916 and 1918 and are generally regarded as his masterpieces. The glorious anthem 'I was glad', composed for the coronation of King Edward VII and on its first performance sung twice because the time of the king's arrival at Westminster Abbey had been misjudged, now seems an immoveable part of the coronation rite, as well as a grand element for other ceremonial occasions elsewhere. Parry's tune for the hymn 'O praise ye the Lord', originally written as conclusion to his fine anthem 'Hear my words, ye people', composed for a Salisbury diocesan festival, has never been seriously challenged, though it was offered as a second choice in the 1922 standard edition of *Hymns Ancient and Modern*. The tune for

'Dear Lord and Father of mankind', which he adapted from his oratorio *Judith*, continues to maintain his influence far beyond the confines of the churches. Even more so, 'Jerusalem', set to William Blake's mystical poem for a 'Fight for Right' meeting in London's Queen's Hall, and sung again at a great meeting in the Albert Hall in 1918 to mark the granting of votes for women, has become a second national anthem. This guarantees Parry the somewhat dubious honour of a permanent place in the programme of 'The Last Night of the Proms' when 'Jerusalem' is roared by thousands in the Albert Hall. Its adoption by the Women's Institute and rejection by fastidious clergy suggests that the religious content is questionable. None of his other handful of hymn tunes ever caught on, which may have more to do with the words than with the music, but some of his organ music, all of fine quality, is still regularly played. His haunting *Elegy* is perfect before a funeral or a service of thanksgiving.

Charles Villiers Stanford

It is not necessary to believe with Professor Arthur Hutchings that Stanford was the first important church musician since seventeenth-century Henry Purcell in order to recognize that he made a major and lasting contribution to Anglican worship and set a standard against which the work of other composers has subsequently been judged. Church music was in fact only a small part of Stanford's astonishingly large output, but it has survived best and is still constantly used in cathedrals and other large churches.

In contrast with the Victorian church musicians, Stanford's work exhibited an uplifting brilliance. He was exceptionally well versed in the work of the great European composers. He was a master of melody, created anthems and service settings with a unified structure, rather than a sequence of individual items, and knew how to relate notes to words in a way that was illuminating, rather than confusing. The result is a distinctive style that is immediately recognizable and invariably welcome.

Charles Villiers Stanford was born in Dublin in 1852. His father was an eminent lawyer and both parents were enthusiastic amateur musicians. The home was a centre of Dublin's intellectual and cultural life and young Charles, who displayed precocious musical talent, had access to the leading teachers of the city, most influentially Sir Robert Stewart, the organist of St Patrick's Cathedral. He was also taught by a professional pianist and a singer, and when only nine gave a public piano recital of works by Bach, Handel, Mozart and Beethoven.

Attendance at Dublin's Theatre Royal gave him a lifelong love of opera and visits to London with his parents enabled him to go to concerts at

Crystal Palace and also to receive specialist tuition in composition and the piano. In 1870 he went to Queens' College, Cambridge, as a classical and organ scholar but while, for want of interest and time, he took only a Third in Classics he made such an impression with his music that when still an undergraduate he was appointed organist of Trinity College and in 1873 conductor of the University Musical Society – a position he held for the next 20 years.

By arrangement with Trinity he was free to use part of the years 1874–76 to visit the great music centres of Europe, studying under two distinguished teachers in Leipzig, and also in Berlin. When he reached Cambridge as an undergraduate, he had already composed several short pieces and now began to produce larger works, including his First Symphony, which won second prize in a national competition for British composers in 1876. A year earlier a piano suite and a toccata signalled to the music world that a new talent had appeared.

An oratorio, *The Resurrection*, was followed by incidental music for Tennyson's drama *Queen Mary,* a *Festival Overture* for the Three Choirs' Festival at Gloucester and an opera *The Veiled Prophet of Khorassan,* which was first performed in Hanover in 1881. In Cambridge the reputation of the University Musical Society was considerably advanced under his leadership – he had organizational as well as musical skills – and the first performances in Britain of Brahms's work took place under his baton. He also attracted to Cambridge leading composers and performers from various parts of Europe and the Society was used for first performances of his own new works.

In 1882 he resigned from his Trinity College post because of the other heavy demands on his time and in the following year was appointed Professor of Composition and Orchestral Playing at the Royal College of Music and also conductor of the College orchestra – posts he held until 1912. He was conductor of the Bach Choir from 1885 to 1902, and in 1887, still only 35, he was appointed Professor of Music at Cambridge, occupying the chair until his death in 1924 and managing to persuade the university authorities to require residence of those taking the MusBac.

His own output of music, extending to about two hundred works, included seven symphonies, three piano concertos, two violin and one clarinet concertos, five operas, eight string quartets, forty choral works, much other chamber music, many songs, five collections of Irish folk melodies and a great deal of piano and organ music. Many of the first performances of his works were given by leading players and none was of less than the highest quality, but they never really caught on and as the twentieth century progressed his style went out of fashion; apart from his church music, little is heard of them today. One of his symphonies was, however, included in the 2008 BBC Prom concerts.

Opera was his first and last love and he regarded his own operas as his most important work. These were highly regarded in his own time and some were performed in European capitals but, again, none is in the current operatic repertory and all await a revival of their style. He started an opera class at the Royal College of Music and tried to get the London County Council to inaugurate a National Opera, but in this he was too far ahead of his time and remained disappointed.

Stanford's influence over his pupils must be regarded as his greatest legacy. He was utterly intolerant of anything related to music that could be judged careless or second-rate and offenders quickly became aware of his sharp tongue. On the other hand, he could show students great kindness and took unusual pains with those who combined talent with a willingness to work. Among these were most of the great twentieth-century musicians, who carried forward the creative movement he had been largely responsible for initiating – Charles Wood, Frank Bridge (the teacher of Benjamin Britten), Walford Davies, Herbert Howells, Gustav Holst, John Ireland and Ralph Vaughan Williams, all of whom acknowledged their indebtedness to him.

As with some other musicians of his time, it is his church music that has continued to be valued and kept in use. His Evening Service in B flat never fails to thrill and inspire and, in company with Charles Wood's Service in D, seems to many to represent the epitome of Church of England worship. He composed it in 1879 for use by the choir of Trinity College, Cambridge, and it immediately set a new, and much higher, standard for cathedral choirs and other churches with adequate choral resources.

A lovely anthem, 'The Lord is my Shepherd', and three beautiful motets, 'Justorum animae', 'Coelos ascendit' and 'Beati quorum' – all composed for use as graces in Trinity College Hall – soon followed. A magnificent Evening Service in A, first sung in the college chapel, is still standard in the cathedral repertory. It was next sung with an orchestral accompaniment at an annual Festival of the Sons of the Clergy in St Paul's. The brilliant Services in G and C came much later. A superb setting of the 'Gloria in excelsis', composed for the coronation of King George V in 1911, was used again at the coronations of George VI and the present Queen. The anthems 'O for a closer walk with God', 'Ye choirs of new Jerusalem' and 'How beauteous are their feet' are still regularly sung by many cathedral choirs, as is his setting for the Eucharist in C. His hymn tunes were perhaps too highbrow ever to become popular, and the 1904 edition of *Hymns Ancient and Modern*, on the musical committee of which he sat in company with Walter Parratt and Charles Wood, was a spectacular failure.

Unbelievably, he found time to write a number of important books – a biography of Brahms (1912), a much-used textbook *Musical Composition*

(1911), *Pages from an Unknown Diary* (1914), *A History of Music* (1916) and two collections of essays. Besides these he contributed innumerable articles and essays to periodicals and reviews.

It would be good to complete this brief life by recording that Stanford exuded charm and made delightful company, but this is not possible. He was not popular. Tall, short-sighted, possessed of a sharp mind and a coruscating wit, and always conscious of his Irish identity, he had a fiery temperament and was notoriously intolerant, especially of modern music. He was once described as 'the most hated man in the country'. But he was awarded doctorates by Oxford, Cambridge, Durham and Leeds universities and by Trinity College, Dublin.

Charles Wood

There was nothing remotely showy or prima donna-like about Charles Wood, who was one of the finest and most prolific musicians of his time. For much of his life he was overshadowed by Stanford, whose star pupil he had been at the infant Royal College of Music in the 1880s. This did not trouble him. The teaching of music was an integral part of his vocation and, since Stanford was, for many years, a largely absentee Professor of Music at Cambridge, it fell to Wood to carry the burden of music teaching in the university. He was also responsible for the development of musical studies, but when eventually he succeeded Stanford in the chair in 1924 he was already in failing health and died two years later.

His influence on the development of English music was profound. Among his pupils in Cambridge and at the Royal College of Music, where he also taught, were Thomas Beecham, Herbert Howells, Ralph Vaughan Williams and Michael Tippett. In an affectionate tribute to him in a volume of essays on English Church Music published by the Royal School of Church Music in 1966, Herbert Howells wrote:

> Even when a man has had the luck to have studied with Stanford, Parratt, Walford Davies and less 'officially', with Parry, Holst and Vaughan Williams, he could still find it possible to rate Charles Wood the most completely equipped teacher in his experience. On the day of my entering the R.C.M. as 'the new composition scholar', in 1912, Sir Hubert Parry greeted me with what he bluntly called 'surprisingly good news'. He told me that he had arranged my going to Wood 'for counterpoint'. So it was.

Woods' work as a composer was by no means confined to church music. He composed some string quartets and his output of songs and part songs was enormous. Towards the end of his life he composed a regimental march for the Royal Corps of Signals. But it is for his church music that he is best remembered and some of his work remains in regular use by every cathedral choir and those parish churches with adequate resources for its performance. (His eight-part setting of John Keble's translation of a third-century Greek hymn 'Hail, gladdening light' is a perfect example of this.) He had a deep sensitivity to what kind of music would best serve the church's liturgy and an instinctive feel for what would sound right in an English cathedral.

A casual attender at Choral Evensong who was fortunate enough to encounter the setting Wood in D, and his glorious anthem 'O Thou the central orb', could hardly fail to believe that he or she had experienced something quite special. No less memorable, but totally different in atmosphere, would have been the combination of Wood in E minor and the exquisite 'Expectans expectavi', in which the composer is reacting to the tragic deaths in the 1914–18 war of both his own eldest son and that of a close personal friend, Charles Hamilton Sorley, whose poetry provided the words for his anthem. Again, had the cathedral visitor chosen Easter Day, Wood's anthem ''Tis the day of resurrection' would have left him or her in no doubt as to the significance of that day's celebrations. He composed over 20 Evensong settings of which, besides that in D, double choir settings in F (written for King's College, Cambridge) and G are the most important. His beautiful Communion settings are little used.

Charles Wood, the fifth of 14 children, was born in Armagh, Northern Ireland, in 1866. His father, also Charles, was a lay clerk of St Patrick's Cathedral and became diocesan registrar and private secretary to the archbishop. It was a musical household, all the boys sang in the cathedral choir and two other members of the family became professional musicians.

Young Charles was taught piano, organ, harmony and counterpoint at the cathedral choir school, and in 1882 he won a foundation scholarship to the Royal College of Music in London, which had recently been created from the National Training School for Music. Shortly before his seventeenth birthday he began to study composition with Parry and Stanford, and counterpoint with Frank Bridge. He also learned to play the French horn and the piano, and later adopted the organ as his second co-instrument.

The influence on him of Parry and Stanford was considerable but at the personal level he was closest to Sir George Grove, the founding Director of the College. He worked hard, formed a string quartet and was soon recognized as a gifted composer. When only 19 he composed 'O Lord, rebuke me not' – the first of several anthems based on sixteenth- and seventeenth-century metrical psalms – and this has been sung by cathedral choirs ever since. In the following year he composed a piano concerto.

In 1888 he went to Selwyn College, Cambridge, as organ scholar, but 12 months later moved to a better organ scholarship at Gonville and Caius College. He continued to attend the Royal College of Music, however, to benefit from Stanford's teaching. He also became involved in the Cambridge University Musical Society, acted as bandmaster for the University Volunteers and established a position in the Cambridge music world that rapidly developed and extended over the next 38 years.

Following his graduation as BA and MusB in 1890, he was appointed college organist of Caius and in 1894 was elected to a Fellowship – the first occasion on which a Cambridge college had elected a Fellow in Music. In the same year he was awarded a MusD, and at the conferring of the degree the choir of Caius, which was now second only to King's in its reputation, sang his composition for the Greek play of that year. A college orchestra, founded in 1896, gave the first performance of his *Symphonic Variations on an Irish Air*. He was appointed university lecturer in harmony and counterpoint and in 1898 married Charlotte Wells-Sandford, also a musician.

The remainder of his life was spent in Cambridge – teaching, examining and composing – but he returned once a week to the Royal College of Music, which he had not really left since he entered its doors as a young student. He greatly valued as a colleague and friend Ralph Vaughan Williams, one of his former pupils. Harmony and counterpoint were always his chief teaching subjects, of which he became the professor, but he developed an interest in Tudor music, which he was pleased to share with others and which had some influence on his own composition.

Wood's original intention had been to compose for the concert hall and the stage and most of his earliest work was in those fields, but for some reason – possibly his busy teaching life or maybe the constant demand for choral works – he did not continue in these directions. His one substantial orchestral work, *Patrick Sarsfield: Symphonic Variations on an Irish Air,* was followed by a series of string quartets but none of these compositions made a lasting impact.

His most substantial contribution to church music was his *St Mark Passion,* the idea for which came from Eric Milner-White, who was at that time the Dean of King's College, Cambridge, and in a nursing home recovering from an appendix operation. He was looking for an alternative to the Bach Passions, which he believed to be unsuitable for the King's chapel and choir, and devised a libretto based on St Mark's Passion narrative. Instead of arias, as in Bach, he envisaged after each of the five sections a chorus and a congregational hymn. Wood readily collaborated with Milner-White in the production of a Passion that they believed would be valued, not only by King's but also by good parish church choirs seeking a change from Stainer's *Crucifixion.* In spite of its very high quality, however, it has yet to become widely performed, choral societies and other larger forces being recruited to render Bach or sometimes, as an alternative, Handel's *Messiah*. This is a loss, as also is the fact that very little of Wood's music has been recorded.

Another fruitful partnership was with the Revd G. R. Woodward, a scholar parish priest, who in the 1890s pioneered the revival of the carol. The two men became close friends, and Wood contributed harmonizations to many of the traditional carols published in new collections, notably 'This joyful Eastertide', 'Ding dong merrily on high', 'Shepherds in the field abiding', and 'Past three o'clock'. He was co-editor of the *Cowley Carol Book* and of the *Cambridge Carol Book* (1924). He was also a member of the music committee of the 1904 edition of *Hymns Ancient and Modern* and composed many hymn tunes, though few of these achieved any degree of popularity.

Wood's knowledge of music was encyclopaedic and musicologists seeking to check a fact or a reference never turned to him in vain. A dapper little man, who was prematurely bald, he wore a substantial moustache and, as he grew older, became increasingly shy and somewhat eccentric. Those closest to him said that he never recovered from the wartime death of his elder son, and his brief tenure of the Cambridge Chair of Music was dogged by ill-health until his death from cancer in 1926. In a personal memoir in the *Musical Times* one of his pupils, Margaret Hayes Nesik, wrote: 'Charles Wood did not shine like a sun on the international scene. He was one of those steadfast, true musicians of whom England has produced so many to her glory, who shone their light on those around them.'

11

The Abbey Comes Alive – Frederick Bridge

Frederick Bridge was at Westminster Abbey from 1875 to 1918 and during this time not only brought the Abbey's music into the modern world but also helped to raise the status of the professional organist in the eyes of both the church and the realm of music. His close friend, John Stainer, was making a similar impact at St Paul's, and during the Edwardian era Bridge became a highly regarded member of the English Establishment, showered with honours, and a familiar figure in London aristocratic circles, as well as a leader of its musical life.

When he was appointed to the Abbey at the early age of 31, he found the music at a very low ebb. His predecessor, James Turle, had been there for 44 years (60 if his time as an organ pupil and assistant is counted) and although a fine organist, albeit of the legato eighteenth-century style, he had been quite unable to raise the standard of the choir from the trough into which it had descended during the previous 100 years. Nonetheless, some of his psalm chants are still in use, as is one of his hymn tunes, 'Westminster', usually sung to 'My God, how wonderful thou art'.

The Dean of Westminster, Arthur Penrhyn Stanley, responsible for Bridge's appointment, was one of the great Victorian churchmen and a reformer. He introduced the performance of oratorios into the Abbey, and led the way in initiating special services for important events and commemorations, but had little interest in the music used in the regular round of daily worship. Much more alarming than this, however, was the irregular attendance and total lack of discipline of the lay vicars, some of whom also sang at the Chapel Royal. The four who sang at the daily Evensong were inclined to leave Abbey services before these ended in order to discharge their other responsibilities. Throughout the nineteenth century Westminster Abbey, St Paul's Cathedral and the Chapel Royal shared what was in fact a single choir, this being augmented by a large number of deputies who appeared in the different buildings to substitute for the official absentees. Part of the explanation of this was the meagre pay of lay vicars, who needed several appointments to make ends meet, and, since they held freehold offices with neither compulsory retirement age nor pension, many of them appeared in the choir stalls long after their voices had seriously declined. One of their number, approaching 70, had for many years been apportioned a solo part in Handel's *Messiah* and, when Bridge suggested diplomatically that he might give way to a younger voice, he aroused the anger of the old soloist, who was supported by the precentor, the dean and other members of the choir. Another lay vicar, who as a boy had sung at the funeral of King William IV in 1837, was still in the choir at the coronation of King Edward VII in 1902.

The choristers inherited by Bridge were, in fact, well trained, but they were day boys, there being no choirhouse, and their education, entrusted to one schoolmaster, was only fair. There were other problems, including the deplorable condition of the organ and the fact that for the first 20 years of his reign Bridge had no assistant and was bound to discharge his responsibilities single-handed. And this in spite of the fact that he needed to undertake many outside engagements to augment his meagre salary.

Fortunately, Bridge had inexhaustible energy, as well as burning ambition. No less fortunate was the fact that his arrival at the Abbey coincided with a turning of the tide in the direction of reform throughout the church. Dean Stanley, who was at Westminster from 1864 to 1881, breathed new life into the Abbey, opening its doors to people of every class and faith and making it a national institution that embodied and expressed the religious aspirations of all. Later, in 1899, the Revd Jocelyn Perkins became sacrist of the Abbey and stayed for 59 years, during which his forceful personality raised the standard of ceremonial and furnishings to a level that made Westminster Abbey the exemplar of decently ordered worship in every part of the Anglican world. He and Bridge were entirely responsible for this, sometimes in the face of strong resistance by the dean and chapter.

Another stroke of good fortune came with the need to mount major national ceremonies in connection with the Golden Jubilee of Queen Victoria's reign and the coronations of King Edward VII and King George V. The coronation of Queen Victoria had, by common consent, been a ceremonial disaster. The Order of Service used by the then sub-dean, Lord John Thynne, bears a pencilled comment, 'There must be a rehearsal next time.' Fifty years later there was a determination to make the Golden Jubilee service both spectacular and devotionally inspiring. Bridge recruited a large choir as well as a band and timpani to augment the organ. Trumpets sounded a fanfare from the top of the choir screen. Bridge composed an anthem that incorporated the National Anthem (there being at that time no tradition of singing this in the Abbey) and some weeks before the event Bridge took a group of choristers and lay vicars to Osborne to sing the chosen music to the Queen in order to obtain her approval. The result of all the preparation was said to be akin to a minor coronation and Bridge received the personal thanks of the Queen as well as an MVO. Ten years later, when the Diamond Jubilee was celebrated at St Paul's, he was given a knighthood in company with a dozen other prominent figures in public life.

At the coronation of Edward VII in 1902 Bridge became the first Abbey organist since Henry Purcell in the seventeenth century to be given responsibility for the music. He responded by recruiting a choir of 200, drawn from cathedrals and collegiate churches throughout the country as well as from the Chapel Royal. The veteran Abbey lay vicar, who had sung at William IV's funeral, was joined by another, a lay vicar from Wells, who had sung at this king's coronation in 1830, and one more who had been in the choir at Queen Victoria's coronation seven years later.

Bridge marked the beginning of the new reign, which came not long after the turn of a new century, by organizing a veritable feast of English church music, starting with Merbecke and Tallis of the sixteenth century, moving to Orlando Gibbons and Henry Purcell of the seventeenth, George Frederick Handel's great anthem 'Zadok the Priest' of the eighteenth, and Samuel Sebastian Wesley, Arthur Sullivan, John Stainer and Charles Villiers Stanford representing the nineteenth. His friend Hubert Parry was roped in to provide an anthem and rose to the occasion with 'I was glad when they said unto me, We will go into the house of the Lord'. This was sung as the King and Queen entered the Abbey and was so successful in incorporating the traditional 'Vivats' shouted by the scholars of Westminster School that it now appears to be an integral part of the coronation rite itself. Bridge's own anthem was much less memorable.

The last minute postponement of the coronation, when the King was struck down by appendicitis, was a great blow to Bridge, who received the news when conducting one of the final rehearsals. Even worse, when following the King's recovery, the preparations were resumed, he was informed by officials of the Court that, owing to the King's frail condition, the music would have to be seriously curtailed in order to shorten the ceremony. Fortunately news of this instruction reached the king's ears and, to Bridge's great relief, he insisted that the full programme of music be performed.

The coronation of George V came only nine years later and Bridge and Perkins had kept careful records about the ordering of the ceremonies and the disposition of the choir and the band, which those responsible for the whole event found very useful. Bridge was again appointed director of the music and commissioned new work from Hubert Parry, Edward Elgar, Charles Villiers Stanford and his own gifted assistant Walter Alcock. Elgar also contributed an orchestral march and among the other composers of orchestral music were Walford Davies and Edward German. Everyone was pleased with the result, including the new king, who appointed Bridge CVO. Earlier he had chosen five funeral marches for the national memorial service for King Edward VII in the Abbey and directed the music at his lying in state in Westminster.

The success of these spectacular national events encouraged the use of the Abbey for even more commemorations and celebrations – not on the large scale that developed during the latter decades of the twentieth century, but significantly more than in its previous history. To each, Bridge devoted considerable care as well as a newly composed anthem, and, for many people, attending the Abbey for a great service was a new and edifying experience. One of these which gave him special satisfaction was a commemoration of the birth of Samuel Sebastian Wesley held later in 1910. A choir of almost 400 included representatives of cathedrals and other churches from all over the country and the selection of music included some of Wesley's finest works. Bridge believed him to have 'raised the anthem to the highest form it has yet attained' and Wesley's family showed their gratitude for the occasion by presenting him with a pair of silver decanter stands which their father always had on his table on great occasions. Wesley was denied a place along with Purcell and other great composers in the 'Musicians Aisle' of the Abbey for want of money to pay for a memorial stone.

John Frederick Bridge was born at Oldbury, Worcestershire on 5 December 1844. His father, who sang as a tenor in the local church choir, subsequently became a lay vicar at Rochester Cathedral and young Frederick was admitted to a choristership there. He recalled helping a verger to toll the bell on the day of the funeral of the Duke of Wellington in 1852 and also noted that seven choristers of his time became cathedral organists, three of these also professors of music.

Having made good progress with the piano, and been recruited on a number of occasions to help pump the cathedral organ, he felt drawn to learn the organ and was articled to the organist – this being the normal method of professional training. Before long he was accompanying weekday services in the cathedral and on Sundays walked to a nearby village to play for the services. On some Sundays he observed Charles Dickens out walking near his home at Gad's Hill and recalled this 15 years later when composing an anthem for Dickens' funeral in Westminster Abbey.

While at Rochester he also played the cornet in the band of the 9th Kent Volunteers, completed his articles, and studied composition under John Goss of St Paul's. He described him as 'a painstaking teacher'. When aged 20, F. D. Maurice, the great theologian, offered him the post of organist at St Peter's, Vere Street, in London's West End, but he went instead to Holy Trinity Church, Windsor, favouring its cathedral-style services and the opportunity to attend nearby St George's Chapel in the castle. He also seized the opportunity to teach at Eton. It was during his Windsor years that he established what became a lifelong friendship with John Stainer; his daughter would marry one of Stainer's sons.

Bridge took his FRCO in 1867 but was disappointed when he failed to win an organ scholarship at Oxford. Undaunted, however, he completed an Oxford BMus, residence in the university not being required for this. In the following year he was appointed organist at Manchester Cathedral. As elsewhere, the music was at a low ebb. Only four lay vicars were employed and the 16 choristers were trained by the precentor, who normally deputed this task to a double-bass player.

The dean and canons, although becoming increasingly wealthy by means of their extensive land and property holdings in a rapidly developing city, were unwilling to devote additional resources to the cathedral's music. A wealthy businessman did, however, finance the building of a new organ. While more than welcome, this did not make the directing of the music any easier on Sunday mornings since the cathedral, being also the only parish church in central Manchester, held mass weddings in the quire while Mattins was being sung in the nave. Nonetheless Bridge managed to raise the standard of performance significantly and he conducted many local choral societies, as well as teaching harmony at Owen's College, the embryonic Manchester University.

In 1874 he took a DMus at Oxford and a few months later was appointed successor to James Turle at Westminster Abbey. One of his first tasks was to initiate full-choir rehearsals – there was no tradition of the men and the boys practising together – but this was firmly resisted by the men who complained that it was 'contrary to the laudable customs of the Abbey'. When the dean and chapter agreed to pay them for the additional time involved they relented. Bridge was himself a fine trainer of boys' voices and eventually he managed to increase the number of choristers from 16 to 24. The organ was rebuilt in 1884 and an electric motor replaced the physical efforts of three old men who had for many years pumped the instrument. They had frequently complained because Bridge played voluntaries before and after the weekday services. Dean Stanley had some sympathy for them and requested that the voluntaries should not be 'too long'.

When Bridge arrived at the Abbey he was astonished to discover that, even though hymn singing was becoming a normal and popular element in the church's worship, no hymns were sung at any of the services apart from the special Sunday evening service in the nave when Dean Stanley might occasionally introduce one to encourage congregational participation. He was led to understand that hymn singing was undignified and therefore inappropriate in the Abbey. When the precentor, Dr Troutbeck, began to introduce a hymn at Sunday Evensong, the previous organist, James Turle, complained to Bridge, 'I thought I was in a parish church.'

Change came with the arrival of Dean Bradley in 1881. He stayed for 21 years and authorized Bridge and Troutbeck to compile a *Book of Hymns and Tunes* for the Abbey. Thereafter hymns were used regularly and Bridge confessed that he enjoyed playing a good tune to a fine hymn more than accompanying an anthem. His appointment as musical editor of the new edition of the *Methodist Hymn Book* indicated his standing in the world of church music, though the Methodists knew what they wanted of hymn tunes so his influence over choices was limited. For some inexplicable reason he was not asked to help with *Hymns Ancient and Modern*.

Bridge knew all the great English musicians of his time and many others in Europe, including Grieg, Dvořák, Tchaikovsky and Saint-Saëns. He called on Gounod in Paris and he was generous in supporting enterprises and institutions devoted to music. Some of his external commitments were related to the need to augment his modest salary at the Abbey – a professorship at the Royal College of Music and the Gresham Professorship of Music, which led him over the years to give an astonishing 350 lectures – but most of his other activities were unpaid.

Chief among these was the College of Organists. William Davidge Limpus conceived the idea of the College as an examining body in 1864 and Bridge, who became one of its first Fellows three years later, devoted a good deal of time to building up its reputation and expanding its influence. In 1893 it was granted a royal charter and in the following year was strong enough to move to premises in Kensington vacated by the Royal College of Music. He was also Chairman of the Board of the Trinity College of Music, a Director of the Royal Philharmonic Society and for a short time Director of the Carl Rosa Opera Company. He was conductor of the Royal Choral Society from 1896 to 1918.

Of special concern to Bridge was the plight of many organists who were so poorly paid that, in order to live, they had to devote most of their time to what he described as 'the unremitting drudgery' of teaching. As they became older their powers began to fail, they could no longer retain their pupils and were in consequence 'faced with grinding poverty'. He suggested therefore the formation of an organists' Benevolent League, which was taken up by the Royal College of organists and became a great success. There was no annual subscription but organists undertook to give regularly, yearly if possible, a recital or some other musical performance, the proceeds of which were donated to the League. As the fund grew it became possible to award small pensions to needy organists and in some instances to give financial help to daughters who had not been provided for. Many of his own pupils became parish church organists, and he pressed hard for an improvement in their status and remuneration, as he did for cathedral lay vicars whom he believed to be grossly undervalued and underpaid. He also pressed for them to have a retirement age, with a pension.

The suggestion of an Archbishops' Committee on Church Music that the times and character of daily services should be altered in order to accommodate the educational needs of choristers aroused his anger. It was proposed that they should not be required to attend Mattins, so that they might be free to attend secondary school, leaving the lay vicars to lead the service in plainsong. Evensong should be held at a later hour, to suit school timetables. But Bridge strongly objected to the regular use of plainsong, which he said was distasteful to most members of Anglican congregations, and he did not see why service times should be altered to suit choristers at the expense of congregations. He wondered if 'it is the choirboy, and not the dean and chapter, to whom in the future we shall look as the final seat of authority in such matters'.

Bridge composed a great deal of music, often for special services in the Abbey, but he was not a gifted composer and hardly any of his work remains in use. He was nonetheless the right man, in the right place, at the right time and worked wonders for the music of Westminster Abbey and the church more widely. He was a flamboyant character, the subject of a SPY cartoon titled 'Westminster Bridge', had a fishing lodge in Scotland and was greatly valued by his many friends. He was married three times and, like his predecessor, retained his house in the Abbey's Little Cloister after his retirement and until his death in 1924. He was buried in Scotland, in the valley of McGlass where he had enjoyed fishing, and has a memorial stone in the Abbey's main cloisters.

12

Much-Loved Uncle Ralph Vaughan Williams

For over fifty years Ralph Vaughan Williams was at the centre of the English musical world and became its most revered figure. He is one of the three greatest and most influential twentieth-century British composers – the others being Edward Elgar and Benjamin Britten. Internationally, he is numbered among the top four or five symphonists. His music represented a distinct break with the traditional style of the Victorian era – the dissonant Fourth Symphony caused a considerable shock when first performed in 1935 – but he did not venture as far as the atonal music that some British composers employed from about 1970 onwards. It owed a great deal to his interest in Tudor church music, announced with a flourish by his *Fantasia on a Theme by Thomas Tallis*, one of his earliest and most frequently performed compositions. His subsequent influence on the music of his younger contemporaries – Herbert Howells, Gerald Finzi, Edmund Rubbra and, to a lesser extent, Michael Tippett and Benjamin Britten – was considerable.

The range of Vaughan Williams's own music, which embraced a great visionary symphony performed on a world stage, as well as a simple piece composed at the request of a village school, was an expression of his deep character and fascinating personality. His music was essentially British in character and he had an extraordinary facility to articulate the national mood at the time. He made a magnificent contribution to the national wider culture, and albeit reluctantly became a prominent member of the English Establishment. With a leonine head, large, heavy frame and lumbering gait, he looked the part, mixing almost daily with the great and the good. Yet he never lost his sympathetic concern for the poor and the needy and always voted Labour at general elections, except in 1945 when he believed that Churchill's wartime coalition government should remain in office for the peacetime reconstruction. Following his rise to fame he became fairly wealthy, but towards the end of his life he set up a trust to receive all his performing rights' dues and to use the fund to support young musicians and local music festivals.

He was in constant demand as a conductor, particularly of his own compositions, in the leading concert halls of Britain and America, yet for 35 consecutive years found time to prepare for performance, then conduct, either Bach's *St Matthew* or *St John Passion* in a parish church in Dorking in Holy Week. He composed some profoundly religious music, including a Mass in G minor which went as far afield as the Benedictine Abbey at Monserrat in Spain; he was the musical editor of *The English Hymnal*, which transformed hymn singing in the Anglican Church; and he devoted many years to the creation of an opera based on John Bunyan's *Pilgrim's Progress*. Throughout his life, however, he was 'a cheerful agnostic' and attended church services only for special commemorations in Westminster Abbey. He refused a knighthood and a peerage but finally accepted the Order of Merit. Until the end of his life he enjoyed the company of pretty women.

Ralph (he always insisted that it be pronounced Rafe) Vaughan Williams was born in 1872 at Down Ampney in Gloucestershire where his father was the vicar. The mixed family background was distinguished, with leading lawyers on his father's side and notables such as Charles Darwin, the scientist, and Josiah Wedgewood, the potter, on his mother's. When he was only three, however, his father died and his mother took her children to Leith Hill Place, her family home in Surrey. Young Ralph was sent to a preparatory school in Sussex and from there went to Charterhouse, where he played the violin in the school orchestra. Earlier an aunt had introduced him to composition, and, having studied Stainer's *Harmony*, he took the advanced examination of an Edinburgh University correspondence course, when he was only eight. At home he learned to play the piano and the organ, and although he did not display outstanding promise, he insisted, against the wishes of his family, on going from Charterhouse to the Royal College of Music.

There he studied composition under Hubert Parry – who declared himself unable to believe that an entrant to the college could know so little music – and the organ under Walter Parratt, the teacher of many future distinguished organists. After two years Vaughan Williams, who had made good, but not particularly notable, progress, went to Trinity College, Cambridge to read History and to take a MusB. His intellectual gifts now emerged – he later became a stimulating lecturer on musical subjects – and he formed lifelong friendships with members of Cambridge intellectual circles who included Bertrand Russell, G. M. Trevelyan and G. E. Moore. He also studied under Charles Wood and returned to the RCM once a week to continue his work with Parry.

Having completed his MusB and taken a second in history in 1895, he became once again a full-time student under Charles Villiers Stanford who shared with Parry pre-eminence in the musical life of that time. But he did not get on with Stanford who severely criticized his compositions. 'Damnably ugly, my boy. Why do you write such things? They're not music', was his comment on one piece. His verdict on a movement of a quartet, to which Vaughan Williams had devoted hours of agony, was 'All rot, my boy'. But the wounded student later acknowledged, 'With Stanford I always felt I was in the presence of a loveable, powerful and enthralling mind. This helped me more than any amount of technical instruction.' During this time he paid his way by serving as organist of St Barnabas Church, South Lambeth, but the services bored him and most of the Victorian hymns appalled him. The atheism of his university years had been modified to agnosticism, but when a new vicar insisted that the organist should receive Holy Communion he refused and resigned. Later he said that this short experience of practical music-making had been of some importance in helping him to recognize that compositions had to be performed.

In 1897 Vaughan Williams married Adeline Fisher, a sister of H. A. L. Fisher, a distinguished historian, and herself a talented pianist, possessed of a lively wit. The honeymoon was spent in Berlin, and a modest private income enabled them to stay for several weeks while he studied composition under the great Max Bruch. Soon after their return to London he took his FRCO (he completed a Cambridge MusD in 1901) and embarked on a variety of related activities – writing and teaching, and all the time struggling to find a distinctive language in which to embark on his career as a composer. At Cambridge he established what was to become a close friendship with Gustav Holst who, although two years his junior, was, according to Vaughan Williams, 'the greatest influence on my music'. It was a grievous blow when Holst died in 1934, aged 60; thereafter a former pupil and a close friend, Gerald Finzi, took his place.

During the winter of 1902 Vaughan Williams gave a course of university extension lectures on music in Bournemouth, and devoted one of these to English folk songs. He had become interested in this subject when neighbours at Leith Hill Place had published two books, *Sussex Songs* and *English County Songs*. The favourable reception given to his lecture, repeated in Gloucester, led him to start his own collection of songs and during the next few years he sought these out while on country holidays or visiting friends. In pubs he encouraged men to sing the traditional songs of the neighbourhood, the words and tunes of which he copied into a notebook. At Salisbury he went into the workhouse and found old people who were delighted to sing to him; a letter to the *Morning Post* brought in many more. In the end he accumulated 800 and joined Cecil Sharp, the pioneering spirit of the folk-song revival, in membership of the English Folk Dance and Song Society, eventually becoming its president and invariably conducting an annual gathering of enthusiasts in London's Albert Hall.

For some years Vaughan Williams and his wife rented a small house in Barton Street, close to Westminster Abbey. One day in 1904 a cab drove up to the door and 'Mr Dearmer' was announced. Vaughan Williams later recalled:

> I just knew his name vaguely as a parson who invited tramps to sleep in his drawing room; but he had not come to me about tramps. He went straight to the point and asked me to edit the music of a hymn book. I protested that I knew very little about hymns but he explained to me that Cecil Sharp had suggested my name, and I found out afterwards that Canon Scott Holland had also suggested me as a possible editor, and the final clinch was given when I understood that if I did not do the job it would be offered to a well-known Church musician (this was Henry Walford Davies) with whose musical ideas I was much out of sympathy. At this opening interview Dearmer told me that the new book was being sponsored by a committee of eight clerics who were dissatisfied with the new *Hymns Ancient and Modern*. He told me that these eight founders had put down five pounds each for expenses, and that my part of the work would probably take about two months.

It is not clear how much time every day Vaughan Williams was expected to devote to evaluating the 600 or so hymns in *A & M* and to finding new tunes for the many that needed replacing, as well as incorporating other hymns which the editors of *A & M* had neglected. But the suggested two months was hopelessly unrealistic and in the event the task took two years and Vaughan Williams's clerical expenses alone came to £250. The result was a massive achievement, and *The English Hymnal*, substantially revised in 1986, remains one of the highest-quality hymn books in the English-speaking world.

Significant though Vaughan Williams's contribution to the hymnal turned out to be, it represented only a small and relatively unimportant part of his massive musical output. His reputation was built largely, though not exclusively, on nine major symphonies, the first two of which, *A Sea Symphony* and *A London Symphony*, were first performed during the years immediately prior to the outbreak of war in 1914. By this time the influence of Maurice Ravel, with whom he had studied in Paris, was evident and *A Sea Symphony* was said to have converted the younger generation to the fact that they lived in an age when music did not belong to the past. It was, however, in no sense avant garde.

Soon after war was declared he enrolled as a Special Constable and quickly became a sergeant, but a few weeks later he enlisted in the ranks in the Royal Army Medical Corps. In 1916 he went to France as a wagon orderly, which involved moving to the front line of battle every night to bring back the wounded to one of the main dressing stations. He had many harrowing experiences, and it was during these dark days that *A Pastoral Symphony* began to shape in his mind. The long trumpet cadenza in the second movement of the symphony was inspired by the sound of a bugler who used to practise every evening near the dressing station, and the sadness of much of the music suggested an epitaph for the war. Vaughan Williams formed a choir from among the soldiers of his unit and did the same when he was posted to Salonika, delighting in the fact that on Christmas Eve they were able to sing carols on snow-capped Mount Olympus. He was commissioned in the Royal Garrison Artillery just as the war was ending in 1918 and for a short time had charge of 200 horses near the front line at Rouen. After the Armistice had been signed he was made Director of Music for the BEF in France and, by the time of his demobilization three months later, he had formed nine choral societies, three music classes, an orchestra and a band.

On his return to civilian life Vaughan Williams became Professor of Composition at the Royal College of Music – a post he held for the next 20 years – and became known as Uncle Ralph. Oxford honoured him with a DMus. But the wartime experience deeply affected him and it was not until 1922 that he completed *A Pastoral Symphony* – first performed by the Royal Philharmonic Orchestra under Adrian Boult. His Mass in G minor had its first performance in the same year, and in the previous year he had succeeded Hugh Allen as conductor of the Bach Choir, of which he had been a member since 1903. He believed that Bach's cantatas were best performed by a small choir in a small building, but in the circumstances of the time 'it had to be 300 voices or no cantatas'.

In 1910 he was commissioned to compose something for the Three Choirs Festival, which was being held that year at Gloucester. This was the origin of *Fantasia on a theme by Thomas Tallis,* which he conducted immediately before Edward Elgar conducted his *Dream of Gerontius.* The two composers came to know each other well. Thereafter Vaughan Williams rarely missed this annual event and sometimes conducted performances of other new compositions. His own included *Five Mystical Songs* based on George Herbert poems, at Hereford in 1911, and a Magnificat at Worcester in 1932. On many other occasions he conducted his *Pastoral Symphony* and the music for the ballet *Job* was heard at Gloucester in 1953. On all these and other occasions he greatly enjoyed himself in the company of old friends and other composers, and in the end became a revered figure at the Festival.

Nearer home, the annual Leith Hill Musical Festival, which he helped to inaugurate in 1905, claimed more of his time than most distinguished musicians would have been prepared to give. He was its conductor, devoting much time to the rehearsals of amateurs until 1953, then became guest conductor. He composed a Te Deum for the Coronation of George VI in 1937. Then once more found himself caught up in the ramifications of world war. His music was placed on Hitler's blacklist in 1939 and he was on the committee responsible for the National Gallery lunchtime concerts, made famous by Myra Hess's piano recitals. He also conducted numerous concerts in various parts of the country, completed his Fifth Symphony in D major, conducting its first performance at a Promenade concert in 1943, and composed music for films, including the wartime propaganda film *Coastal Command*. Later he expanded his music for the film *Scott of the Antarctic* to create *Symphonia Antarctica*. His seventieth birthday in 1942 was a national event.

The post-war years produced four more symphonies – the last of these completed shortly before his death in 1958 – and he continued to be at the centre of the English music world, though a new generation of musicians began to react against his style. His personal life now took a new and, to those who were not in the know, a surprising turn. In 1953, two years after the death of Adeline, to whom he had been married for 54 years, and who played an important part in his career, he married Ursula Wood, his glamorous assistant and future biographer, who was 40 years his junior. Although devoted to Adeline to the end, she had not been able to meet all his needs and he had been conducting a *ménage à trois* for the previous 13 years, though this was not made public until after Ursula's death in 2007. Some believe that the more passionate character of his later work owes much to this liaison.

The five remaining years of Vaughan Williams's life included long holidays and much travelling, as well as the composition of two more symphonies. Shortly before his sudden death in 1958 he expressed in simple terms his understanding of the significance of music:

> To the boys and girls of the Primary School, Swaffham. I am very much pleased to think that one of your houses is to bear my name. I am myself a musician, and I believe that all the arts, and especially music, are necessary to a full life. The practical side of living, of course, is important, and this, I feel sure, is well taught in your school; such things teach you how to make your living. But music will enable you to see past facts to the very essence of things in a way which science cannot do. The arts are the means by which we can look through the magic casements and see what lies beyond.

The English Hymnal and *Songs of Praise*

Percy Dearmer's choice of Vaughan Williams for the musical editorship of *The English Hymnal* some years before he had become famous was a masterstroke. No musician of the time, nor many others subsequently, could have done it better and the fact that an agnostic played such a critical part in the transformation of hymn singing, and therefore of the quality of the church's worship, as well as composing outstanding music of religious depth, raises interesting questions about sources of inspiration.

The hymnal was conceived by Dearmer and a few colleagues as an antidote to the poor quality of words and music employed by much Victorian hymnody and made too readily available in the highly popular *Hymns Ancient and Modern*. They also believed that a hymn book should be closely related to the pattern of worship provided by the Book of Common Prayer, with provision for all the saints' days, and recognition of the centrality of the Eucharist. Material was needed for churches employing antiphons and processions. The use of plainsong was encouraged and this was handled by J. H. Arnold.

In an essay on the music of the new hymnal, included as part of its preface, Vaughan Williams displayed considerable writing skill and was candid in his assessment of the quality of many Victorian hymns: 'More often than not they are positively harmful to those who sing and hear them.' He confessed to a problem over the proposed inclusion of a number of these which had become popular with congregations, but went on to record, 'The problem solved itself in a happy and unforeseen manner because the insertion of several of the tunes in question was not allowed by the owners of the copyright.' He added, 'Nothing but gain can result from the exclusion of certain tunes, which are worthy neither of the congregations who sing them, the occasions on which they are sung, nor the composers who wrote them.' Driving his point even deeper, he stated:

> It is indeed a moral rather than a musical issue. No doubt it requires a certain effort to tune oneself to the moral atmosphere implied by a fine melody; and it is far easier to dwell in the miasma of the languishing and sentimental hymn tunes which so often disfigure our services. Such poverty of heart may not be uncommon, but at least it should not be encouraged by those who direct the services of the Church; it ought no longer to be true anywhere that the most exalted moments of a church-goer's week are associated with music that would not be tolerated in any place of secular entertainment.

His starting point was that the music should be essentially congregational in character and the pitch of each tune kept as low as consistent with the melody. Familiarity was important, therefore the 'specially composed tune – that bane of many a hymnal – has been avoided as far as possible'. He searched widely for singable tunes of a high standard, claiming a good deal from J. S. Bach, the German Psalter and other continental services, as well as 13 items from Orlando Gibbons, 15 from the Scottish Psalter and 15 Welsh hymn melodies. A new source for hymnody was provided by English traditional melodies and carols of which, from his own extensive knowledge, he chose about 50, making adjustments where necessary.

George Herbert's poem 'Teach me, my God and King', which had been reworked by John Wesley, was allocated a traditional air that had originally been set to a 27–verse carol. 'Fight the good fight' was given an adapted version of a folk song, 'Tarry Trousers'. 'Who would true valour see' from Bunyan's *Pilgrims' Progress* was given a traditional folk song that Vaughan Williams had picked up in the Sussex village of Monks Gate. 'Father, hear the prayer we offer' benefited from another Sussex folk melody, and G. K. Chesterton's 'O God of earth and altar' – one of the best national hymns – was appropriately set to an English folk melody. A jolly May Day carol was prescribed for St Philip and St James' Day (1 May). The challenge to Vaughan Williams was to locate among folk-music tunes appropriate to the words, and he rarely failed, though not everyone approved of his use of this essentially secular music. Some considered it frivolous.

For four hymns he was driven by necessity to compose new tunes himself. Three were outstanding. The Whitsun hymn 'Come down, O Love divine', a translation of an Italian medieval poem, had not previously been much used, but Vaughan Williams's tune 'Down Ampney', described by Erik Routley as 'perhaps the most beautiful hymn tune composed since 'Old Hundreth' in the 16th century', soon became, and remains, a favourite. Joseph Barnby's tune for Bishop Walsham How's great hymn 'For all the Saints' was popular and had to be given space in *The English Hymnal* appendix, but it could not complete with Vaughan Williams's magnificent 'Sine Nomine' without which no celebration of All Saints' Day now seems complete. It is frequently used also at funerals and memorial services. Again, the plainsong optimistically provided for 'Hail thee, Festival Day', a medieval processional hymn for Easter Day, Ascension Day and Whitsunday, did not stand a chance when challenged by Vaughan Williams's exciting 'Salva Festa Dies'.

Although the use of *The English Hymnal* tended to be confined at first to churches of a moderately High Church tradition, its success had by 1925 encouraged Percy Dearmer to embark on a totally different kind of hymnal, which he called *Songs of Praise*. In his preface he explained:

In this book we have endeavoured to make a national collection of hymns for use in public worship, and also of such 'spiritual songs' as are akin to hymns and suitable for certain kinds of services in church, as well as for schools, lecture meetings, and other public gatherings.

Vaughan Williams was pressed into service again as music editor and Martin Shaw entrusted with the plainsong. The choice of hymns and songs was ecumenical and considerably influenced by the outlook of the modernist/Liberal Evangelical movement, then gathering strength in the Church of England. On its appearance, however, it was apparent, surprisingly, that Dearmer had forsaken the standards that had led him with justice to describe *The English Hymnal* as 'a collection of the best hymns in the English language'. Much fine material, some of it new, was included but this was seriously diluted by items which should not be sung by anyone, anywhere.

One of the worst offenders was Dearmer himself, who felt moved by what he perceived to be gaps in the book's range of subjects to provide 23 new hymns. But he was no poet and hardly any of his work has survived. This is true of most of the other inferior items and it is unfortunate that, for want of other suitable tunes, Vaughan William was driven to compose for some of these, with the result that a number of his own fine tunes have never become known and valued.

In spite of its evident weaknesses, however, *Songs of Praise* was recognized as having broken new ground in hymnody and for some years was widely used in schools and in parish churches where its religious stance was valued. In 1929 a conference to discuss a possible enlargement of the book attracted over 1,200 participants. This was followed by a series of meetings in the North of England at which 89 clergy discussed the hymns in common use and voted on their preferences. Through no fault of Vaughan Williams and Martin Shaw, the resulting enlargement contained even more hymns of poor quality and in the post-war church it became virtually unusable.

The Oxford Book of Carols

Most of the older Christmas carols were created during the fifteenth century, when they were permitted to make the only contribution in English to the Latin service, replacing the old Office hymns. They flourished until the time of the Commonwealth and the 1647 Act of Parliament which abolished the observance of Christmas and the other festivals of the Christian year. And the Restoration of the Monarchy in 1660 did not lead to their revival, though they were still sung 'underground' in some rural areas, particularly in the north and west of the country.

By the beginning of the nineteenth century carols were said to be a thing of the past, but as the century advanced sporadic attempts were made to bring them back. A turning point came in 1871 with the publication of *Christmas Carols Old and New*, edited by H. R. Bramley, Fellow of Magdalen College, Oxford, and John Stainer, the celebrated organist of St Paul's. This collection included 13 of the traditional and 29 of new carols, virtually all of the latter being of little merit.

Other collections followed and, as with the hymns of the time, there was a flood of material of poor quality. Nonetheless, carol singing again became popular and this revival coincided with the scholarly recovery of a considerable number of old English folk songs in which Ralph Vaughan Williams played a leading part. Among the songs there were carols, but it was not until the 1920s, and after the favourable reception given to *The English Hymnal*, that Percy Dearmer embarked on the tasks of compiling in a single volume the best of the available materials. Once again Vaughan Williams and Martin Shaw were recruited as music editors and 1928 saw the publication of *The Oxford Book of Carols*.

This comprised 197 carols, of which 21 were carefully selected modern carols, and a number drawn from other European sources. A few Easter carols were also included and in a valuable preface Dearmer recommended that the singing of carols in church should become an all round the year element in the worship – replacing the anthem when the choir was below standard. The volume was immediately recognized as the standard collection and has remained so, running to about 40 impressions. *The New Oxford Book of Carols*, edited by Hugh Keyte and Andrew Parrott, and published in 1998, was designed as a supplement to the original. It contains 201 carols, spanning seven centuries, together with comprehensive notes on the source and variants of every carol.

13

Sydney Nicholson and the Royal School of Church Music

Sydney Nicholson succeeded Frederick Bridge at Westminster Abbey in 1919 – a challenging assignment at any time, and especially so when his predecessor had held the office for 43 years and become not only the most distinguished member of the Abbey community, but also a leading light in London's musical life and won high praise for his contribution to two coronations and other national events.

Nicholson was not, by his own admission, a top-class organist. He was, however, an unusually gifted trainer of boys' voices and a highly competent administrator who maintained and developed the already high standard of the Abbey's music. And, being unafraid of innovation, he was ready to move in new directions, which led him to resign from his post in 1928 in order to found the School of English Church Music.

The outstanding success of this project, which later became the Royal School of Church Music, was his greatest achievement and was largely responsible for the widespread raising of the standard of parish church music during the twentieth century. He was editor of the *Standard Edition of Hymns Ancient and Modern* (1922) and lived long enough to edit the Revised Edition, though he died three years before its publication in 1950. Of his own hymn tunes, only two have remained in common use – 'Bow Brickhill' for 'We sing the praise of him who died' and 'Crucifer' for 'Lift high the cross' – but these are of the highest quality. Of special importance was his editing of *The Parish Psalter* (1928) which applied to all the psalms the speech-rhythm pioneered by Robert Bridges the Poet Laureate. This was first used at the Temple Church, under Sir Walford Davies, and it gradually replaced in most parishes the cumbersome and often ludicrous pointing of the *Cathedral* and *New Cathedral* Psalters.

Sydney Hugo Nicholson was born in London's West End in 1875. His father, a baronet, was a physician and for many years a prominent figure in Australia's public life, and his two brothers both achieved notable success in the artistic sphere, one as a conservation architect who also designed about ten new churches in Southwark diocese, as well as extensions to Sheffield Cathedral; the other as a stained-glass artist who designed the memorial window to Edward Elgar in Worcester Cathedral. Young Sydney went to Rugby School, then to New College, Oxford, to read English. At Oxford he had his first encounter with serious church music in the chapels of New College and Magdalen College, and also in Christ Church Cathedral. By the time he came down his skill as an organist was becoming evident and, against the wishes of his father, he went to the Royal College of Music to study under Walter Parratt, one of the notable organists of that time, and Charles Villiers Stanford, the composer. He gained the Oxford BMus in 1902.

Nicholson's first professional appointment was that of organist of Chipping Barnet Parish Church, which he held from 1897 to 1903. Within the parish was the Nicholson family seat. During this time he trained a fine choir, conducted oratorios and organized festivals that involved other local choirs. His church became noted as a centre of fine music and was near enough to London for his talent to be noted more widely. He was also for a short time organist of the Lower Chapel at Eton, before spending a year at the conservatory in Frankfurt am Main in Germany. In 1904 he became acting organist of Carlisle Cathedral where the organist, though incapable of performing his duties, retained the freehold office.

Next came the offer of the organist post at Canterbury Cathedral, which he accepted, but from which, to the astonishment of many, he then withdrew when the opportunity came to go to Manchester Cathedral. There, as at Carlisle, he raised the standard of the music and extended his influence by organizing diocesan music societies to bring together parish choirs to sing in music festivals. At Manchester the society had 4,000 members and eight branches.

Shortly after the end of the 1914–18 war he moved to Westminster where, after Bridge's long reign, several matters required attention. Some of the elderly lay vicars, whose voices had long been past their best, retained freeholds and had to be persuaded to retire. Another long-standing problem, that of regular rehearsals, required a firm hand for its solution. It was also apparent to Nicholson, who had a close rapport with boys, that excessive demands were being made on the choristers, to the detriment of both their performances and their educational needs. So he persuaded the dean and chapter to finance the doubling of their number to reduce the pressure.

Nicholson's cathedral experience confirmed his belief in the value of associating amateur singers with professional choral foundations, so at Westminster he founded a Special Choir of 100 men and 100 boys (including the Abbey choristers) from parish choirs in all parts of London. This was entrusted with an annual performance of Bach's *St Matthew Passion*; other oratorios were added later. The choir continued until the

1980s when it finally ran out of steam, largely as a result of the decline of amateur parish church choirs in the capital.

Unlike many of his professional colleagues, Nicholson recognized that, although the cathedrals and other great churches had a responsibility for maintaining the highest standards, the overall quality, and the future of English church music, could not be confined to their own rarefied atmosphere. For parish churches, ranging from those in large towns with impressive resources to those in small villages with a handful of enthusiasts, he published *Church Music: A practical handbook* (1920) and, jointly with G. L. H. Garner, *A Manual of English Church Music* (1923). He also gladly collaborated with the BBC over the first broadcast of Choral Evensong in 1926, believing, against the advice of many, that only good could result from wider knowledge of Anglican choral worship at its best and from the challenge of a high standard.

Nicholson was well aware that nothing worthwhile could be achieved without adequate training and in the year following the broadcast he conceived the idea of a new institution dedicated to the training of church musicians and the propagation of good practice. A meeting of leading church musicians was therefore convened in Westminster Abbey's Jerusalem Chamber on St Nicholas's Day, 6 December 1927, a decision was made to launch an English School of Church Music and, in confirmation of Nicholson's enthusiasm and efficiency, a provisional council met a fortnight later. In the following year an ideal property was located and bought (with his own money) in Chislehurst, Kent.

This was named the College of St Nicolas. Ten choristers (seven of them from a recently closed choir school in Nottinghamshire) were recruited and arrangements were made for them to attend a nearby preparatory school. The first four students arrived in January 1929 and their contribution to the daily services in the chapel was augmented on Thursdays and Sundays by a number of former Westminster Abbey choristers. The music of the services varied to represent choirs of differing ability in order that students might experience the full range of Anglican worship.

From the outset it was determined to recruit affiliated choirs and in May 1929 400 members of these choirs in the London area took part in a service in the Church of the Holy Sepulchre in Holborn. Another 400 came from ten other dioceses in December of the same year, by which time about 300 choirs had affiliated. It was not intended at this stage that Nicholson and his small specialist staff should visit choirs in their own parishes, but rather that church musicians should attend the College for short periods, perhaps as little as a day, to receive some training. The recruiting of full-time students was, however, slow and, in spite of Nicholson's own generous financial support and regular donations by the proprietors of *Hymns Ancient and Modern*, financial problems began to create anxiety. A public appeal brought in only £2,748.

A breakthrough came in 1930 when the *Daily Mail*, which had been following with interest the progress of the project, offered to sponsor a great festival of church music in the Royal Albert Hall. Twelve hundred singers came from 180 affiliated choirs, including four from Scotland and two from Ireland, and the *Daily Mail* covered all their travelling expenses. The chosen music was suitable for parish church choirs and, although Nicholson compared his task as conductor to that of 'taking a jellyfish for a walk on an elastic lead', the result was good enough to meet the standard for the radio broadcast. A choirbook of the music was published for use by choirs in their own parishes, and in 1931 six 10-inch gramophone records were made to demonstrate to choirs what might be achieved. Thus began what became a very considerable publishing enterprise designed to provide parish churches with high-quality music in manageable form and at affordable cost. By 1932 there were sufficient affiliated choirs to require the formation of diocesan branches. In the following year, short residential courses for boys and others, and summer schools for all, were started at the College, and a second national festival, this time at the Crystal Palace, attracted 4,000 voices.

This rapid expansion continued. In 1935 the number of affiliated choirs rose to 1,137, and Ernest Bullock, the organist of Westminster Abbey, became director of studies at the college in order to release Nicholson to travel the country to help parish choirs. During the next two years he visited 400 choirs, some of them overseas, and in 1938 his work was recognized by the conferring of a knighthood. The outbreak of war in 1939 led, however, to the closure of the College, for want of students. Numbers had never been large – a total of 89 had attended the longer courses, 170 for the shorter – but the results had been impressive, especially among young organists, one of whom was David Willcocks, who spent a year there and later became the distinguished organist and director of music at King's College, Cambridge.

Nicholson moved the rest of the school to St Michael's College, Tenbury (in 1943 it was moved again to the more conveniently located Leamington Spa), and during the war years he continued to visit the parishes, using an autocycle to maximize the limited petrol ration. In the absence of men from the choirs, he concentrated on boys' voices and, although the growth in the number of affiliated choirs was inevitably much slower, it had reached 2,000 by 1945. It became the RSCM in 1945.

When the war ended, the headquarters was moved to the precincts of Canterbury Cathedral, and the College was reopened, but without a residential choir school. Instead, boys were recruited from local parishes for the daily services held in the cathedral's crypt. Gerald Knight, the cathedral organist, became warden of the College, Nicholson remaining as director and continuing to visit choirs and conduct festivals until his death in 1947. On any reckoning, his was a massive achievement. Sometimes he was criticized for showing too little concern for congregational involvement in worship, and there was some truth in this, though the days of increased participation, especially in the Eucharist, were still some distance in the future. The church's debt to him was, and remains, enormous.

Following Nicholson's death, two other distinguished musicians, John Dykes Bower of St Paul's and William McKie of Westminster Abbey, joined Gerald Knight to make a trio of honorary directors and these held the fort until Knight became the full-time director in 1953. A year later the RSCM moved to the grand location of Addington Palace – at one time the country home of the Archbishop of Canterbury, near Croydon.

It was a tangible tribute to Nicholson's achievement that the next 35 years of the School's existence was spent under the leadership of two outstanding directors who recognized the importance of its work and were ready to leave major cathedrals in order to move it forward. Knight, who became known as 'The Apostle of Church Music', was responsible for establishing and developing the work at Addington Palace, and he devoted 20 years to this. The building was large enough to accommodate not only the College of St Nicolas, but also a variety of residential courses of varying length which attracted students from many different parts of the world. It became even more apparent, however, that the main thrust of education and training must be in the parishes, and to facilitate this a number of regional commissioners were appointed. These were usually the organists of cathedrals and other major churches, who had the time to visit parishes to hear their choirs and to offer practical advice. Annual diocesan choral festivals, on particular Christian themes and with prescribed music, provided an enjoyable challenge and on the day the cathedral organist conducted the final rehearsal and the service. Members of affiliated choirs wore a medallion of St Nicholas on a ribbon over their surplices and a chorister training programme led to the award of other medallions to indicate levels of achievement.

The appointment of Lionel Dakers of Exeter Cathedral as Knight's successor in 1972 brought renewed energy and enthusiasm and considerable flair. He had been a pupil of Edward Bairstow at York Minister and before going to Exeter was at Ripon. Earlier he was a parish church organist, and had also been assistant at St George's, Windsor. At Exeter he had devoted a great deal of time to the parish church choirs and before diocesan festivals in the cathedral would spend nearly every evening for four or five weeks taking regional rehearsals. He also encouraged deanery festivals. His move to Addington Palace was timely inasmuch as the Church of England was now well into a period of unprecedented change, most noticeably in its forms of worship. New experimental services required a different approach and new musical material.

Dakers, who always saw worship as an integral part of the church's witness, had a high regard for tradition, but was open to liturgical reform, believing this to be essential after three centuries of stagnation. He also recognized the importance of congregational participation in worship and told the organists that their main task was to accompany the singing in such a way that all would compulsively *want* to sing. He could be scathing in his attacks on conservatism, though he warned that change must not be allowed to bring a lowering of standards or a loss of the sense of awe in worship. He often pointed out that necessary change could be effected by better use of existing resources in hymns and psalms. His *Church Music at the Crossroads: A Forward-Looking Guide* (1970) became an invaluable handbook for many years.

On taking up the appointment Dakers reaffirmed the main objectives of the RSCM – instructional courses, publications and advice – and soon afterwards the College of St Nicolas was closed because of financial problems and the declining number of good students. More attention was now given to shorter courses either at Addington Palace or at centres throughout the country. These proliferated and covered every conceivable aspect of church music, ranging from the ordinary 'bread and butter' work of parish church choirs in every kind of location to specialist courses for clergy and (always popular) 'the reluctant organist'. Girls' choirs were welcomed. Besides the diocesan festivals, Dakers also introduced local hymn-singing festivals in which choirs, congregations and clergy were brought together to learn how to sing more effectively and enjoyably, and to learn new hymns, including the best of those emanating from Evangelical circles.

As at Exeter, Dakers was indefatigable in visiting parishes and undertook overseas tours that took him to virtually every part of the Anglican Communion. And no less important than the expert advice he offered, always tailored to the possibilities in local conditions, was the encouragement he gave and the enthusiasm he engendered. The number of affiliated choirs continued to grow and by the time of his retirement in 1989 had reached 8,000. He was appointed CBE in 1983 and also awarded a Lambeth DMus.

Dakers was succeeded by another highly talented musician, Harry Bramma, the organist of All Saints, Margaret Street, who had previously been at Southwark Cathedral. He continued the work of his predecessors but widened its scope. The area festivals were augmented by annual celebration days in different parts of the country, at which specially devised services were sung by several hundred singers from affiliated choirs in the region. A 'Year of the Small Choir' initiative focused attention on the many churches with no formal choir. These were offered specialist publications and advice, while renewed encouragement and advice was given to the 'reluctant organist'.

Another series of publications included arrangements of contemporary worship songs, arranged for organ and choir in harmony, and these went a good way towards bridging the gap between the different styles. Geoff Weaver was appointed director of studies and brought wide-ranging knowledge of all types of church music, particularly songs from the world church, while Robin Sheldon, founder and first Director of the Music and Worship Foundation, joined the part-time staff to contribute his experience of the Evangelical tradition.

Although the RSCM is now an ecumenical organization, its roots are within the Anglican Church, and, following a recommendation of the 1992 Archbishops' Commission report *In Tune with Heaven*, it became the Church of England's official music agency, while wisely retaining its independence. This led to the publication of a quarterly, *Sunday by Sunday*, a planner used by many clergy and organists responsible for the choice of music. The established *Church Music Quarterly* remains widely read and respected.

During Bramma's time as director, the lease on Addington Palace approached expiry and the RSCM accepted the gift of Cleveland Lodge, the former home of Lady Susi Jeans, the organist. This became the new headquarters in 1996 and Bramma masterminded a major appeal to finance the adaptation of the building.

John Harper, who took over from Harry Bramma in 1998, brought different gifts and skills. He was a music and liturgy scholar who had been director of music at St Chad's Roman Catholic Cathedral in Birmingham, university lecturer and Informator Choristarum at Magdalen College, Oxford, and, immediately prior to his appointment at the RSCM, Professor of Music at the University of Wales, Bangor. He also had vision and managerial skills, which he applied to a substantial reorganization of the RSCM's administration.

A new educational programme was introduced. The established Chorister Training Scheme became Voice for Life, and made appropriate for all ages, with handbooks for singers at three different levels (these indicated by light blue, dark blue and red ribbons worn by choristers with the RSCM medallion), and a comprehensive handbook for choir trainers. Appropriate music was also published. Another strand in the programme was the provision, under the title Skills of the Church Musician, of practical schemes of study for parish organists, keyboard players, music groups and choir directors, as well as cantors. For the more advanced, collaboration between the RSCM and the university at Bangor introduced a course, Sacred Music Studies, rooted in music and liturgy and leading to formal RSCM qualifications, including diplomas.

The appointment of Harper to the Liturgical Commission signalled a new acknowledgement of the place of music in worship and this led to consultations between liturgists and church music composers at the time of the production of *Common Worship*. The RSCM produced a comprehensive series of music publications to meet the new need. By 2006, however, it was apparent that Cleveland Lodge had become too expensive to maintain, and the central administration was moved to Sarum College, in the Close at Salisbury.

Lindsay Gray, who became director in 2008, came from the headmastership of Llandaff Cathedral School, where he had also founded and directed the girls' choir at Llandaff Cathedral. He is particularly committed to the encouragement of young singers in church, school and community choirs, and to increasing the membership, which presently exceeds 8,000. There are autonomous RSCM divisions in Australia, New Zealand, Canada, South Africa and the USA.

The vision of Sydney Nicholson has produced remarkable results. His basic aims and methods remain unchanged and the need for the RSCM's insights and experience has become more, not less, important.

14

The Choristers

During the early decades of the nineteenth century choristers were among the victims of the general malaise then affecting cathedral life. Their conditions varied from cathedral to cathedral but, whereas prior to 1700 they were boarded within the Close and cared for within the life of a community, so now they were in most places required to stay with their families (fathers were often lay clerks) or with others who would take them in. The boys' non-musical education was, except in a handful of places, virtually non-existent. The days of the monastic school and its successor grammar school were long past and the boys were left on their own for long periods. In marked contrast to this, their musical training was generally very good – undertaken by a senior lay clerk – but almost everywhere their numbers were seriously depleted, sometimes because dean and chapters were unwilling to spend even the small amount of money required, often because no one was prepared to recruit them; organists were not normally responsible for cathedral choirs, only for playing the organ.

The gradual improvement in their conditions during the nineteenth century owed much to the devoted efforts of Maria Hackett, 'The Choristers' Friend'. Born in Birmingham in 1783, she eventually moved with her twice-widowed mother to London where they settled near St Paul's and she became a regular worshipper. She was not rich, but she had some private income and was generous in her use of it. When 27 she became the guardian of the seven-year-old son of a relative and, in the expectation of securing him a good education, obtained for him a choristership at St Paul's. She was soon disillusioned and wrote to the Bishop of London to express her concern:

> The neglected situation of the children belonging to St Paul's choir has for some time been a subject of general animadversion. In the earlier ages of the church, they with other members of the church formed a part of the dean's household; and till within a few years, they were maintained and educated from the funds of this richly-endowed cathedral; but the sum allowed to the almoner for their board became, through the depreciation of money, totally inadequate for their support. The

almoner who held the situation of music master, applied to the Chapter for an augmentation; but instead of complying with this request the Chapter declined making any addition to the sum anciently assigned for the maintenance of the choristers, and the almoner was under the necessity of dismissing them from his protection, dividing among them their trifling salary.

In consequence of this arrangement, many of the children reside at a considerable distance from the church and from the singing master and a great proportion of the day is consumed in loitering about the streets, having no one to call them into account for the employment of their time. If they appear in their places at the hour of service, no thought is bestowed upon their conduct for the rest of the day – and, let me add, the night also.

To remunerate their singing master for his trouble, the children are hired out to public concerts, and are exposed, unprotected, to the contagion of any society they meet within those nocturnal assemblies. No one, on these occasions, is appointed to have an eye upon their conduct; no one to return them safely to their friends. After the conclusion of the concert, these youths are committed to their own discretion, are left to walk the streets alone and at midnight, and to find their way home as they can. What effect this vagabond life, at so early an age, is likely to have upon their morals, in most instances, may be easily imagined. Nor is their education less neglected; and except that they attend a singing master for the requisite lessons to enable them to get through the choral service, and that they are called upon a very few times in the year to repeat the *catechism*, they are literally kept without instruction.

The Bishop sent the letter to the Dean who was rarely present at the cathedral, being also Bishop of Llandaff, and he failed to respond. Four months later she wrote angrily to one of the canons, but received no reply, then to all of the canons, one of whom replied evasively. Meanwhile she discovered from research into the archives of St Paul's, lodged in the British Museum, that the dean and chapter had a statutory duty to feed, clothe, educate and care for the choristers. In 1814, with the help of her uncle and his half-brother, she began a legal action to secure for the choristers their statutory rights, but this became too expensive to pursue to a judgement. Undaunted, she continued to press the dean and chapter until they purchased a house in the Strand for the choristers, who were joined by the ten children of the Chapel Royal, and a new almoner, William Howes, was appointed at an increased salary to conduct their education and generally care for them. With the arrival of a new dean in 1828 his salary was increased further to £400 per annum, but since this was intended to cover the entire cost of the establishment and was insufficient, Howes had to continue to hire out the boys for banquets and secular concerts. It was not until 1876 that Dean Church and his reforming chapter opened a choir school for 40 boys in Carter Lane. By now Maria Hackett was 93 and she visited the new school a few weeks before her death.

St Paul's was, however, only one, albeit the most important, of her chorister concerns. Following her initial battle with its dean and chapter she embarked on what became a lifelong commitment to promoting the welfare of choristers in all the English and Welsh cathedrals. Every autumn for more than fifty years she went on a tour which enabled her to visit every choral foundation at least once every three years. In a meticulously kept notebook she recorded the name and progress of every boy and each received a gift – often a new shilling, a book and a purse, though Frederick Bridge, the future organist of Westminster, recalls receiving from her a small gift of money and a sugar bun when he was a chorister at Rochester. Her greatest beneficiary was John Stainer, who was to transform the music and the conditions of the choristers at St Paul's, and whose organ lessons she paid for after he had left the cathedral choir. She also endowed a Gresham prize for cathedral composition.

Just how great was Maria Hackett's influence on the improvement of choristers' conditions is not easy to assess. Her book *A Brief Account of Cathedral and Collegiate Schools, with an Abstract of their Statutes and Endowments*, published in 1827, went to every dean and chapter, and must have made some impact but it was not until the cathedrals moved into an era of general reform that substantial progress was made. Nonetheless a few years after her death a memorial, describing her as 'The Choristers' Friend' was erected in the crypt of St Paul's, its cost having been met by subscriptions from past and present choristers of every cathedral.

In many parishes the increasing influence of the Oxford Movement, with its emphasis on the importance of well-ordered worship, led to the formation of surpliced choirs in a high proportion of parish churches. Thomas Helmore, a gifted musician, established at St Mark's College, Chelsea, a pattern of choral worship that its students took to the parishes where they became school teachers. This development was by no means confined to those places where there was a new emphasis on the centrality of the Eucharist. The model provided by the renewed cathedral choral foundations was hugely influential in churches where Mattins and Evensong remained the chief diet of Sunday worship, and in a few places there were choir schools and daily choral services, most notably Leeds Parish Church, All Saints, Margaret Street in London and St James's, Grimsby, the sole survivor of these into the present century.

Everywhere the choirs became an important element in the life of the congregation. They demanded a commitment from their members and stimulated enthusiasm that led to increased knowledge of church music.

The boys were given a stake in the church's life and a sense of companion-ship, as well as a small income gained from singing at weddings. Many of them went on to become the choirs' altos, tenors and basses.

Among the thousands of boys who had an early introduction to discip-lined singing, as well as to the church's liturgy, there were, as might have been expected, many of special talent. Some of these found their way into cathedral choirs and a number had outstanding musical careers. During the 1920s there appeared a new phenomenon – the boy soprano – who was not always a member of a church choir but who had good training and was employed to perform songs and arias in secular settings, concert halls, banquets and the like, reminiscent of the activities of the St Paul's choristers a century earlier.

The most famous of the boy sopranos, Ernest Lough, was in fact a member of the highly professional choir of the Temple Church in Lon-don's legal enclave. There he benefited from the guidance of the organist George Thalben-Ball, one of the outstanding trainers of boys' voices of all time and a notable organist who was at the Temple for nearly 60 years. Lough was born in Forest Gate, south London, in 1911 and sang in the choir of his local St Peter's Church. His uncle, Albert Frisby, was a bass in Southwark Cathedral choir and took him for an audition for his choir. He was, however, turned down and then taken to the Temple Church where, in spite of being somewhat older than most of the other probationers, he was accepted and developed so quickly that he soon became head choris-ter. He also won a place at the nearby City of London School.

One Sunday morning Lord Justice Eldon Banks, a resident of the Tem-ple and a strong supporter of the choir, was so impressed by the anthem, Mendelssohn's 'Hear my prayer' (more widely known for its middle section as 'O for the wings of a dove'), that he said afterwards that it was a pity so beautiful a performance could not be preserved. Recording was then still in its early stages and confined to special studios, but when Thalben-Ball discussed the possibilities with HMV they decided to take their recently acquired mobile recording van into the Temple precincts and record the choir singing 'Hear my prayer' in the church. Here an element of good fortune intervened, for only a few weeks earlier E. H. Fellowes and the choir of St George's Chapel had agreed to record 'Hear my prayer' for Columbia but had gone on a tour of Canada before the recording could be made. Ernest Lough, now 15, was chosen for the solo part. He recalled 60 years later in a *Daily Telegraph* interview:

We did four or five 'takes'. One was discarded because a child was whistling outside, another because the Temple clock chimed. I wasn't aware that I was making history. I was so small I had to stand on a couple of Bibles so the microphone would pick up my voice.

The record was released a few weeks later and was a sensational success, eventually selling five million copies worldwide, and became one of the outstanding bestsellers of gramophone history. Sir Compton Mackenzie wrote in the *Gramophone* magazine in July of that year: 'I am quite sure that no boy's voice has ever been recorded nearly as well as this, and I am equally sure that I have never heard such a beautiful voice.' In 1962 Lough, who became a baritone in the choir, in which he sang until 1971, was awarded a golden disc to mark the success of 'Hear my prayer'.

Other recordings inevitably followed and, although not achieving quite the same success, were nevertheless remarkable in their popularity, with Handel's 'I know that my Redeemer liveth' and 'I waited for the Lord' predictably well to the fore. Lough's own favourite recording was of 'Hear ye, Israel' from Mendelssohn's *Elijah*. This was an after-thought at the end of a recording session when some waxes were still unused. Thalben-Ball offered to produce 'Hear ye, Israel' to fill this and since Lough did not know the piece, he taught him to sing it there and then in about half an hour.

One consequence of the boy's fame was that people in London from all parts of the world attended the Temple services to hear him and the choir sing. Another was the circulation of strange rumours about him – that he had fallen and broken his skull while playing a football game at the Temple; that he had burst a blood vessel near his heart while singing and never recovered; that he had been kidnapped by a rival choirmaster and so on.

But Lough was never spoiled by his fame, neither did it bring him a fortune. The royalties went to the Inner Temple and half of these were shared by Thalben-Ball and the 24 members of the choir who had all been involved in the recordings. He was presented with a pair of cufflinks after singing Schubert's songs 'Where is Sylvia?' and 'Hark, hark the lark' at a Royal Command performance. On leaving school he joined, as a tea-boy, a leading advertising agency with which he remained for the whole of his working life, and when finally he retired from the Temple Church choir in 1971, he sang for another ten years in the Bach Choir, under Sir David Willcocks. His three sons all became choristers – two at the Temple Church, the other at the Chapel Royal, which took him, in company with his father, to sing at the coronation of Queen Elizabeth II.

Hardly less well endowed and no less well trained was Denis Barthel who was born in 1916 and joined the choir of St Stephen's Church, Rochester Row, Westminster, when he was eight. The organist and choirmaster, Dr William Bunney, became aware of an unusual talent and three years later took him to the Temple Church for an audition by George Thalben-Ball. He was accepted and became a probationer at the time when Ernest Lough was the head chorister. Barthel later acknowledged how kind and helpful Lough had been to him during his early days in the choir.

In 1931 he became head chorister and principal soloist and made a number of outstanding recordings that were received with critical acclaim. On Armistice Day 1931 he sang solo 'O valiant heart' at the first broadcast of the Festival of Remembrance in the Royal Albert Hall in the presence of King George V and Queen Mary, and, after a career in insurance, won an MBE while serving as a major in the wartime army. Ronald Mallet, who sometimes recorded with Lough, served in the war, but was shot while trying to escape from a prisoner-of-war camp in Germany.

The war years not only had a devastating effect on parish church choirs, particularly the recruitment of boy choristers, but opened the way to new and more widely appreciated forms of music in society. The days of the 'star' boy soprano therefore seemed to have ended until towards the end of the century broadcasters, especially in television, discovered that a very fine boy's voice, singing serious popular music, still had the power to attract huge audiences and sell records. The latter-day successor of Ernest Lough was Aled Jones, who was born in 1970 in North Wales and showed early promise as a singer. When only six he sang a solo in the local parish church hall and four years later BBC Wales broadcast his singing of a lullaby carol under the school Christmas tree. In the following year he had the leading part in a school production of the Lloyd Webber/Rice musical *Joseph and the Amazing Technicolour Dreamcoat*. Subsequently he won prizes in local Eisteddfod.

Aled's entry into the choir of Bangor Cathedral was almost accidental. He had initially gone to the organist and master of the choristers, Andrew Goodwin, for piano lessons, but Goodwin once asked him to sing and, recognizing an unusual talent, invited him to join the choir. Before long he was the chief soloist and received coaching from Elizabeth Le Grove, the organ scholar, who taught him to sing Mendelssohn's 'Hear my prayer' and items from *Elijah*. Commenting on Aled's ability as a chorister, George Guest, Organist and Master of the Choristers at St John's College, Cambridge, and a leading choir-trainer, said:

> He is one of the best trebles I have ever heard. I think the thing about treble singing is that you have to have three attributes – a very good voice, of course many boys have got good voices, but you also have to have an innate kind of musicianship, and then the third attribute is being virtually nerveless when performing in public. Many boys have one or two of these characteristics. Aled had all three and that is really the reason why he became such an outstanding treble.

On leaving the choir Aled received specialist vocal training, gave an increasing number of public performances in Wales and in 1984 made a record for a small Welsh recording company. This chanced to be heard by Richard Baker, then a highly respected BBC presenter, who included some of it in his radio programme *Baker's Dozen*. He said later: 'I was convinced that here was a boy's voice of exceptional quality ... comparisons with the legendary Ernest Lough quickly came to mind.' A further record followed and this chanced to be heard by Neville Marriner who, having been let down by a boy soloist for a recording of Handel's *Jephtha* at St David's Hall, Cardiff, with the BBC Welsh Symphony Orchestra and Chorus, engaged Aled at a fortnight's notice as a replacement.

His professional career now took off and was considerably enhanced when a recorded programme, *Born in Bethlehem*, made in Israel, was broadcast on Christmas Eve and Christmas Day 1984 on BBC 2. Thereafter he appeared frequently on television and in the concert hall. These demands became incompatible with those of a cathedral chorister, so, with great sadness, he left the choir. A documentary film, *The Treble*, on a year of his life was acclaimed in Britain and won an Emmy Award for its makers in America. A recording of the song 'Walking in the air' from Howard Blake's *The Snowman*, released in time for Christmas 1985, reached number five in the popularity charts, and the album of which it was a part won a Golden Disc. Shortly before Christmas he made his first appearance on *Top of the Pops* and among the hundreds of cards received on his fifteenth birthday on 29 December was one signed by every member of the Liverpool Football Club.

So it went on. He was now a national celebrity with a host of fans in many other parts of the world. Virtually everything he sang was of the popular genre and his remarkable voice was expressed through a gentle, attractive personality. Inevitably this came to an end when his voice broke and although he developed a good tenor voice this did not lead to further stardom. He did, however, become a popular presenter of radio and television music programmes. Other 'stars' of the period included Paul Miles Kingston of Winchester Cathedral and Anthony Way of St Paul's, but their fame was relatively short-lived. A national Chorister of the Year award brings recognition and considerable publicity to young singers from every sort of choir.

Meanwhile, away from the broadcasting studios and concert platforms, the number of choristers occupying the stalls in parish churches declined inexorably. Various explanations for this have been offered. The general decline in churchgoing and the inability of most churches to attract or retain the allegiance of young people undoubtedly has a good deal to do with it. The great explosion of music that came in the 1960s offered young people other forms of song that made traditional church music 'uncool'. There are now many alternative activities to the weekly choir practice and church services twice on Sunday.

Yet, in reasonably large centres of population, where some sense of community remains and there is an enthusiastic and capable musician on hand, boys' choirs of a high standard are still to be found. Elsewhere girls and women have accepted responsibility for the soprano line, often with good results.

During the second half of the twentieth century cathedral choristers flourished in ways that Maria Hackett could never have dreamt of. The renewal of cathedral life generally, stimulated by the reconsecration of Coventry Cathedral in 1962, and the demand for much higher standards of music everywhere, stimulated by broadcasting, led to a new recognition of the importance of cathedral choirs. Former Oxbridge choral scholars began in increasing numbers to replace older lay clerks who had other occupations in or near the cathedral city, and local boys, often the sons of lay clerks, were soon replaced by the sons of middle-class families who recognized the value of a disciplined musical education, at reduced fees, in what had become well-run residential preparatory schools. The overall effect of these changes was to raise the standard of cathedral music to an unprecedentedly high level and although the recruitment of choristers had, for a variety of reasons, become less easy by the end of the century, there are no signs of decline.

Indeed, the opportunities offered to choristers, including overseas tours, broadcasting and high-profile public performances, led to recognition that girls should not be denied such privileges. Recognizing that boys' and girls' voices do not happily mix, many cathedrals, led by Salisbury, established separate girls' choirs which now have a share in the singing of Sunday and weekday services – to the great benefit of the cathedral as well as of the girls.

Virtually every cathedral is now involved in a national 'Sing Up' project, designed to encourage more and better singing by children in state and other primary schools. The government provided an initial £10 million to finance this and £1 million was allocated to cathedrals. Co-ordinated by the Cathedral Choir Schools Association, grants enable directors of music and choristers to engage in 'outreach' activity that takes them into the schools of their regions, and also welcomes them into the cathedral for singing festivals. By the beginning of 2009 over 30,000 children, some from very deprived backgrounds, had become involved nationally in 'Sing Up', with the cathedrals making an increasingly significant contribution.

15

The Viennese and Parisian Innovators

During the early years of the twentieth century, when Edward Elgar was leading a revival of English music, developments in continental Europe were taking music in a very different direction. Brahms, Wagner and Mendelssohn could no longer be allowed to predominate. The origins of atonal, 12-tone serialist, modernist music, using the descriptions usually employed, are often disputed. Claude Debussy (1862–1918) – one of the greatest French composers – is the prime suspect, though some say that it goes back further to Liszt, who was thought by Wagner to be displaying signs of 'budding insanity'. But the movement that took music outside the major- and minor-key system into the mainstream originated without doubt in Vienna.

Arnold Schönberg

Arnold Schönberg, whose shopkeeper father was of German-speaking Jewish background, was born in 1874 and brought up in Vienna in a home that did not even possess a piano. He learnt much of the classical repertory from a military band that played in a coffee house, taught himself to play several instruments and learned composition from an encyclopaedia.

After working for a short time as a bank clerk, he embarked on a career as a freelance musician, advertising for pupils and, like other artists, establishing himself in one of the coffee houses, attracting his own coterie.

Schönberg's early compositions displayed only fleeting signs of dissonance, but from 1907 onwards he moved further and further away from traditional compositional techniques until public performances of his works created outrage and heavy criticism, not only from the ultra-orthodox but also from others who were generally sympathetic to new styles. Nevertheless he pressed on, attracting a few disciples, among them Alban Berg, who had been one of his first pupils and became a leading composer in Germany. Another of the early pupils was Anton Webern who developed the 12-tone technique to extremes and became even more controversial through his enthusiastic support for Hitler. He was accidentally killed in 1945 by the American military.

Schönberg had during the early years formed a Society for Creative Musicians in Vienna, of which Richard Strauss accepted honorary membership, expressing the hope that it would 'blessedly light up many minds darkened by decades of malice and stupidity'. How far it fulfilled his hope will always divide opinion, but of its profound influence on twentieth-century music there can be no doubt. It continued to develop in many different ways, and the catastrophe of the human scene in the 1930s and 40s drove some composers to extremes in their attempts to express the terror. The church, by and large, was able to accept and use it only in heavily diluted forms.

France, as always, went its own way and, significantly, its innovators were nearly all church musicians. It is a curious paradox that while the early decades of the twentieth century were witnessing the decline, virtually to the point of extinction, of the choral tradition of the French Roman Catholic Church, some of the organ lofts in Paris were occupied by musicians of outstanding brilliance and creativity.

Gabriel Fauré

Fauré, who was a contemporary of Debussy, was nurtured in the classical, flowery, Romantic style, but as his career developed his style became more simple and, although there was nothing radical about any of it, there are sometimes hints of dissonance. Overall, it represented something new, and among his pupils was another great French composer, Maurice Ravel. He was a prolific composer in several fields and from 1874 to 1905 was largely responsible for the music at the great Parisian Church of the Madeleine. His contribution to church music took the form of a series of motets, many of which are still in use in Anglican churches, and one of these, 'Cantique de Jean Racine', together with a Requiem in D minor, are among the most beautiful and most popular works in the church's choral repertory. They are also frequently performed by secular choral societies.

Fauré's secular vocal music also became widely popular in his own time – it was new, but not startlingly so – and he is often described as the master of the French art song. His chamber music is generally considered to be his best work, but his contribution to music for the piano – his favoured instrument – is hardly less important. Shortly before his death he destroyed most of his orchestral work, believing it to be of inferior standard. An early ambition to compose an opera was abandoned for want of a suitable libretto, though he produced some music for the stage.

From humble beginnings, Gabriel Fauré rose to become the most notable musical figure in Paris and appointment as Director of the Conservatoire gave him considerable prestige throughout France. He was born in 1845 in Pamiers, in the South of France, not far from the Pyrenees, and from an early age displayed unusual musical talent. When only nine he went, with the help of a scholarship from the Bishop of Pamiers, to the Ecole Niedermeyer in Paris – a school for the training of church organists and choirmasters. There he became a brilliant pianist, less good on the organ, and among his teachers was Camille Saint-Saëns, who introduced him to the music of Franz Liszt and Robert Schumann. Saint-Saëns was ten years his senior, but they became lifelong friends. Fauré spent 11 years at the school, and it was towards the end of his time there that he composed 'Cantique de Jean Racine', winning first prize for it in a competition. He left in 1866 to become organist of the church in Rennes where he found provincial life dull and the musical life of the town virtually non-existent. Relief came in 1870 through enlistment in the army during the Franco-Prussian war, and he was present at the raising of the Siege of Paris.

On demobilization he taught for a short time at the Ecole Niedermeyer when it had moved to Switzerland to escape the Paris Commune. But he returned to the capital in October 1871 to become assistant to Charles-Marie Widor, the organist of the Church of Saint Sulpice. He also helped to found the Société National de Musique and in 1874 began to deputize for Saint-Saëns at the Madeleine during his absences for national and international engagements. When Saint-Saëns retired he was succeeded by Théodore Dubois (yet another outstanding musician) and Fauré was appointed choirmaster, remaining at the church until 1905, succeeding Dubois as organist in 1896.

The choirmaster post was something of a chore involving responsibility for the daily services in Paris's most fashionable church, but having recently married he needed the money. The 20 boy choristers ('my geese', he called them) were often difficult to manage, and members of the small orchestra – enlarged for big occasions – were not always co-operative. Much worse were the clergy, who tried to keep their fashionable congregation happy with the operatic style of music then in vogue, leaving no scope for new compositions.

In 1888 Fauré ventured to use his Requiem for its first public performance, at the funeral of a well-known Paris architect. After the service he was summoned to the sacristy and asked by the parish priest, 'What was that Mass for the dead you have just conducted?' 'It was a requiem of my own composition,' Fauré replied. 'Monsieure Fauré,' responded the priest, 'we don't need all these novelties, the Madeleine's repertory is quite rich enough; just content yourself with that.' Soon, however, it was being performed all over Europe.

It has sometimes been suggested that the Requiem was composed during a time of sadness caused by the deaths of both Fauré's parents, but this seems not to have been the case. He said in 1902 that it was 'an attempt to compose something new and different. That's how I see death – as a joyful deliverance, as aspiration towards happiness beyond the grave, rather than a painful experience.' It was also unusual in that it left out the *Dies Irae* and the Benedictus from the normal Requiem and he substituted some funeral texts, including 'In Paradisum', which was usually spoken at the graveside. The work took over 20 years to complete in its various forms. The 'In Paradisum' and the 'Pie Jesu' are frequently performed separately as motets. An 'Ave Maria' and an 'Ave verum corpus' are also among his popular motets.

It was many years before Fauré achieved fame since his style was not acceptable to the French musical establishment. Until then he was invariably short of money; the birth of two sons required him to augment his modest salary from the Madeleine with much teaching of piano and harmony. Unwisely, he sold the copyright of his early works to a publisher for a mere 50 francs each, and during this period of his life he was able to compose only in the summer holidays.

All this and what had proved to be an unsatisfactory marriage left him often depressed. He had an attractive personality, a soft voice and a charming manner. The casual, delicate way he moved, and the charm of his music, led his friends to call him 'the Cat', and in the early 1890s he established a liaison with Emma Bardac who would later marry Claude Debussy. She had a young daughter, Dolly, of her previous marriage and this inspired Fauré to compose a *Dolly Suite,* the *berceuse* from which was played as the opening and closing music for the BBC's *Listen with Mother* radio programme from 1950 to 1982.

In 1900, the relationship with Emma having ended, he fell in love with Marguerite Masselmans, who was only 24 but already married. Divorce being socially out of the question, she became his mistress and brought him great happiness until his death in 1924. From 1902 onwards, however, he began to suffer from hearing problems and, although he continued to compose for some more years, he was in the end able to hear his music only in his head. This deafness was concealed from all but a few friends and he remained Director of the Conservatoire until 1920, when his retirement was marked by the conferring of the Grand-Croix of the Légion d'Honneur – a rare honour for a musician. Death came four years later and the Requiem was performed at his state funeral in the Madeleine.

Olivier Messiaen

Messiaen was the most important French composer of the twentieth century and the first to make a complete break with the classical Western tradition. In 1937 he complained:

> Twentieth century music is miserably, continuously laggard! This is normal. It has always been so: but never has the gap (between music and the other arts) been so scandalous as it is now. This is why we must support with all our energy those – a ridiculously small company – three or four in the whole world – who are trying to regain a little of the lost ground.

His definition of successful music was that it must be 'interesting, beautiful to listen to and touch the listener'. He was radical without being doctrinaire. His style, with its intense colour and irregular rhythms, is immediately recognizable. A good deal of his music also includes birdsong, since he was a keen ornithologist as well as a composer, and he described birds as 'the greatest musicians'. Other features of his environment influenced him. Encounters with Hindu, Balinese, Javanese and Japanese cultures during visits to the East left their mark, especially the Indonesian gamelan – a form of tuned percussion that Benjamin Britten and some other composers adopted much later. A newly created electronic instrument, the *ondes Martenot*, which makes an eerie, haunting sound, akin to Hindu music, found a use in his *Turangalîla Symphonie* (1948).

All these elements in Messiaen's generous output undoubtedly require of those unacquainted with more modern styles a degree of perseverance for it to be fully appreciated. It doesn't always disclose its secrets immediately and it is unforgiving of incompetent performance. When it was first performed in Britain in the late 1950s, it created a sensation. But, unlike the more avant-garde composers, including his own pupils, Karlheinz Stockhausen and Boulez, he was committed to the supremacy of the melody.

A devout man, and probably a mystic, though he disliked the term, Messiaen was the twentieth century's most theological composer. The American critic Alex Ross makes this point in a striking contrast of his work with that of Schönberg:

> The difference between Schönberg and Messiaen is ultimately theological. Schönberg believed that God is unrepresentable, that his presence could be indicated only by placing a taboo on the familiar. Messiaen felt that God was present everywhere and in all sound. Therefore there was no need for the new to supersede the old: God's creation gathered magnificence as it opened up in space and time.

As he grew older, Messiaen's formal attachment to the Roman Catholic Church weakened, yet a great deal of his work is an expression of the great doctrines of the Catholic faith. It is infused with an awareness of the divine love, the miracle of human redemption and the experience of joy. Sadly, most of his essentially liturgical works had for many years to be performed in concert halls rather than in churches. Not now. In 1998 his motet 'O sacrum convivium' was used in almost one-third of English Anglican cathedrals. Some also used 'Le banquet céleste', 'Les images' (from *La Nativité du Seigneur)*, his *Solemn Mass* and his *Mass for Pentecost*. But most churchgoers encounter Messiaen through his great organ music which is in the repertory of every cathedral, and the best parish church, organist.

He was born into a literary family in Avignon in 1908. After teaching himself to play the piano, he had lessons from Paul Dukas, who was also the teacher of Duruflé. Turning to composition, he became interested in the ground-breaking work of Debussy and Ravel, and when the family moved to Paris in 1919 he entered the Conservatoire. There he was taught by two great organists, Widor and Marcel Dupré, who introduced him to the French organist tradition. Maurice Emmanuel, his composition teacher, 'converted' him to modal-style music.

Having deputized for several years for the often sick organist of La Trinité Church in Paris, Messiaen succeeded to his post in 1931. Appointment was agreed only after he had given an assurance that he would not 'disturb the piety of the faithful with overly anarchic chords'. How far he was able to honour this has not been recorded, but he remained at La Trinité until his death in 1992. Meanwhile in 1932 he married Claire Delbos, a composer and violinist, and in the following year joined three other young composers in the forming of *La Jeune France*. This survived for only a short time, but enabled them to explore music together. While still only a student he had himself published *Eight Preludes for Piano* (1929), using a distinctive modal technique which suggested a highly original musical talent. He was for many years able to compose only as the spirit moved him and not for commissions. In 1934 he produced *L'Ascension*, a massive, deeply religious work for orchestra, and this was quickly followed by *O sacrum convivium* (1935) for organ and solo voice, and an organ cycle *La nativité du Seigneur* (1935) which is now regarded as one of the great organ works of the twentieth century.

In 1936 Messiaen began to teach at the Ecole Normale de Musique and the Schola Cantorum, and three years later published another organ cycle, *Le Corps glorieux*. But on the outbreak of war in 1939 he was conscripted as a medical auxiliary in the French army (he had poor eyesight which ruled out combatant duties) and in 1940 was captured at Verdun and sent to a prisoner-of-war camp in Silesia. There he relieved hunger and intense cold by composing and performing, and produced *Quatuor pour la fin du temps* for a poorly tuned piano, cello, violin and clarinet. This was first performed, out of doors in January, for 5,000 prisoners and guards, and the score was prefaced with a text, 'There shall be time no longer' (Revelation 10.6). Later it came to be regarded as a masterpiece.

Following his release in 1942, Messiaen returned to Paris where he became Professor of Harmony at the Conservatoire and resumed his duties at La Trinité. The grim conditions in wartime Paris were not conducive to inspired composition, but he attracted a group of highly talented young composers who were to become leaders of the avant-garde. Among these was a brilliant young pianist, Yvonne Loriod, who became his second wife and exercised a great influence on his work. He composed several pieces for her, including a two-and-a-half-hour work, *Vingt regards sur l'Enfant Jésus* (1944), which received international acclaim.

During the 1950s Messiaen's work was mainly based on adaptations of birdsong. This was not an original concept – Dukas had urged all his students to 'listen to the birds' – and other composers had, with varying degrees of success, tried to make use of their music. But Messiaen introduced their natural sound, most effectively in *Catalogue d'Oiseaux* for piano (1956–58) which included pieces for particular birds, including curlew, garden warbler, buzzard, wheatear and thrush. Birdsong was also used in his orchestral work and he rarely composed anything without including it.

After a decade of this, and one in which his gifts and special contribution had become widely recognized, he returned to major religious themes. *La transfiguration* (1968–69), in 14 movements, was designed for a 100-voice, 10-part choir, several solo instruments and a large orchestra. *Méditations sur le mystère de la Sainte Trinité* (1969) is a major organ work, while *Saint-François d'Assise* (1975–79) is an opera inspired by reading a life of the saint. This was performed in the Royal Festival Hall, London, in 1988 to celebrate Messiaen's eightieth birthday. Themes related to life after death increasingly engaged him.

His final years were, however, seriously affected by back problems that required frequent operations, and, following his death in 1992, it was left to his wife to complete his *Treatise on Rhythm, Colour and Birdsong* – a multi-volume work on musical theory, the title of which summarized his own distinctive contribution to twentieth-century music. He had been awarded many honours in several countries, and the highest rank of France's Légion d'Honneur. The centenary of his birth in 2008 was marked in Britain by performances of his work in many cathedrals and concert halls, and the special attention of BBC Radio 3.

Francis Poulenc

Although much less well known in Britain, and the composer of only a small amount of church music, Francis Poulenc made an important and distinctive contribution to the development of twentieth-century music. Writing shortly after his death in 1963, Lennox Berkeley said, 'There are many passages in his religious music that are strangely haunting – moments that reveal a touching tenderness and simplicity of heart, and that remain in the memory.'

His Mass in G (1937) represented something quite new in French music and, like his subsequent religious compositions, was a deliberate attempt to break with the German Romantic style which he believed had dominated the liturgy in French cathedrals and major parish churches for far too long. By 1998 his Mass was being performed in about eight per cent of British cathedrals and choral foundations, and there was a wider appreciation among them of his anthems and motets. Of these, 'Videntes stellam' registered 20 per cent, 'Seigneur Je vous en prie' 18 per cent, 'Vinea mea electa' 15 per cent, 'Quem vidistis' and 'O magnum mysterium' both 14 per cent. In total, about 20 of his works were used that year.

Poulenc belonged to a group of young composers, *Les Six*, who reacted against Debussy's style and identified themselves with a burgeoning Parisian artistic movement. His own music, which extended to opera, ballet, song, oratorio, chamber and orchestral as well as organ, is characterized by clear rhythms, wonderful harmonies and, as with Messiaen, priority to melody. There is also something of Fauré's inventiveness. In his religious work, however, some musicologists claim to have detected what they believe to have been a struggle to come to terms with the conflict between his homosexual life and his Catholic faith. He was in fact bisexual and, besides relationships with various musicians, writers and a painter, was involved with several women. A Paris critic once described him as 'le moine et le voyeur' (half monk, half scallywag) – a comment on his music, as well as on his lifestyle – and he suffered long periods of depression.

He was born into a musical family in Paris in 1899. His father was a devout Catholic but his mother, who taught him to play the piano, was a free-thinker. From an early age he displayed unusual talent and when 14 was so deeply impressed by a recital given by Edward Risler, a leading pianist of the time, that he announced his intention to be a composer. During the years of the 1914–18 war he was influenced by a number of leading Parisian musicians and later acknowledged a debt to Igor Stravinsky. As a composer, however, Poulenc was largely self-taught, which, as in the case of other twentieth-century innovators, may explain his originality.

It was during National Service with the army in 1918 that he began to compose short pieces and a number of piano sonatas aroused much interest. His first success, when only 18, was achieved without his having had a single lesson. Later he studied with Charles Koechlin, a leading teacher, who encouraged the development of an individual style which would for some years make him the *enfant terrible* of the French musical establishment. In 1936, however, the deaths of several close friends led him to make a pilgrimage to Rocamdour in south-central France, where he had a vivid personal experience at the shrine of the Black Virgin. This led to his recovery of the Catholic faith from which he had lapsed, and made some of his future music more sombre. *Litanies à la Vierge Noire* (1936) was the first indication of this, though eventually he contributed to church music a refreshing combination of profundity and high spirits. His *Stabat Mater* (1951) is probably the best known of his religious compositions, his magnificent Gloria (1961) the most uplifting. There are many motets, and a brilliant organ concerto (1938) is widely believed to be among the finest of the century. His death, following a heart attack in 1963, caused great sorrow in the musical world where he was a popular figure.

Maurice Duruflé

Maurice Duruflé, who was organist of St Etienne-du-Mont in Paris from 1929 until the end of his life in 1986, composed only 14 pieces of choral music, but virtually all of these are now performed in one or other of the British cathedrals and choral foundations. Three of them – his Requiem Mass and the motets 'Ubi caritas et amor', 'Tantum ergo sacramentum' – are among the best loved of the entire choral repertory. All are firmly based in Gregorian chant and display none of the adventurous spirit of Duruflé's distinguished contemporaries. But each has its own distinctive content – no one else could have composed them – and most are the fruits of numerous revisions, some after their first publication.

He was born in Louviers in Normandy in 1902 and when aged ten became a chorister at Rouen Cathedral, attending its then flourishing choir school. There he studied piano, organ and musical theory, and was greatly influenced by the traditional Catholic music of the cathedral. When the family moved to Paris, young Maurice entered the Conservatoire mainly to concentrate on the organ and was fortunate enough to be taught by César Franck. But he also studied piano accompaniment, composition and harmony, and carried off the first prizes in all his four subjects. For several years he was deputy organist at the Basilica of St Clotilde and influenced by the teaching of Louis Vierne at the Conservatoire. In 1927 Duruflé became assistant at Notre Dame and two years later was appointed organist of St Etienne-du-Mont in Paris – a post he retained until the end of his life in 1986. Soon after this he married his assistant, Marie-Madeleine

Chevalier, who was 12 years younger than himself. In 1943 he started to teach at the Conservatoire and became at the same time Director of the Gregorian Institute.

His Requiem, composed for choir, soloists, organ and orchestra, was first published in 1947 and later appeared in versions for organ only and organ with small orchestral accompaniment. In 1998 it was used, often on All Souls' Day, by 23 per cent of British cathedrals and choral foundations, a substantial increase on the nine per cent in 1986. His *Messe cum jubilo* (1972) was also used in 17 per cent of these places in 1998, an increase from seven per cent. Duruflé was, however, primarily an organist and a composer of fine organ music. He premiered Poulenc's organ concerto in 1939, and in the 1960s and 70s toured extensively with his second wife (also a gifted player) as an organ duo. But this came to an end in 1975 when he was seriously injured in a car accident and had to give up performing. His wife took over at St Etienne-du-Mont, though he retained the organist title.

Jean Langlais

Jean Langlais, another musician greatly influenced by Messiaen, was blind from the age of two, but from 1945 to 1987 was the organist of the Basilica of St Clotilde in Paris, where César Franck was among his predecessors. Before that he had had a long spell at the Church of St Pierre-de-Montrouge. Born in 1907 in a village near Mont St Michel, he was educated in Paris. Evident musical talent took him to the Conservatoire where he was a pupil of Marcel Dupré for organ and Paul Dukas for composition. Messiaen was also a student there at the same time.

Langlais taught at the Conservatoire from 1961 to 1976 as well as at the Schola Cantorum where he was said to be the best teacher of improvization in the world. Students from many different parts of the world travelled to Paris to learn under him. During this period of his life he composed no fewer than 254 works, many of which display his own high-spirited approach, and all of which are typical of mid-twentieth-century music – free tonal and varied rhythms. His style is much less distinctive than that of Messiaen, and in the field of secular music he is much less significant.

About a dozen of his anthems were, however, performed in one or other of Britain's cathedrals and choral foundations in 1998, none of them frequently, though four per cent of these churches used as a motet the Agnus Dei from his *Missa in Simplicitate*, composed for solo voice and organ. About 43 per cent of them used his *Messe Solennelle*, almost double the use in 1986. It had achieved immediate popularity following its first performance in Paris, and it displays clearly the influence of plainsong, which Langlais had studied closely.

As with Poulenc, much more is heard of Langlais through his lively organ music. Most of this requires an organist of the very highest competence for its best performance. He was himself a brilliant performer, who toured extensively in Europe and America, and also a colourful character. He was married, but kept a mistress, whom he later married and who presented him with a son when he was 73. He died in 1991.

16

Mid-Twentieth-Century Explorers

By about 1950 the modernist atonal composers of Western Europe and America were still seeking to extend the boundaries of dissonant music. In Britain, however, the Church of England was, for the most part, still luxuriating in the glorious, uplifting works of Elgar and Vaughan Williams. Herbert Howells had made a significant mark with a highly distinctive style that gently broke new ground, but, because of its feeling for melody, would in no sense be regarded as avant-garde. It also seemed as if he now had nothing new to say, though what he said was still worth hearing and using.

Benjamin Britten was well known in serious classical music circles, and some cathedrals were bold enough to use his relatively small amount of church music. But recognition as equal to Elgar and Vaughan Williams in importance still lay in the future and, although the performance of his masterpiece *War Requiem* in Coventry Cathedral in 1962 would create a sensation, he was, and remained, an essentially conservative composer who owed nothing to Schönberg and Webern, but a very great deal to Henry Purcell, who had treated harmony with a freedom that would have been unthinkable after the end of the seventeenth century.

There were nonetheless some English composers who were taking the modernist movement seriously and trying, in their own distinctive voice, to interpret and develop this in ways that might gain for it an appreciative hearing in the more adventurous concert halls and even, perhaps, in those most conservative bastions of music – the cathedrals. None of them achieved great international fame, but all were important contributors to the music of twentieth-century Britain.

William Walton

William Walton is best known for his stirring music for ceremonial occasions and for some iconic wartime films, but none of this is fully representative of his style, and although his contribution to church music was small it remains significant. Like Elgar, he was largely self-taught and, astonishingly, was still only a schoolboy when he composed an unaccompanied setting of a poem by Phineas Fletcher which begins 'Drop, drop slow tears' and was later published as 'A Litany'. It is still widely used by cathedrals. National recognition also came early with an orchestral work, *Façade*, which occupied him for much of the 1920s. This broke new ground and was booed and hissed at the end of its first performance in 1929. But it soon came to be seen as a work of considerable importance, incorporating some of the dissonance he had imbibed during a previous flirtation with the continental atonal school but also lively modern jazz.

Soon after this (1930–31) a full-scale cantata, *Belshazzar's Feast*, commissioned by the BBC, also created a stir with its use of violent music to express the atmosphere and action of an Old Testament story. Not yet 30, Walton was established as a composer of note. Symphonies, operas, chamber music, concertos and much else, including 15 film scores, followed but, having made a precocious start, his later years were much less productive.

William Walton was born in Oldham, Lancashire, in 1902 and into a family where there was little money. His father, a baritone, eked out a living as a music teacher and organist of a local church; his mother earned a little as a contralto. Young William joined his father's choir, which was a good one, and at the age of ten won a choristership at Christ Church, Oxford, which set him on the path to a great musical career. The Dean of Christ Church at the time was T. B. (Tommy) Strong, who had unusual administrative gifts and was also a highly competent organist. During his own time as an undergraduate at the college he played the organ for Evensong on Thursdays when Dr Corfe, the organist, was out hunting and could not get back in time. As dean, he was happiest when in the company of undergraduates and did his best to stamp out snobbery in the 'House'. So, having taken Walton under his wing when he was a chorister, he contrived to get him into the university when he was just 16 and virtually financed his years as an undergraduate at Christ Church.

These years were not very profitable in terms of musical tuition, though he received some help from Hugh Allen, the organist of Christ Church and Professor of Music in the university. He did, however, spend a good deal of time in the library studying the scores of Debussy, Ravel, Prokoviev and Stravinsky. This led to the composition of an experimental string quartet which was published in 1922 and praised by the arch-atonalist Alban Berg, but later withdrawn by Walton because, as he put it, 'It is full of undigested Bartok and Schönberg.'

He successfully completed both parts of the BMus but, having three times failed Reponsions (a basic test imposed on all undergraduates at that time), left Oxford without a degree.

This did not matter. He was immediately befriended by Osbert and Edith

Sitwell, who took him into their London home, introduced him to their cultural circle, and gave him financial support so that he might be free to compose. When he left, ten years later, this support was taken over by T. B. Strong, who had become a wholly ineffective bishop, Lord Berners and Siegfried Sassoon. It was augmented in the 1930s by a bequest from Elizabeth Courtauld which guaranteed him an income of £500 a year for life. All of which was put to good use, leading to a considerable output of music which, while not actually avant-garde, had enough early twentieth-century influence to indicate a distinctive voice and an openness to new ideas. These were suppressed somewhat in 1937, when he was invited to compose a march for the coronation of King George VI. During his early years he had absorbed sufficient Anglican music to enable him to judge what would sound right in Westminster Abbey, and, possibly sensing that the grim times required a march to raise the spirits, looked back to Elgar and produced *Crown Imperial*. This was a huge success and continues to be used on ceremonial and other less formal occasions.

In the following year, and in complete contrast, he composed for a wedding a short anthem, 'Set me a seal upon thy heart', which again remains immensely popular, and not only at weddings. Most cathedrals include it in their repertory. For the coronation of the present Queen in 1953 he was an automatic choice for appropriate music and produced another stirring march, *Orb and Sceptre*. But it was his electrifying Te Deum that outshone the rest of a notable offering of music.

Walton's involvement in film scores began in 1934 and continued steadily until the outbreak of war in 1939. He was exempted from military service and attached to a unit responsible for the production of what might broadly be described as propaganda films. The first of these, *The First of the Few* – relating to the Battle of Britain – was the most memorable and his *Spitfire* Prelude and Fugue is still in use, mainly by the RAF. Several more war films followed and also fine music for Laurence Olivier's film adaptations of Shakespeare's *Henry V* (1944), *Hamlet* (1947) and *Richard III*. At a quite different level, the composition of music for a grand opera, *Troilus and Cressida,* proved to be a great personal struggle, partly because of his aversion to anything short of perfection. And, even though it was well received at Covent Garden and in New York and San Francisco, when it eventually appeared in 1954, it was deemed a failure at La Scala, Milan.

This was a devastating blow, compounded 15 years later when his music for a new film on the Battle of Britain was rejected on the grounds that it was too short for a long-playing record. Without being given the chance to remedy this, a new composer was engaged. Olivier protested and threatened to remove his name from the film credits; eventually a short piece of Walton's composition was included. These rejections, allied to the fact that his music went out of fashion in the post-war years, had a destructive effect on his creativity, though his Second Symphony (1960) is generally considered to be one of his best works. And it was during this time that most of his valuable choral music was produced. Gloria (1961), for chorus and orchestra, was commissioned by the Huddersfield Choral Society. *The Twelve* (1965) is to a text by W. H. Auden, and for choir and organ. There is a much-used *Missa Brevis* (1966) and an even more popular *Chichester Service*. A Jubilate Deo (1972) is another favourite.

Walton's personal life during his early years was as turbulent and colourful as that of most others in the Sitwell circle. A liaison with the impecunious Baroness Imma Doenberg was something of a disaster but led, it was said, to the splendidly stormy music of his First Symphony. Later he entered into a long and happy marriage to the Argentinian Susana Gil Passo, most of which was spent on the Mediterranean island of Ischia. He was the recipient of many honours, which included a knighthood, but his death in 1983 came far too soon for him to be aware of the renewed appreciation of his music at the end of the century.

Lennox Berkeley

Lennox Berkeley composed a great deal of fine music that is generally underrated. This is, perhaps, because for the most part he stood outside the English tradition. There is nothing in his work to suggest that he ever heard any of the music of Elgar and Vaughan Williams, but much to indicate that he had been schooled in Paris by Ravel and Boulanger; yet his influence on English music was important. He was Professor of Composition at the Royal Academy of Music from 1946 to 1968, and among his pupils were John Tavener and Richard Rodney Bennett. Worshippers in cathedrals are almost certain to hear some of his music during the course of the year.

He was born into an aristocratic family in Oxford in 1903 and, had there not been an irregularity in his father's marriage, he would have eventually become the Earl of Berkeley and the occupant of Berkeley Castle. The effect of this on his future work as a composer can only be a matter for speculation. From the Dragon School, Oxford, he went to Gresham's School, Holt, in Norfolk (remarkably, the school also of W. H. Auden and Benjamin Britten), but had to leave when he was 15 owing to ill-health.

After a period of home-tutoring, he resumed his education at St George's School, Windsor, where the first public performance of his music was given at a school concert. At Merton College, Oxford, he read French, Old French and philology, but, more significantly, he met the French composer Maurice Ravel, who was impressed by his music and suggested that he should, after Oxford, go to Paris to study with Nadia Boulanger. By the time he arrived in Paris one of his small orchestral works had already been heard on the BBC and, during the next few years, he not only imbibed much of his teacher's style, but also established a friendship with Ravel and met Stravinsky, Fauré and Poulenc. Hardly less influential was his conversion to Roman Catholicism, the effects of which coloured a good deal of his subsequent music.

He then spent four years on the French Riviera, caring for his frail parents, enjoying a lively social life in the company of a neighbour, Somerset Maugham, composing a violin sonata and starting on an oratorio, *Jonah*. A visit to the ISCM festival in Barcelona in 1936 led to a meeting with Benjamin Britten. A close friendship resulted, and he lived for a time with Britten in a converted windmill at Snape, near Aldeburgh. But the relationship cooled considerably after Britten went with Peter Pears to America in 1939.

Three years later, during the darkest days of the war, Berkeley joined the BBC as a talks producer but was soon moved to the music department to be an orchestral programme planner. In 1943 he conducted the London Philharmonic Orchestra at the Proms in the premiere of his own Symphony No. 1, and the same year saw the premiere of his *Divertimento*.

Soon after the end of the war he married Freda Bernstein, his BBC secretary, and began a long, happy and musically creative partnership with her. Their son Michael also became a composer. He also began his long teaching career at the Royal Academy of Music. Thereafter his life as a composer continued to flourish and he added three more symphonies, choral, chamber, opera, piano and guitar music. All of this is unmistakeable in its attractive, robust, yet melodic style, though there are some atonal elements and not all is deemed to be of the highest quality.

Berkeley's real strength lies in his vocal and choral music, of which the *Four Poems of St Teresa of Avila* (composed for the great contralto Kathleen Ferrier, in 1947) is outstanding. The church has also benefited greatly from his genius. The *Missa Brevis* (1960) is one of the most frequently performed Mass settings in cathedrals. But a *Mass for Five Voices* (1964) has never caught on. An anthem, 'The Lord is my Shepherd' (1975), has a strong following, and the canticles of the *Chichester Service*, commissioned by the cultured and always perceptive Dean Walter Hussey, are a distinguished twentieth-century contribution to cathedral music. Two other anthems, 'I sing of a maiden' and 'Look up, sweet babe', are popular and, looking beyond acts of worship, there is a *Stabat Mater*, which he dedicated to Benjamin Britten, when he became a godfather to Michael, and an opera *Ruth* (1956).

Although he had an attractive personality, was generous and encouraging to others, and was an important composer, Berkeley never moved into the musical establishment of his time. He was nonetheless widely honoured and given a knighthood in 1974. He unveiled a memorial stone to Benjamin Britten in Westminster Abbey in 1978, and a year later began his last opera, *Faldon Park*, commissioned by English National Opera. But from 1985 onwards he was increasingly disabled by Alzheimer's disease and died a few days before the end of 1989. A memorial Mass was celebrated in Westminster Cathedral by Cardinal Basil Hume, and broadcast on BBC Radio 3.

Michael Tippett

The music of Michael Tippett, one of the twentieth century's foremost English composers, is no less complex than that of his own personality. Moreover, having lived through virtually the whole of the century (1905–98), he was deeply influenced by the changes and chances of what now appears to have been the most turbulent, innovative, destructive period of human experience. It cannot be surprising that something of this is expressed in the music of a sensitive composer such as Tippett. What makes his work especially interesting is that not only its content but also its style changed with the passage of time.

He was nothing like as prolific a composer as were most of his contemporaries and he started much later in life than virtually all of them. More than they, he tended to look back, and be influenced by the work of some of his most significant predecessors. Since these included composers as diverse as Elgar and Stravinsky, with also space for jazz and blues, the result was a singular twentieth-century voice that is not always easy to listen to and sometimes taxes the skill of even the most accomplished performer. Yet its importance was recognized by many honours, including a knighthood in 1966 and admission to the Order of Merit in 1983.

Although born in London, Tippett's early childhood was spent mainly in Suffolk. At Stamford Grammar School in Lincolnshire he learned to play the piano and decided that he wanted to be a composer. Life for him was not, however, straightforward. His parents were driven by financial problems to reside in France, he had some unhappy personal experiences as a school boarder, and discovered his own homosexuality. About this he subsequently made no secret.

He went to the Royal College of Music to study composition with Charles Wood, whose teaching was of lasting influence, and conducting with Adrian Boult and Malcolm Sargent. On leaving the College at the end of 1928 he went to live in Oxted, Surrey, where he made a modest start to a musical career before returning to the RCM for two further years of study.

Involvement with some of the social consequences of the 1930s economic depression encouraged a left-wing outlook which took him in 1935 into membership of the Communist Party. This did not last long, however, since, as a Trotskyist, he was strongly opposed to the Stalinist stance of his branch. He also parted company, though for different reasons, with his homosexual partner. This led to a major personal crisis and consultation with a Jungian analyst.

The next crisis arose from his pacificism and membership of the Peace Pledge Union. On the outbreak of war in 1939 he registered as a conscientious objector, but refused to accept agricultural work that would have involved relinquishing his teaching post at Morley College. He was therefore sent to prison for three months, and towards the end of his life unveiled in London a stone commemorating conscientious objectors. Following his release from prison he was allowed to resume his work at Morley College. For several years, starting in the late 1960s, he conducted the Leicester Schools Symphony Orchestra, concentrating mainly on twentieth-century music and raising its standard to radio and recording level.

For the most part, however, he combined the life of a composer with that of a cultured intellectual, and became involved in another turbulent homosexual relationship which lasted for 17 years before ending in tears. During this time he entered into an additional liaison with Meirion Bowen, which survived until the end of his life in 1998. Besides offering emotional support, Bowen served him as a personal assistant, dealing with his correspondence, negotiating commissions and acting as an influential sounding-board for his compositions.

Tippett's music embraced opera, orchestral, chamber, piano sonata and choral/vocal music, and of his choral music, the earliest, an oratorio, *A Child of our Time* (1941), is arguably the most important. Like many other composers, he was an agnostic, and this oratorio cannot be accounted church music. But its content was deeply spiritual, as well as intensely humanist. It was started during the early days of the 1939–45 war, soon after he had completed dream therapy, and prompted by a pogrom of Polish Jews carried out by German Nazis the previous November.

At the suggestion of T. S. Eliot, Tippett wrote the libretto himself and the music of the text was interspersed with interpretations of Negro Spirituals, such as 'Deep river' and 'Go down Moses'. (These are now frequently performed as church anthems.) The impact of the work was considerable and it is possible to believe that it provided a model for Benjamin Britten's *War Requiem*, in which the poetry of Wilfred Owen plays an important part. Britten and Tippett admired each other's music and were close friends.

In the preface to another, later, oratorio, *The Mask of Time* (1982), Tippett said that it 'deals with those fundamental matters that bear upon man, his relationship with Time, his place in the world as we know it and in the mysterious universe at large'. Agnostic humanism did not, however, prevent him from composing, at the request of George Guest, a magnificent set of Evensong canticles for the choir of St John's College, Cambridge.

Kenneth Leighton

Kenneth Leighton is different again. In common with Lennox Berkeley, he drew more on modern continental sources than on twentieth-century British music, but as an academic (he was Professor of Music at Edinburgh University from 1970 to 1988) his compositions are all marked by a distinctive intellectual rigour.

From the beginning of his musical career he was an explorer, concerned to discover new styles of music and evaluate their significance. For many years the radical atonal style of the Viennese school, especially that of Alban Berg, heavily influenced him and made his work less accessible to most ordinary music lovers. But later, and without losing its 'edge', a more relaxed, even lyrical, element brought his music closer to that of Messiaen. And, although much of his life was spent in Scotland, he became a notable contributor to Anglican church music. This owed a good deal to his early education.

Born in Wakefield in 1929, he became a chorister at Wakefield Cathedral, and, displaying unusual talent as a pianist, took the LRAM when only 17. A scholarship to Queen's College, Oxford, enabled him to take a degree in classics, and he stayed on to study for a BMus under the supervision of Bernard Rose. He then went to Rome on the Mendelssohn Scholarship to study with the Italian avant-garde composer Goffredo Petrassi.

On his return to England in 1952 Leighton became, somewhat improbably it might be thought, Professor of Theory at the Royal Marine School of Music at Deal. A year later, however, he won a fellowship in music at Leeds University. By this time his output, which would eventually extend to over 100 items, was growing rapidly. It included an opera (*Columba*), symphonies, sonatas, concertos, organ music and fine piano works, besides church music, of which two cantatas, *The Light Invisible* (1958) and *Crucifixus Nobis* (1961), made a distinguished start.

In the following year an extended anthem, 'Alleluia, Amen', displayed a sensitive use of the organ, as might have been expected of a professional keyboard player. He was capable of performing his own work on BBC Radio 3. Four of his anthems, 'Let all the world', 'Drop, drop slow tears', 'God is ascended' and 'Solus ad victimam', are more widely used, and two of his sets of canticles, *Collegium Magdalena Oxoniensis* (also known as 'in G') and *Second Service*, are very popular. His Eucharist in D is specially useful when only men's voices are available, and best known of all are his *Preces and Responses* which can be guaranteed to rouse any somnolent congregation.

Leighton's academic career took him from Leeds to Edinburgh where he was Lecturer then Reader in Music from 1956 to 1968. He was in Oxford, briefly, as a Fellow of Worcester College and university Lecturer in Music, before returning to Edinburgh as Professor. So long and distinguished a career in teaching inevitably had a considerable influence on successive generations of students, among whom were James MacMillan and Stephen Oliver. Leighton died in 1988.

17

The Oxbridge Choirs

Although the public profile of the Oxford choirs in the twentieth century never came near to that of King's College, Cambridge, this was as much to do with architecture as it was with music. The quality of the music at New College, Magdalen College, and, later, Christ Church, was no less high.

Kenneth Andrews

The revival at New College started with the appointment of Kenneth Andrews as organist in 1938. He had previously spent four years at Beverley Minster, where he inspired great loyalty in his choristers (at least one of whom is still attending the Minster 70 years later), and, having private means, he paid some of the songmen, that is, lay clerks, of York Minster to sing for him at Sunday Evensong. At New College he also subsidized the six lay clerks, which pleased the bursar but created problems for his successors. He soon raised the standard of the choir to a higher level than that of any other Oxford college and made a number of distinguished recordings, though the war years inevitably brought problems.

Andrews, being notably eccentric, attracted many stories about his attitudes and activities – most of them true. He would apparently lock the chapel doors from time to time to keep the congregation out, lest they disturb his music. He hated large-scale community occasions, such as the annual carol service, which he always conducted with his plus-fours conspicuously displayed under his surplice. He also carried a written resignation in his pocket, which, as the service progressed, he transferred, first to his music desk, then to his hand, before giving it to a lay clerk who also worked in the bursary – 'Speakman, hand this to the Precentor tomorrow morning.' At the end of the service, however, he carefully retrieved the letter, though legend has it that he once forgot to do this and his resignation was announced and implemented the following day.

Another story, which may be apocryphal, relates to the BBC's wartime practice of recording broadcast Choral Evensong on four consecutive weeks from the same location. For security reasons the service was always announced as coming from 'somewhere in England'. New College choir took its turn at a time when Westminster Abbey was seeking a new organist and master of the choristers and, mistakenly supposing that the service was coming impressively from Magdalen College, appointed its organist, William McKie, to the post.

Andrews, an acknowledged authority on the music of William Byrd, was also open to the work of modern composers and welcomed Herbert Howells to the first use of his *New College* canticles. Howells followed the choir into the vestry after the service and congratulated them on the beautiful singing of his music. To which Andrews made the whispered response, 'Just shows what he knows about it.' Following his retirement from New College he continued to play occasionally in other college chapels, and his death, when it came in 1965, could not have been more dramatic or, perhaps, appropriate. He was helping at Trinity College and died while playing the Nunc Dimittis. His body slumped over the manuals, causing the organ to play loud and long until an ambulance crew lowered his huge frame on a stretcher over the side of the organ loft.

David Lumsden

David Lumsden went to New College, Oxford, from Southwell Minster in 1959. The choir at that time consisted of only six lay clerks and a dozen choristers. His predecessor, Meredith Davies, was a distinguished conductor who had held the post for only four years, during which he had been largely preoccupied with his work with the City of Birmingham Symphony Orchestra. The choir's repertory was exceedingly limited.

Lumsden recalls, modestly, 'It was easy to make a favourable impression', and Kenneth Andrews, who attended the chapel, but only when invited, remarked to him, 'Nice to hear the choir singing in tune again, but we must do something about that tenor.' A good deal was done with the whole choir. After tough negotiations with the college over money, the number of men was raised to 12 by the recruitment of academical clerks (choral scholars), and the salaries of the lay clerks were increased.

An important turning point came in 1960 with the arrival, from Ely, of the first academical clerk – James Bowman, the future renowned countertenor. His outstanding voice and musicianship set new standards, and Lumsden rebuilt the choir around him. The long-term effects of this are still evident. Another influential event was a disastrous broadcast of Choral Evensong when the singing chaplain, who was shared with Christ Church, pitched the opening versicles too low. Enterprising members of the choir sought to remedy this, but in three different ways, thus creating a cacophony, until an alert organ scholar played the right note and the chaplain and choir started again. A new spirit was born in the choir from that day on.

Yet another factor in the revival was the choir's rivalry with Magdalen College, ultimately to the great benefit of both. Neither Lumsden nor Bernard Rose discouraged this – they were part of it – and they became the closest of colleagues and friends. Sometimes, when a New College regular bass was unavoidably absent, Rose would deputize for him; the two organists played together in a wind ensemble. The combined choirs recorded BBC concerts and performed together on many occasions elsewhere, most memorably in 1965 at the 900th anniversary of Westminster Abbey's foundation.

Overseas tours were then something new, and not encouraged by the college, but Lumsden recognized the benefits to the choir, as well as to the reputation of the college, of occasional visits to America and Europe. For the first time ever in the 600 years of the college's history the choir sang outside Britain – in Miami Cathedral. Recordings also became important, exploiting a greatly widened repertory. This was far more adventurous and embraced the works of Britten, Stravinsky and other modern composers. The recorded works of Kenneth Leighton, with whom Lumsden had a close affinity, were specially acclaimed. But Tudor music was not neglected and, again, there were highly rated recordings.

The repertory was changed considerably, however, when a decision was made to replace the worn-out organ. This had been resisted for many years on grounds of cost, until A. J. (Freddie) Ayer, the famous linguistic philosopher and notorious atheist, declared at a crucial college meeting, 'You know my view on the chapel (in which he had never set foot), but the statutes say we must have a choir, and any decent choir requires a decent organ, so we must have the best we can provide.' The financial problem was solved by the sale of a coal mine in the North of England. The building of the very fine new organ took three years. During this time a small chamber organ was used, sometimes a piano, string quartet and wind ensemble, so that the music of New College often seemed, apart from the acoustic, akin to that of St Mark's, Venice, at the time of Gabrieli.

Lumsden was a gifted trainer of treble voices and, although the strictly disciplined boys treated him with something approaching awe, a warm friendly atmosphere prevailed throughout his years at the college. His restrained style, unlike that of Rose at Magdalen, never approached the flamboyant, and, combined with the austere spirituality of the dean, Gareth Bennett, helped to produce acts of worship that were of great beauty as well as uplifting to those who attended them. The chapel was often full.

David Lumsden was born in Newcastle-upon-Tyne in 1928. He studied organ with Conrad Eden at Durham Cathedral and David Willcocks at

Salisbury, then won an organ scholarship to Selwyn College, Cambridge, where he came under the influence of Boris Ord. He took the MusB in 1951 and four years later completed a PhD with a dissertation on Elizabethan lute music – a subject on which he became an authority. An Oxford doctorate by incorporation followed in 1959.

Before Cambridge, National Service intervened, and he became, as he often described it, organist of Stonehenge, that is, of the nearby Royal Artillery camp. Assistant to George Guest at St John's College, Cambridge, led to appointment as Nottingham University organist, combined with that of organist and choirmaster of St Mary's, Nottingham, where he founded the Nottingham Bach Society. In 1956 he became Rector Chori of Southwell Minster, combining this with Director of Music at what later became Keele University. His move to New College came after the college choir committee, then seeking a successor to Meredith Davies, saw a television broadcast from Southwell Minster, and they liked what they saw and heard.

During the next 17 years Lumsden influenced many future professional musicians besides James Bowman, and three future bishops also owed something to him. In 1976, however, he felt it would not be right to spend the remainder of his career at New College so he became Principal of the Royal Scottish Academy of Music and Drama, and after six years in Glasgow moved to London to be Principal of the Royal Academy of Music. There he established a joint faculty with the Royal College of Music and the first performance-based undergraduate course between the RAM and King's College, London. He was knighted in 1985 and retired in 1993, still recognized as a notable organist and Bach specialist.

Edward Higginbottom was only 29 when he succeeded David Lumsden in 1976 and has now completed 33 years of service. Over the course of half a century, therefore, New College has known only two organists. Besides maintaining the choir's high standard, made more difficult by the abandoning of boarding choristers in favour of local day boys, he has introduced a French dimension to its life. A lover of French culture and with a considerable knowledge of its music, much of which the choir has recorded, he has organized many European tours and received an honour for his personal contribution to the revival of a number of French choir schools.

Bernard Rose

Bernard Rose went to Magdalen in 1957 with substantial academic credentials after some years as official Fellow in Music at Queen's College. He found the chapel music at a low ebb, though his first senior chorister was Stainer's great-grandson. With the support of the president, Tom Boase, who attended Evensong every day, the first priority was to phase out the salaried lay clerks and establish a full number of choral scholars, or academical clerks, as they were called. In the end the last lay clerk was paid to stay away. By then the standard of music at Evensong had been dramatically raised. The meticulous singing of the psalms, with special attention to the clear enunciation of the words, was the basis of every service, while the repertory of anthems and motets became one of the widest in the country. Evensong at Magdalen was soon known far beyond Oxford for its distinctive quality.

Rose was undoubtedly highly strung, an exacting taskmaster and totally intolerant of anything that fell short of perfection. But he controlled his anger, remaining icily polite, for example, in his contempt for the incompetence of the departing lay clerks. At the same time, he could be not unsympathetic towards the limitations of some of his younger singers. He inspired intense loyalty from his choir. Many 'academics' became his personal friends, and all had enjoyed the unstinted hospitality offered by him and his wife in their home just outside Oxford. Nor was it only choir members who shared this largesse. His other pupils, who competed for the 12 o'clock tutorial, enjoyed, as Rose did, an ample gin and tonic when the work was done. Roderick Dunnett, a former academical clerk and now a music critic, recalls how his beautiful rooms in the cloisters were 'peppered alternately with guffaws, biting sarcasm and unmentionable oaths'. Rose's first organ scholar was Dudley Moore, whose skills as a musician were combined with those of actor and cabaret artist to make him one of the stars of mass entertainment in the final decades of the century.

Bernard Rose was born in Hertfordshire in 1916. His father died when he was only three and his mother took him to Salisbury, where he later became a chorister under Walter Alcock. Recognizing a beautiful voice and musical talent, Alcock secured him a place at the Royal College of Music to study with Boris Ord and Patrick Hadley. This led to an organ scholarship at St Catharine's College, Cambridge, and the conductorship of the University Music Society. After Cambridge he went to Queen's College, Oxford, as organist and tutor in music, but almost immediately war broke out. He enlisted in the County of London Yeomanry (Sharpshooters) in 1941, serving with the 'Desert Rats' at the Battle of El Alamein. Later, as adjutant, he took part in the D-Day landings, only to be taken prisoner six days later. He spent the rest of the war in a POW camp at Brunswick.

On demobilization he returned to Oxford, and was awarded a fellowship of Queen's in 1949. A university lectureship in music soon followed and his career continued to combine the academic and creative sides of music. Among his most distinguished former pupils was Kenneth Leighton, Professor of Music at Edinburgh University and a notable pioneering composer of church and secular music. As conductor of the Eaglesfield Music Society Rose was entrusted with premieres of works by Vaughan Williams and Edmund Rubbra, a colleague and close friend.

His own specialism was English polyphonic church music, which includes the works of Tallis, Byrd, Gibbons and others. During his Magdalen years (1957–81) the choir made some classic recordings of these. He edited three volumes of the standard *Early English Church Music* and also the anthems of Thomas Tomkins. About 18 of his own anthems are sung here and there, the most popular being 'Morning glory, starlit sky', and many cathedrals sing his Canticles in E and C minor. Most popular of all are his *Preces and Responses*, the first to abandon the traditional inflexions of the cantor's part, following a request from the Dean of Divinity at Magdalen for a 'more interesting part to sing'. It is probable that the 'Rose Responses' are more widely used than any beside those of Tallis. His dissonant chants have seldom been heard outside the college.

He served twice as Vice-President of Magdalen, was awarded an Oxford Doctorate of Music in 1955 and appointed OBE in 1980. His influence today is found in the music of a number of important groups, including The Sixteen, The Clerkes of Oxenforde and the Tallis Scholars. He died in 1996.

Rose was succeeded by John Harper who stayed for 11 years before moving to become Professor of Music in the University of Wales. His interest in music for the new liturgical texts and the parishes subsequently led him to a nine-year term as Director General of the Royal School of Church Music. Since 2007 the Magdalen Choir has been directed by Bill Ives, a composer and a diminutive counter-tenor who achieved considerable popularity with the King's Singers in the 1980s.

Simon Preston

Simon Preston took Christ Church by storm and transformed its music almost overnight, demonstrating dramatically the crucial role played by choir directors in the setting of standards. Born in Bournemouth in 1938, he went from Canford School to the Royal Academy of Music to study organ under the renowned C. H. Trevor. He then won the A. H. Mann Organ Scholarship to King's College, Cambridge, which brought him under the tutelage of David Willcocks who earlier had, solely on grounds of age, turned him down for a choristership at Salisbury Cathedral. He continued, however, to go to Trevor.

On leaving Cambridge in 1962 his talent was recognized by appointment as sub-organist of Westminster Abbey. By this time he had already recorded some of the music of Orlando Gibbons and was soon to make his first appearance in a Prom at the Royal Albert Hall – to perform with the BBC Symphony Orchestra Saint-Saëns' Organ Symphony. His position at Westminster Abbey did not allow him to have much influence on its fairly undistinguished choir, but his organ playing (then in its early fiery phase) made a considerable impact. There were also milestone recordings of Messiaen's *La nativité* and Reubke's *Sonata on the 94th Psalm*.

Five years at Westminster was followed by a short spell as acting organist of St Albans Abbey, before beginning in 1970 his notable career at Christ Church. The remarkable skills as an organist, which brought him world fame, were accompanied by no less skill as a choir director. Those who have sung under him sometimes speak of an 'almost magical' touch that enabled individuals to reach heights they had previously thought unattainable and choirs to give out of the ordinary performances that were both demanding and exhilarating for all involved.

For just over a decade, Oxford's musical life was thus enriched. Acclaimed recordings were made by choir and organist, and he was also a university lecturer in music. In 1981, however, he returned to Westminster as organist and master of the choristers and, again, there was an overnight transformation, though it took somewhat longer than this for Preston to be satisfied with the standard. Deutsche Grammophon made recordings that won worldwide recognition and all the time Preston's star as an organist and conductor was rising. In 1987 he left the Abbey to devote himself entirely to his international role in music.

At Christ Church he had been succeeded by his assistant, Francis Grier, who was driven by ill-health to resign after only four years. He recovered to become an eminent concert pianist and a composer, much of his work in the field of church music. Stephen Darlington, who took over from him in 1985, has maintained the choir at a very high standard, made many recordings and opened the doors to close and fruitful collaboration with several contemporary composers.

Nine Lessons and Carols

It is not commonly known that the Service of Nine Lessons and Carols held in the chapel of King's College, Cambridge, on Christmas Eve, and broadcast worldwide, dates no further back than the early 1920s, and that it originated in Truro Cathedral. When Edward White Benson became Bishop of Truro in 1877, he began the task of building a new cathedral that would incorporate an aisle of the town's parish church. This required the demolition of the remainder of the church and the erection of a temporary wooden structure to accommodate 400 people and serve as a cathedral until the first stage of the new building was completed.

This was obviously a long way from ideal, but Benson, who had been Chancellor of Lincoln Cathedral, was determined that the quality of the worship should be in no way inferior to that of the great historic cathedrals. A 17-year-old organist, Robert Sinclair, was appointed to lay the foundations of a choral tradition, but he was inevitably much under Benson's authority – 'I was a sort of prefect,' he said, 'with the bishop (who was also the dean) as headmaster.' Nonetheless he developed to become one of the distinguished organists of the late nineteenth century and was a close friend of Edward Elgar, who dedicated one of his 'Enigma Variations' to him.

Before this, however, Benson, with Sinclair's assistance, devised a Christmas service of lessons and carols, consisting of Bible readings tracing the path of human salvation from the creation to the incarnation, interspersed with carols and hymns. A chorister read the first lesson and other members of the embryonic cathedral community read the rest, in order of seniority. The service was held at 10 p.m. on Christmas Eve in order to get men out of Truro's pubs. It remained a local observance but became known to Eric Milner White who on his return from war service in 1918 became Dean of King's, where he remained for 23 years until his appointment as Dean of York. He introduced the service at King's, refining it in various ways and adding a bidding prayer that reflected his own spirituality and feel for language. The BBC, still in the early days of broadcasting, picked it up and, such was its immediate popularity, it became a fixture on the Christmas programme schedule. Before long it spread, often in shortened form, to parish churches so that it is now one of the best attended services of the year not only in Britain but in many other parts of the English-speaking world.

Arthur Henry Mann

Milner-White inherited at King's 'Daddy' Mann, who had already been the organist for 42 years and during this time transformed the choir from a very low standard to become one of the leading choral foundations in the country. He had been a chorister at Norwich Cathedral in the 1850s and spent a year as organist of Beverley Minster before going to King's in 1876. He stayed there until 1927 and is numbered among the second generation of Victorian musicians who helped to bring about a revolution in the Church of England's worship.

Boris Ord

Bernhard (but always known as Boris) Ord, who succeeded Mann, took the music of King's forward several steps. Born into a musical family (his mother was German) in Bristol in 1897, he was one of the first truly professional organists and choir directors who brought to these tasks not only considerable musical talent, but also top-class training. He was educated at Clifton College, took the ARCO when only 17, and won an organ scholarship to the Royal College of Music where he studied under Sir Walter Parratt, a distinguished organist of St George's Chapel, Windsor.

His studies were, however, interrupted by the 1914–18 war in which he served as a pilot in the Royal Flying Corps, but when the war ended he returned to the RCM for a year before winning an organ scholarship to Corpus Christi College, Cambridge. While there he took a MusB, founded the University's Madrigal Society, and was elected to a fellowship of King's, it being understood that he would succeed Mann (now 73) when he eventually retired. This came after four years, one of which Ord spent with the Cologne Opera to gain wider experience. When he took over from Mann his impact was immediate and the annual Christmas Eve carol service soon made the wider world aware that the choir of King's had moved into a class of its own. Tudor polyphony was added to the repertory. He also started overseas tours. But his only composition was a setting of the medieval carol 'Adam lay y-bounden', which is still widely used.

In a presidential address to the Royal College of Organists, George Guest, who had been an organ scholar at St John's College, recalled:

In the late 1940s some of us in Cambridge used to watch Boris Ord rehearsing his choir with little less than awe. We admired his technique but, above all, we were electrified by his personality, of course, which inspired his choir. It was partly to do with his choice of words, partly to do with the particularly characteristic sound of his voice, partly to do with the precision and rhythmic vitality of his gesture, but, above, all, to do with his eyes – it is in the eyes of a conductor that a member of a choir finds inspiration.

David Willcocks, who succeeded Ord, said, 'He taught me everything I know about training a choir.' Besides his work with the choir, which was interrupted from 1941 to 1945 by service in the RAF in an administrative role (he was now deemed too old to fly), he was conductor of many notable performances by the Cambridge University Musical Society, including Vaughan Williams's *Pilgrim's Progress,* attended by the composer.

Ord was also a university lecturer in music and, besides his work in Cambridge, sometimes conducted concerts at the Festival Hall in London.

But during the early 1950s he was afflicted by disseminated sclerosis and in 1958 driven to retirement. In the same year he was appointed CBE and among his other honours were doctorates in music from Cambridge and Durham. He died at the end of 1961.

David Willcocks

David Willcocks, who succeeded Boris Ord at King's in 1957 and remained there until 1973, devoted the whole of his professional life to choral music and had a very considerable influence on the standard of music attained by the choirs of the English cathedrals and on the content of Christmas carol services in almost every parish church.

He inherited a fine choir at King's, albeit one that was feeling the effects of Ord's declining years, and raised it to a level where, for a choir of its kind, it was without rival in the world. A man of great warmth and charm, and always with a twinkle in his eye (and happily still alive), his standards were nevertheless exacting and he was intolerant of inaccuracy and anything suggesting sloppiness. His rapport with choristers, who loved him, was extraordinary and he exerted a magic over his choirs that was probably unique. The Psalms became a special feature at Evensong.

His influence beyond Cambridge was mainly, but not exclusively, due to the extension during his time at King's of radio and television broadcasting, and the development in the 1960s of the LP record. The Christmas Eve carol service had been broadcast on radio since the 1920s and there had been some records of other choral music, but now television cameras were admitted to reveal the glory of the chapel setting, and the sale of very large numbers of fine recordings made the choir's music well known worldwide. The effect of this was to set a new, and higher, standard for other choirs to emulate, one by which these choirs could be judged. At the same time, King's and the other Oxbridge choral foundations began to supply the cathedrals with a stream of highly accomplished ex-organ and ex-choral scholars who would assist in the raising of standards and the provision of the next generation of cathedral musicians. Simon Preston was the most notable of his organists. Others who found fame in the concert hall included the conductor Sir Andrew Davis, and the singers Robert Tear, Charles Brett, Michael Chance and Simon Keenlyside.

Willcocks's influence on parish church music came by a different route. At the 1958 carol service he decided to enliven the hymns 'O come all ye faithful' and 'Hark the herald-angels sing' by adding his own descants. At the same time he inserted a simple setting of 'Away in a manger'. The descants were widely appreciated and the Oxford University Press asked if they could publish them. Large sales led to a further request that he edit a book of new arrangements of 50 carols, but he felt able to manage only 25, so Reginald Jacques, the conductor of the Bach Choir, was recruited to do the rest. *Carols for Choirs* was so successful that the Oxford University Press requested another volume of 50. By this time, however, Jacques had died and Willcocks suggested that his new collaborator should be a gifted Cambridge undergraduate named John Rutter. He would deal with new carols and new arrangements of carols while Willcocks would deal with the old hymns. In the end a total of five volumes were published and it is now rare to attend a Christmas carol service without finding the names of David Willcocks and John Rutter attached to one or more of the items. He became general editor of church music for the Oxford University Press in 1961.

David Willcocks was born in 1919. His father was a bank manager and his mother the daughter of a country parson. He went to Westminster Abbey as a chorister in 1929, where he was greatly influenced by Ernest Bullock who gave him organ lessons. He only narrowly escaped expulsion from the choir, however, for smoking. At Clifton College he came under the influence of Douglas Fox, a brilliant one-arm pianist, and at the end of his time there completed the FRCO.

He then spent a year at the RSCM's College of St Nicolas at Chislehurst, and also took the opportunity to study at the Royal College of Music before becoming organ scholar at King's College, Cambridge, under Boris Ord, in 1939. The outbreak of war quickly brought this to an end, for in 1940 he enlisted in the Duke of Cornwall's Light Infantry in which he became an intelligence officer. During the Normandy Campaign, in 1944, however, he had to take over when the commanding officer was killed in action and he was subsequently awarded the Military Cross for 'his courageous leadership'.

Willcocks returned to King's in 1945 to complete his organ scholarship and to take a degree in music; he was then elected to a fellowship of the college, which he held until 1951. Almost simultaneously with this appointment he was chosen to succeed 85-year-old Sir Walter Alcock as organist of Salisbury Cathedral.

He was happily married and settled there when, in 1950, he was invited to become organist of Worcester Cathedral. He hesitated before accepting, but a telephone call from Sir Adrian Boult, the conductor, convinced him that he should move because of the opportunities provided by the Three Choirs Festival. Again he succeeded an octogenarian, Sir Ivor Atkins, and soon transformed the struggling choir. He also became conductor of the City of Birmingham Choir and developed the skills that made him a remarkable conductor of massed choral societies. On three occasions he was chief conductor of the Three Choirs Festival, building strong collaborative relationships with his colleagues at Hereford (Meredith Davies) and

Gloucester (Herbert Sumsion). He sometimes deputized for Sir Malcolm Sargent with the Royal Choral Society in London.

When in 1957 it became clear that Boris Ord's illness would seriously limit his future at King's, Willcocks was pressed to return to the college as organist, Ord remaining with the new title (for King's) of Director of Music. This placed Willcocks in his former organ-scholar role, but it was understood that he would take over full responsibility for the music when Ord retired, which he did in January 1958. He was also a university lecturer in music, conductor of the university's Musical Society, and responsible for many notable concerts and recitals in Cambridge.

Maurice Duruflé, who had played the organ under Willcocks at the first performance of his Requiem in England at Worcester in 1951, gave an organ recital in the chapel. Benjamin Britten, with whom he worked closely, conducted a performance of *The Dream of Gerontius* in the chapel, and the music of Elgar, of which he was a skilled and sympathetic interpreter, was frequently heard. He had in fact sung under Elgar when the Westminster Abbey choir provided the music at the dedication of a memorial to Queen Alexandra near St James's Park. Later he came to know almost everyone of note on the British choral music scene and was a close friend of Ralph Vaughan Williams and Herbert Howells.

He left King's in 1973, believing that he had taken its music as far as he could, and became Director of the Royal College of Music, a position he occupied for the next ten years. His special concern for choral music brought a renewal of this element in the College's curriculum and his rapport with young people changed its atmosphere. Six years into this appointment he took on the conductorship of the Bach Choir and held this for the next 38 years. This task of stamina, as well as of skill, gave him enormous pleasure, shared fully with a devoted choir and the audiences of 5,000 and more in London's Albert Hall.

Willcocks became a popular national figure whose charm and humanity were not diluted by worldwide fame, and, besides a knighthood in 1977, he received honorary degrees and other honours from more than 50 universities. He was succeeded by another distinguished musician – Philip (later Sir Philip) Ledger – who had become the youngest cathedral organist, when he went to Chelmsford aged 24. Since then he had been Artistic Director of the Aldeburgh Festival, with Benjamin Britten and Peter Pears, and won a high reputation as a pianist, organist and conductor. He maintained the standard at King's, but after eight years moved to Glasgow to succeed David Lumsden as Principal of the Royal Scottish Academy of Music and Drama.

Since then Stephen Cleobury, who had been sub-organist of Westminster Abbey, then master of the music at Westminster Cathedral, has enhanced the reputation of King's by combining its traditional regard for

Tudor music with boldness in commissioning work from many contemporary composers.

George Guest

The choir of St John's College, Cambridge, has never received the same public attention as that of its neighbour, King's College. This is undoubtedly because it sings in a much less glorious chapel and also because it has never achieved through broadcasting such a close association with the traditional observance of Christmas. Yet, as a result of the work of George Guest, who was organist and director of music from 1951 to 1991, its influence has perhaps been even more significant.

Guest was the first, and for a long time the only, Anglican choir trainer to appreciate the ground-breaking work of George Malcolm who trained the choristers of Westminster Roman Catholic Cathedral in what was known as the 'continental' tone. This is a more robust, forthright style than the somewhat hooting sound that had come to characterize the singing of English trebles, and it requires a different breathing technique. Guest's initial attraction to the different approach was reinforced by the experience of the music he heard in other Roman Catholic cathedrals when on holiday in Europe, and he decided to adopt it at St John's. This was not done on a whim, or out of a desire to make the music of St John's different from that of King's, but out of a deep conviction about the sound of particular forms of music.

In an address to the Royal College of Organists he explained:

> It is a matter of what is appropriate. For polyphonic music you need rounder sound than you do for contrapuntal music. Of course, you do not want Spanish brilliance in English music, but equally Vittoria would have been shocked at the way his music is sung in many cathedrals. A lot of the time I encourage the use of a gentle vibrato of the sort you would expect from a top-class string player, to bring emotion into the music that would be incongruous to sing in a dry, technical fashion. You have to answer the question 'Do I want to admire the choir or be moved by it?' We aim for the latter.

He also made a special point of demanding clear enunciation on the grounds that 'the words are more important than the music'.

All of which became, as a result of years of patient training, the distinguishing feature of the St John's choir, but known only to the relatively small number of those who attended the chapel or heard its broadcasts on Ash Wednesday and Advent Sunday or bought its recordings. Among these, however, were a significant number of highly gifted young men who aspired to be cathedral organists and won organ scholarships at St John's in order to be trained by Guest. Among the most notable are David Hill, John Scott, Stephen Cleobury, Adrian Lucas, Andrew Lumsden, Jonathan Bielby, Andrew Nethsinga, Brian Runnett and Jonathan Rennert. Sir David Lumsden was also one of his pupils.

His retirement in 1991 was marked by a service in Ely Cathedral led by the choir of St John's and three other choirs directed by former pupils – King's College, Cambridge, St Paul's Cathedral and Winchester Cathedral. There were many other distinguished organists who were changing the face of choral music in the English cathedrals to reflect what they had learned from Guest. It was a remarkable transformation, largely unnoticed except by the *cognoscenti*.

George Guest was born in 1924 in Bangor, in North Wales, where his father was the amateur organist of a local parish church, often employing his young son as organ blower. And, because he could never fail to be recognized as anyone other than a Welshman, he was always to some extent an outsider in England. He had a great love of the language and culture of Wales and on St David's Day Evensong at St John's was sung in Welsh. And, although he was for years wedded to Cambridge, he was never fully incorporated into its establishment, and was always irritated by arrogance and snobbishness.

As a chorister at Bangor Cathedral he showed clear signs of musical ability and moved to Chester Cathedral to gain experience with a more professional choir. During this time he was also given organ lessons by the sub-organist and completed the FRCO in 1942. He was then conscripted into the wartime RAF, where his brilliant extemporization on the piano kept him busy in off-duty hours and, while serving in India, he was for a time hired to play quiet music in a Bombay nightclub.

On demobilization in 1946 he returned to Chester Cathedral for a year as sub-organist before going to St John's College, Cambridge, as an organ scholar under Robin Orr. During his final year Orr announced his retirement, and Guest was invited to succeed him. By this time he had been deeply influenced by Boris Ord, the organist at King's College, whose rehearsals he often attended. After five years, however, the future of the music at St John's was threatened by the closure of the day school from which its choristers were drawn, but Guest, strongly supported by his predecessor, persuaded the college to found its own choir school.

The choir was raised to a very high standard and its repertory enlarged by the introduction of works by Palestrina, Vittoria and Lassus. Soon the cathedrals began to receive a regular stream of lay clerks who had been choral scholars. Guest was an exacting choir director who could be sharp with those who made mistakes, though, unlike David Willcocks, he was focused more on the broad sweep of the music than on its precise detail. A warm outgoing personality, with a sense of humour and a delight in the bizarre was shared after rehearsals with the Lay Clerks during a convivial hour in a Cambridge pub. His love of whisky became something of a legend.

Many overseas tours were arranged and at one time the choir was better known abroad than it was in Britain. Over 60 LP records and CDs were recorded during Guest's time, including some late-Haydn Masses that came to be regarded as classics. He was also a lecturer in music from 1953 to 1982, served as university organist from 1974 to 1991 and for a short time in the early 1960s Professor of Harmony at the Royal Academy of Music. He was at various times President of the Royal College of Organists and of the Cathedral Organists Association, and was appointed CBE in 1987.

Although Guest was of a liberal mind and had a wide interest in the arts, he was decidedly a traditionalist in matters related to the church's worship. He believed that services should always be dignified and was intolerant of liturgical change. New translations of the Bible and modern hymns aroused his ire. On the other hand, he greatly valued the work of some serious contemporary composers. Sir Michael Tippett and Herbert Howells wrote service settings for the choir, and the distinguished French organist Jean Langlais provided a setting of 'Beatus vir'. Whatever the material in use, Guest never departed from the conviction, 'I cannot take part in a performance without aiming for perfection. Even a simple "Amen" is a performance in itself.' He died in 2002.

A female-led revolution

During the early part of the twentieth century a number of other Oxford and Cambridge colleges had reputable choirs. When Charles Villiers Stanford and Charles Wood were at Cambridge, the choirs of Trinity and Gonville and Caius colleges were good enough to premiere their new compositions. Gradually, however, this tradition went into decline.

Several choir schools were closed and enthusiasm for recruiting local boy choristers waned. Organ and choral scholars were retained but repertories were of necessity limited.

All this changed in the 1980s, when women undergraduates were admitted to most of the previously all-male colleges. Their voices and enthusiasm brought about a revolution in the choral life of the chapels and by the end of the century the resources were such as to attract to certain colleges some of the leading choir directors.

At Cambridge the choirs of Clare and Gonville and Caius colleges are now of a very high standard, while that of Trinity College, under Stephen Layton, is outstanding – one of the best small, mixed choirs in the country. Soon after Easter 2009 seven of the Cambridge choirs, other than those of St John's and King's, combined to sing the BBC's Choral Evensong from Ely Cathedral. The quality of music is attracting many more worshippers to the chapels and, besides the training of 30 organ scholars, there are about 350 choral scholars.

Oxford was a little slower in its response to the new opportunities, but Queen's College, under the scholar-director Owen Rees, now has the finest mixed-voice choir in the university and the city. At the beginning of the 2008/09 academic year Merton College inaugurated a new foundation, with 14 choral scholars and an organ scholar, and attracted the distinguished scholar-conductor Peter Phillips to be its director.

The effects of this revolution on the church's musical life could be considerable.

18

The Minor Canons and Precentors

The office of minor canon is now rarely encountered in the life of a cathedral, but until comparatively recently it played a significant part in the leading of worship in all the ancient cathedrals and in some nineteenth- and twentieth-century foundations. For want of ability or commitment, usually a combination of both, deans and canons delegated responsibility for worship to a number of 'inferior' clergy whose status was indicated by the title 'minor canon'. Their number, duties and privileges were defined by the statutes, and in many cathedrals there might be as many as six of them whose voices augmented those of the lay vicars in the choir. Modestly paid, most also held one or more benefices to ensure an adequate income.

In some places, however, most notably St Paul's, there could be 12 of them, who formed a college with their own organization and officers, and a marked degree of independence. At St Paul's there is still a warden of the college, though the offices of senior cardinal and junior cardinal have gone out of use, and as recently as the 1960s the three remaining minor canons of Westminster Abbey took their dean and chapter as far as the Privy Council to determine whether or not they held freehold offices. Until the reforms of the nineteenth century it was one or other of their number, or a senior lay vicar, rather than the organist, who was responsible for the training of the choir. For the leading of the worship two of them would normally be on duty for, say a month, in the manner of a more senior canon in residence.

While the senior minor canon held the office of precentor in cathedrals of the New Foundation, that is, the former monastic cathedrals that were given statutes by King Henry VIII in the sixteenth century, this was not so in the pre-Reformation collegiate cathedrals, where it was one of the great offices, next in seniority to the dean, held by a member of the chapter. Originally the holder of this office was responsible for the ordering of worship, and may have been qualified to do so, but, as soon as appointments to chapters began to be determined by non-functional factors, the day-to-day duty was delegated to a minor canon known as the succentor or the vicar choral. During the second half of the twentieth century, however, when liturgy and music came to be accorded far greater importance, and financial constraints required a reduction in the number of clergy, only qualified precentors were recruited to serve on the chapters of virtually all the cathedrals. In some other choral establishments the title 'precentor' is given to the leading musician.

Thomas Helmore

In 1840 Thomas Helmore, newly ordained, became a curate at St Michael's Church, Lichfield, and also a Minor Canon of Lichfield Cathedral. He thus began what proved to be the most influential contribution to the development of English choral singing in the first half of the nineteenth century. Born at Kidderminster in 1811, he was the son of a Congregationalist minister who soon moved to Stratford-upon-Avon. On completion of his education at Mill Hill School, he returned home to teach in the chapel school, but came increasingly under the influence of the infant Oxford Movement and was baptized and confirmed in the Church of England. He then felt drawn to holy orders and went to Magdalen Hall, Oxford, where, besides reading for a degree, he studied music under the organist of Christ Church Cathedral. He also attended the choral services at Magdalen and New Colleges.

Thus equipped, he went to Lichfield where he found the standard of worship no higher than that of most other cathedrals of that time and a good deal lower than what he had experienced in Oxford. He began to intone the services but none of the dean and chapter was at all interested in music and he became involved in the recently formed Motet Society (he would later become its precentor) which was concerned to revive the music of Palestrina, Vittoria, Byrd, Gibbons, Tallis and Blow.

The offer in 1842 of the combined post of Vice-Principal and Precentor of St Mark's College, Chelsea, was therefore too good an opportunity to miss. The college had started just a year earlier as the Church of England's first national training college for teachers and from the outset it was intended that daily services, sung by a trained choir, would be held in the soon-to-be-built chapel. For this Helmore would be responsible, together with some teaching of harmony and counterpoint to the more advanced students. The rest would be taught basic music and singing by John Hullah, who had joined the staff some months previously and was known for his pioneering work of introducing into Britain a highly effective French method of teaching boys to sing. The best boy singers from an attached day school were to become the trebles in the chapel choir.

The partnership between Helmore and Hullah began to produce remarkable results, often from distinctly unpromising material – but not without a great deal of hard work by both teachers and students whose programme of study was also tougher than any that might be imposed today. Even the teaching of Tallis's responses occupied several weeks, but the more capable of the singers were introduced to complex canticles and anthems, so that eventually the repertory of the daily services exceeded in breadth and quality that of most cathedrals. These soon began to attract large congregations made up of not only discriminating Chelsea residents but others from much further afield who were concerned to see church music improved. The developments, which included intoned prayers and a surpliced choir, were regarded by some as an insidious expression of the beliefs and practices of the now growing Oxford Movement and this provoked 'No Popery' demonstrations outside.

The college itself grew to accommodate about 80 students and these, on completion of their training, were directed to take what they had learned of music into their schools and parish churches. They were soon in great demand, not least because the principals of the other teacher training colleges then being founded, often close to cathedrals, were strongly opposed to such an emphasis on music. The influence of St Mark's on the development of church music in the first half of the nineteenth century cannot be exaggerated.

In 1846 Helmore became Master of the Children (the choristers) at the Chapel Royal – the first priest to be so appointed since the Reformation. At first he hoped that it might be possible to combine this with his responsibilities at the college, but the state of the music and the cruel conditions imposed on the children at the Chapel soon led to recognition that both needed his full-time attention. Among the children was Arthur Sullivan, the future composer, and once standards were raised Helmore would sometimes lead the children in their picturesque uniform through the streets to join the choir at daily services in the college chapel – to the benefit of both.

Helmore, whose energy was boundless, now found time to compile an edition of the Psalter based on Gregorian tones. Another musician of the time, William Dyce (he was previously a painter, whose frescoes can still be seen on the walls of the Queen's Robing Room in the House of Lords and at All Saints, Margaret Street) had already published *The Order of Daily Service with Plain-tune* (1843). This was a new edition of Merbecke's Book of Common Prayer and led eventually to the widespread use of Merbecke's setting of the Eucharist. Helmore took the rules of pointing derived by Dyce from Merbecke and applied these to the whole Psalter, testing them in St Mark's Chapel in penitential seasons when Anglican chants were not in use. This appeared in 1849 as *The Psalter Noted* and in the following year was enlarged to include *The Canticles – A Brief Directory* (which contained instructions about method), and *Three Appendices*.

Published as *A Manual of Plainsong*, this has never been superseded. Helmore subsequently collaborated with J. M. Neale in the recovery of medieval Latin hymns, published in what became the very influential *Hymnal Noted*.

He was succeeded as precentor of St Mark's College by his brother Frederick, who remained a layman but was no less committed to the cause of church music. Like his brother, he started as a schoolteacher, became an itinerant choir trainer – a 'Musical Missionary' he called himself – then went up to Magdalen Hall, Oxford. There he became concerned for the reform of Anglican choral music and also founded the Oxford University Motet and Madrigal Society, becoming its first conductor. After completing some years at St Mark's, he again took to the road and travelled to most parts of the United Kingdom training choirs. The Prince Consort engaged him to train a choir of 40 to sing in the domestic chapels at Buckingham Palace and Windsor Castle.

Earlier John Hullah had also spread his wings to promote massed singing classes in Exeter Hall, London (one of the participants subsequently became organist of York Minster), and also singing classes in Merton College Hall for undergraduates from all the Oxford colleges. These did not last for long but they created an interest in church music that Frederick Helmore took forward. Writing in 1850 about the influence of Hullah and the Helmore brothers, Charles Dickens said:

> In hundreds of quiet out-of-the-way country churches, an approximation is made to choral services often purely vocal. Hundreds of country clergymen are now qualified, by musical attainment, to superintend the singing of their choirs and congregations, and exert themselves to render it consistent with taste, propriety and devotion.

Walter Kerr Hamilton

Walter Kerr Hamilton, who was Bishop of Salisbury from 1854 to 1869, has a place in church history as one of the nineteenth century's great reformers, comparable with the work of his contemporary, Bishop Samuel Wilberforce at Oxford. His reforming efforts began, however, 14 years earlier when he went to Salisbury as precentor of the cathedral and became one of the first to recognize the urgency of change in all England's great churches.

Born in London in 1808, he was a son of an Archdeacon of Taunton and Prebendary of Lichfield, who had been one of Thomas Arnold's pupils. Walter had a brilliant academic career at Christ Church, Oxford, staying on as a student (that is, a fellow) before moving to Merton College in 1833 as a fellow and tutor. In the following year he was ordained and combined his academic responsibilities with those of a curate at St Peter's-in-the-East Church in the city. There he and the vicar, Edward Denison, worked hard to restore and reorder the church and to improve the worship to, it was said, 'a pitch for that time highly ornate'. When in 1837 Denison left to become Bishop of Salisbury, the parishioners successfully petitioned for Hamilton to succeed him. During the next few years, he came increasingly under the influence of the Oxford Movement and, shortly before accepting an invitation from his former vicar to become a minor canon of Salisbury Cathedral, compiled and published a *Book of Daily Services* for every day of the week for use by his parishioners.

He arrived at Salisbury in 1841 as a convinced High Churchman and was shocked by what awaited him. Bishop Denison had already tried to initiate some reforms in the cathedral, but the canons residentiary were more absent than present and even when there often chose not to attend the services. Enquiry into the reasons for the small congregations at the daily services led to the discovery that during the times of service the clergy were to be seen walking about the Close or paying calls. The attendance of the lay clerks of the choir was hardly better. In theory, four or six of these, plus three supernumeraries, should have been present at every choral service, but this was rarely achieved and Hamilton complained, 'How utterly the musical power of our choir is below what is required for the due celebration of divine Service.' A chilling response came from a lay member of the community: 'Well, sir, I dare say you are right, but you must know that the rule of Salisbury has always been "Let everybody get off everything he can."'

Hamilton's arm was strengthened when, after about a year, he was made canon precentor, with a place on the chapter. But it remained an uphill struggle. He urged his fellow canons to give up their country benefices and concentrate on the work of the cathedral, setting a personal example by declining the offer of the living of Loughton. A new system of choir rules for attendance, with fines for absences, was applied. The choristers, who had previously lodged in various homes in the city, were brought under one roof in the Close, with a resident master, and in order to improve their discipline, a list of fines for misbehaviour was introduced – 2d for attending the cathedral with dirty hands or face, or for running into the cathedral, or for wearing a hat in the building, 3d for arriving late at the song school or services, the same for kicking a boy or throwing a stone. The fines were doubled for offences on Sundays.

He chose all the music with great care, went about in his cassock all day, took pastoral interest in the choristers and lay clerks, gave constant attention to the ordering of the worship and was eventually rewarded with a marked improvement in performance. The teacher training college was regularly visited, he became widely known to people in the city and every

Sunday entertained six or eight poor people to dinner. An outbreak of cholera took him into the homes of its victims without regard for his own safety. The cathedral's archives were reordered. Hamilton had, however, wider ambitions for the cathedral and in 1853 addressed a letter to the Dean urging that steps be taken to turn it into a real centre of education and musical life. This was followed by a pamphlet, *Cathedral Reform*, in which he applied his experience and vision to English cathedral life as a whole.

Following the death of Bishop Denison in 1854, Hamilton was appointed to succeed him – the bishop having urged the Prime Minister, in a letter written from his death bed, to do so. The diocese now claimed his reforming zeal, but he continued to be involved in the life of the cathedral and to urge further reform. A daily 8 a.m. Holy Communion had been instituted in 1849 and he celebrated this every Sunday until his death in 1869. He rarely left the diocese, apart from summer holidays, and his death was believed to be due in no small part to the fact that he had worn himself out.

E. H. Fellowes

E. H. Fellowes (he seems never to have been known by either of his Christian names, Edward Horace) was at St George's Chapel, Windsor, from 1900 until his death in 1951, but the high distinction of being made a Companion of Honour was not for his ministry as a minor canon and precentor. He used the ample leisure afforded by that post – there were three other minor canons on the establishment – to become a pioneering explorer of the work of the composers of the English madrigal during the creative period 1546–1645; also that of the Tudor church musicians, especially William Byrd and Orlando Gibbons. He edited 36 volumes of madrigals, 32 of lute songs, 20 volumes of Byrd's music and 10 volumes of other Tudor choral music.

In the case of the madrigals, while these were known about and used, the manner of their performance had departed a long way from their composers' instructions: the rhythms were wrong, the tempi too slow. The Tudor church music had for the most part lain hidden, and therefore unused, in cathedral libraries all over the country. It was the massive achievement of Fellowes to discover in the British Museum in 1911 an almost complete collection of the scores of the English madrigal composers and then to edit and publish 36 volumes, irregularly barred to indicate varied rhythms and accented to indicate when some irregular rhythms cut across bar lines. Not everyone agrees with the way in which he edited the church music but no one underestimates the degree to which the music of the church, especially its cathedrals, was enriched in the twentieth century by his prodigious, scholarly work.

He was born into a reasonably prosperous family in Paddington in 1870 and, his father having died when he was only 11, was brought up by his mother – a gifted musician and water colourist. He himself displayed early music talent, but was denied an opportunity to study under a celebrated violinist, Joseph Joachim. He went to Winchester College, fresh with hearing Rubenstein, Liszt and Clara Schumann perform, but found the teaching of music at the college substandard. Later he reached professional standard with the violin and taught himself to play the lute in order to accompany rediscovered songs.

At Oriel College, Oxford, he did not shine academically, taking only a fourth in theology, but played a full part in the university's musical life. This included membership of a choir that sang to illustrate Professor John Stainer's lectures and led to a friendship with Stainer that proved to be helpful. In 1894 he became a curate in Wandsworth, South London, and, while useful in training the choir, was not much use pastorally in the slum district of the parish to which he had been allocated. More successful were his musical studies, for, having completed an Oxford BMus in 1896, he left Wandsworth in the following year to become Precentor of Bristol Cathedral.

This was on Stainer's recommendation, but the post was beset with problems. The outgoing precentor had been at loggerheads with the organist and retired in despair. The organist had also been in serious dispute with the dean and chapter – involving an ugly legal action which ended inevitably with his dismissal a year or so after Fellowes had taken over. Fortunately he got on well with the disputatious organist, arranged the enthronement of a new bishop, composed a Morning and Evening Service in D, raised the standard of the choir and trained the choir of St Mary's, Redcliffe, for 18 months. He also became much involved in the city's wider musical life and it was when attending the recitals of the Madrigal Society that he became convinced that the characteristic features of Tudor music had been seriously misunderstood.

After three years, however, and once again on Stainer's recommendation, he left to become a Minor Canon and the Precentor of St George's Chapel, Windsor. Yet again his arrival took him into a dispute, since one of the other minor canons, who thought he should have been appointed, claimed that the statutes required the precentor to be a man older than his colleagues, which Fellowes, still only 30, obviously was not. A lawyer settled the matter when he advised that a certain Latin phrase in the statutes had been mistranslated.

The duties of the precentor were not onerous. Only two of the minor canons were required on duty at services, leaving the others free to augment their small stipends by undertaking Sunday duty in neighbouring parishes. No liturgical reordering was called for, but when the organist, Sir Walter Parratt, retired in 1924 and Walford Davies, then at the Temple Church, declined to succeed him, Fellowes, who had himself a beautiful singing voice, undertook responsibility for the training of the choir. This extended over three years while the chapel was being restored, and during this time he took the opportunity to widen the repertory. In 1925 he went with the choir to the HMV studio at Hayes to make the first ever recording of a complete Choral Evensong. This was followed by several records of anthems and two services for the Columbia Company in the chapel itself, but the recording of a boy's solo voice proved to be impossible because of technical difficulties. When these had been overcome, Fellowes promised this company that when he and the choir returned from a tour of Canada they would make a recording of Mendelssohn's 'Hear my prayer'. While they were away, however, HMV engaged the Temple choir, with its soloist Ernest Lough, to make an identical recording which brought world fame and massive royalties.

In 1927 Walford Davies felt free to accept the still vacant organist's post at St George's, leaving Fellowes with more freedom to visit libraries and cathedral muniment rooms in all parts of the country in his quest for hidden Tudor music. He was an exact, albeit self-trained, scholar (there were no schools of musical research at that time) and he could seem forbidding to those who were just entering his field of study. To some he seemed pedantic, yet he believed passionately that edited music should not be returned to the library to gather a new supply of dust but should be put to use by madrigal singers and church choirs. The choir of St George's led the way. He also shared Stainer's concern to raise the standards of cathedral music and church music generally. Towards the end of his life he became President of the Church Music Society. Choirs were engaged to sing madrigals and in 1920 he conducted the first public performance in modern times of properly interpreted madrigals. Recordings and books about madrigals and their composers followed to further the cause.

It was a measure of Fellowes's skill that when only five parts of Byrd's great anthem *Hosanna* could be found he reconstructed the missing part to enable it to be performed. And when eventually the missing part turned up it was discovered that, apart from two unimportant differences, it was the same as the reconstruction. Tudor church music research had in fact been started by Sir Richard Terry at Westminster Cathedral and he recruited the young Herbert Howells to lend a hand. But when a small group of scholars was formed to extend the work, Terry soon dropped out, leaving Fellowes as the principal editor. The greatest thrill came with his discovery of Byrd's *Great Service* in the library at Durham.

The publication of so much music – Tallis, Weelkes and others were soon added to Byrd and Gibbons, together with organ music – raised serious problems over the financing, since Novello were in no position to run big risks with a pioneering project. Fellowes dealt with this by seeking patronage for both the madrigals and the church music from the leading musicians of the time. The response exceeded all his expectations and money was given by most of the great names in English music and many others in Europe – 400 in all. The resulting editions have remained in print and in frequent use ever since.

There was still time to sort out and catalogue the fine nineteenth-century music library assembled by Sir Frederick Ouseley at St Michael's College, Tenbury. Fellowes was rewarded for his labours there by the discovery of the original score of Purcell's *Dido and Aeneas* and the conducting score for Handel's first performance of *Messiah* in Dublin, as well as thousands of other manuscripts which were then made available to scholars. Lectures in this country and overseas, books, including *English Cathedral Music from Edward VI to Edward VIII*, 50 articles contributed to the new *Grove Dictionary of Music and Musicians*, and much involvement in chamber music concerts also kept him busy.

Back at Windsor he seemed entirely at home as a member of the Court. He had been born, and married, into the gentry and enjoyed the company of the titled and the aristocrat. During his half-century at St George's he was involved in many royal ceremonies, starting with the dramatic funeral of Queen Victoria. He served under five sovereigns, unprecedented for any of the clergy of the chapel, and was involved in the coronations of Edward VII, George V and George VI in Westminster Abbey. Besides the Companionship of Honour, Fellowes was awarded honorary doctorates in music by Oxford, Cambridge and Dublin. An honorary fellowship of Oriel College, Oxford, gave him special pleasure in view of his abysmal academic record while an undergraduate of the college. Curiously, he received no recognition by the church and was disappointed never to have been raised to a full canonry at Windsor or offered one at Westminster Abbey. Either of these would have been appropriate, and neither of them would have hindered his life's main work.

Joseph Poole

Joseph Poole was the first of the modern precentors, and the rebuilding of Coventry Cathedral after its wartime destruction by bombing provided him with unusual opportunities to arrange the Church of England's worship in new and creative ways. He was not, however, one to be seduced by the latest fashion and when his critics sometimes described him as Victorian he would riposte, 'You are wrong. My century is the 17th.' Neither was he a liturgical archaeologist who believed that the content of twentieth-century worship should be determined by what was in use during the fourth.

Poole combined an artistic sensitivity with a flair for staging great acts of worship in a large new building. He was fortunate to have considerable resources at his disposal and a provost, Bill Williams, whose vision of what a cathedral ought to be allowed much scope for innovation. Like many other gifted men, however, Williams was far from easy to work with and not least among Poole's achievements was the development of a close partnership with him. They were well aware of the new liturgical ideas of the time and the Coventry Liturgy incorporated the most important of these – lay involvement, an offertory procession and exchanging of the Peace, and there was coffee afterwards – but it was in some ways more conservative than that of many parish churches.

The new building was itself a serious problem and remains so. A reconstruction committee formed in 1941, not long after the bombing, commissioned Giles Gilbert Scott, the architect of Liverpool Cathedral, to produce a new design, prescribing only the retention of the old ruins. He submitted his plans in 1946 and these were of a church built around a central altar, with a special chapel of unity. The committee was happy with this, but the plans were rejected by the Royal Fine Art Commission, whereupon Gilbert Scott resigned.

A commission chaired by Lord Harlech then held a competition, with a brief that the building should be in the English Gothic tradition. Out of 219 entries that of Basil Spence was the unanimous choice, though it caused vigorous public controversy. There was further controversy, created by other architects and liturgists, when its rectangular shape arose – 'espresso-bar Gothic' one called it – and, although Williams and Poole were initially lavish in their praise, its limitations for the staging of worship and other activities, such as drama and ballet, soon became all too evident. Gothic churches were not designed for active congregational participation and the new cathedral, consecrated in 1962, allowed only rows and rows of people, arranged in military-style order, located at an ever increasing distance from the altar. There was the complaint that in the building it was impossible to see, to hear and even, since the ventilation system was inadequate, to breathe.

It is given to few precentors to be made responsible for the ordering of the worship at the consecration of a new cathedral and this was undoubtedly Poole's finest hour. His rule always was that no detail of language or ceremonial was unimportant enough to be ignored in the devising or execution of a service. The overriding concern, though, was that an act of worship should uplift and inspire those who took part in it, and that this should take priority over theological or liturgical 'correctness'. The Bishop of Coventry and other participants were required on this occasion to attend eight rehearsals so that perfection might be achieved on the great day. To assist good deportment, another of Poole's passions, new penny coins were placed on the floor of processional routes to ensure movement in straight lines. 'Glide like ghosts,' he would say, 'putting one foot in front of the other.'

Reconciliation and resurrection were the overarching themes of a service in which pageantry, fine music, assisted by an orchestra and the choirs of seven other Midlands cathedrals, moments of drama and the contribution of a bishop whose sense of the theatrical was as great as that of the precentor – all combined to create an intense atmosphere of thanksgiving and dedication. The Queen and several other members of the Royal Family were there, in company with the Archbishops of Canterbury and York and many other bishops from across the world. The Prime Minister attended, along with the diplomats from 57 different nations, and a group of young German men and women who had helped to turn the ruined vestries into an International Centre of Reconciliation. Television coverage ensured that the service was experienced worldwide.

This was, however, only the first of a series of events extending over three weeks and constituting a great festival. Besides 29 services, there were performances by the Berlin Philharmonic Orchestra, the Royal Ballet, Covent Garden Opera and most notably the first performance of Benjamin Britten's *War Requiem*. Among the other musicians involved were John Barbirolli, Thomas Beecham, Malcolm Sargent, Peter Pears, George Solti, Yehudi Menuhin and David Willcocks, and the whole event became a national celebration of hope and expectancy at the beginning of the 1960s. While by no means responsible for everything that took place, Poole was a key figure in the planning and on many occasions for the execution.

The same skills and concern for detail he applied to the many hundreds of special services that were held in the cathedral during the next 15 years. Organizations of every kind in the Midlands, as well as in the diocese, were invited to commemorate or celebrate something or other in their corporate life and made each one distinctive and memorable – employing roaring brass at a great celebratory event or the piquant sound of a single flute at the beginning of a memorial service.

Joseph Weston Poole was born in 1909 in Gravesend, Kent, where his father was Vicar of St James's Church. He went from the King's School, Canterbury, to Jesus College, Cambridge, as both an organ scholar and a classical exhibitioner. During his preparation for Holy Orders at Westcott House, Cambridge, he established what became a lifelong friendship with a fellow student, Cuthbert Bardsley, whose later appointment as Bishop of Coventry was directly responsible for the inspired appointment of Poole as canon precentor of his cathedral. 'Cuthbert's choreographer' was Poole's mocking description of himself.

After a curacy in Colchester, he joined the staff of the then flourishing Student Christian Movement in London, but his interest in worship and musical gifts were soon recognized by appointment as sacrist, then precentor, of Canterbury Cathedral. The scope for innovation there was limited but, encouraged by the 'Red Dean' Hewlett Johnson, another theatrical churchman, Poole introduced much colour and new ceremonial to raise the worship to a level appropriate to the mother church of the Anglican Communion. The funerals of Archbishops Temple and Lang were held during his time, as were the enthronements of Temple and Archbishop Fisher. During the war years when the boarder choristers were evacuated to Cornwall, he ran a day-boy choir with great success, and the danger from bombing drew the response, 'Being on the brink of eternity made it so much more fun to be here.' He then spent the years 1949–58 as Rector of Merstham, in Surrey, where he was a valued pastor and put some of his new ideas about worship into practice in the setting of a parish church.

It was from here that he went to Coventry to begin almost two decades of highly creative work, the importance of which has never been fully recognized by the church. His influence was limited, partly by the fact that a more informal, 'matey' approach to worship soon spread like wildfire throughout the church, and partly by the mistaken belief that the resources of a cathedral were necessary for the meeting of his demands. In fact he was always generous in advising all those who were serious in their aims, whether in a great cathedral, a small village church, or in the open air. And inasmuch as the new approach to cathedral life initiated by Provost Williams and his chapter had a profound effect on that of virtually every other cathedral in England, and some far beyond these shores, the influence of Joseph Poole is still alive.

In 1976, a year before his own retirement, Poole arranged a special farewell service for Bishop Bardsley. This included a scout band, banners, and 12 children dressed in the costumes of the countries visited by the Bishop during his episcopate. And in a note to the Bishop's wife before the service he suggested, 'If possible, please wear a garment of heraldic colour.' She obliged with a bright red coat.

19

The York Succession

It is a remarkable fact that between 1913 and 2008 York Minster had only three organists and masters of the music, all of whom were outstanding musicians and together made a significant contribution to English church music.

Edward Bairstow

Edward Bairstow, a legend in his own lifetime and still regarded with something approaching awe by those old enough to have been associated with the Minster prior to 1946, was an important figure in the musical world of the inter-war years. This was a period when organists of the major cathedrals still had an honoured place in wide society. Knighthoods were expected (Bairstow's came in 1932).

For those too young to go back so far, his memory is kept alive by the frequent performances in every cathedral of many beautiful anthems, of which the most popular are 'Blessed city, Heavenly Salem', 'Let all mortal flesh keep silence', 'Save us, O Lord, waking', 'Jesu, the very thought of thee' and 'I sat down under his shadow'. Hardly less popular are his Morning and Evening Canticles in D and E flat, and of his 12 organ pieces, the Sonata in E flat is heard most often.

It is perhaps not surprising that the character of so talented a musician should have contained an irascible element. Born in Huddersfield in 1874, he was a Yorkshireman through and through – opinionated, blunt-spoken, intolerant and fearless. Of his frequent appearances as an adjudicator at Yorkshire music festivals he once said, 'When God gave man a tenor voice he took away his brains.' Contraltos were likened to 'a lot of cows looking over a gate'. Having given an organ recital in Canada in 1928 he informed the audience that the two solo singers who had taken part were not of a high enough standard. Deans tended to be treated differently, but there were rows with the hugely gifted, yet underrated, Herbert Bate, a brilliant pianist, who was at the Minster until 1941 and whose wife reconciled them with the aid of tea and cake. Eric Milner-White his successor was not a dean to be trifled with and was too remote a figure to be drawn into conflict, so they got on well.

Yet Bairstow had a sense of humour, was mostly kind, and untiring in his devotion to his many pupils, all of whom remained for the rest of their days both grateful and proud to have been numbered among them. His admonition, 'Only the best is good enough', uttered in rasping, nasal tones, would never be forgotten, even when not always achieved. He was at heart a deeply religious man, who could be moved to tears during his accompaniment of the psalms.

Bairstow began his organ studies at Balliol College, Oxford, and was then articled to Frederick Bridge, the notable organist and master of the choristers at Westminster Abbey. At the end of his pupilage he stayed on for four years as Bridge's amanuensis and during part of this time was organist of All Saints, Norfolk Square, in London.

In 1899 he returned, for good as it turned out, to the North, first as organist of Wigan Parish Church, then of Leeds Parish Church. He was not the only top-class organist of that time to have a longish spell at an important parish church. Three of his predecessors, including Walter Parratt, had become cathedral organists. At Wigan, Bairstow devoted his outstanding gift as a teacher to the building up of a large teaching practice, with a special emphasis on singing. He also became conductor of the town's Philharmonic Society and other local choral societies. He found time to complete a Durham DMus in 1901.

The same broad pattern of work was continued when he moved to Leeds in 1907, except that the large parish church had daily services of the cathedral type, with a professional choir. His Evening Service in B minor is among the most used today. He was now well on the way to becoming the leading musician of his native Yorkshire, and it was no surprise when, in 1913, he was offered the York post. He hesitated before accepting. For one thing, it involved a reduction in salary; for another, 'I rather dreaded that the two cathedral services a day would tend to cramp my imagination.'

As in many other cathedrals, the Minster's music was in poor shape. Most of the lay clerks were too old to be serviceable and there was no pension provision to encourage their retirement. The outgoing organist, Thomas Tertius Noble, had spent much time in America and had finally been attracted to St Thomas's, Fifth Avenue, in New York, where he stayed for 30 years and established a choral tradition on English cathedral lines. When asked if he would follow his predecessor's example by visiting America, Bairstow replied, 'I would rather go to the devil.' The Minster had acquired a musician who never pulled his punches.

It had also acquired one who had hardly been touched by the early twentieth-century renaissance of English music. He had been trained, and was steeped, in the German romantic tradition of the previous century, especially in the music of Brahms. This would always control his own compositions, though all his works bore his own, unmistakeable personal stamp. The vast open spaces of the Minster also encouraged him to compose in the grand style; hence its continuing utility in other large cathedrals.

Bairstow composed 29 anthems, including large-scale works for choir and organ, and one of his specialisms was the hymn-anthem, several of which are among his most popular works. Of his canticles, chants and hymn tunes, however, few are now in use, but those that are include Morning and Evening Services in D, E flat and G which are very popular. Of special importance is his chant setting of the *Lamentations of Jeremiah* (1942), the fruit of close collaboration with Eric Milner-White, the then Dean of York, whose own artistic gifts complemented those of his organist. This was almost his last work and probably his greatest.

The standard of the Minster choir was raised to a high level after he had solved the problem of the elderly lay vicars and eventually became world famous. In 1928 he was invited to succeed Frederick Bridge at Westminster Abbey, but preferred to remain in Yorkshire, so he recommended one of his former pupils, Ernest Bullock, who was duly appointed.

He had, as in almost everything, strong views on the training of church musicians, believing that this should embrace all aspects of music and not be confined to the sacred. A perfectionist, and a worrier about maintaining high standards at York, he rarely played the organ voluntary after a service. He explained that he did not have sufficient time to practise, so the task was best left to a pupil. His own accompaniment of services was generally a model of the organist's art but could occasionally be startling and not entirely satisfactory, since he would seek to remedy the choir's irregular tempo by means of loud organ blasts, resulting in chaos.

He was, naturally, conductor of the York Musical Society and from 1917 onwards also of the Leeds Philharmonic Choir – a post he held until his death. In 1927 he conducted the Royal Choral Society in London to mark the fiftieth anniversary of the first performance in Britain of Bach's B Minor Mass, and two years later became the non-resident Professor of Music at Durham University. He composed an Introit for the coronation of King George VI in 1937. Early in his career, at the end of a choral work, an elderly man mounted the platform, seized his hand, and said, 'You are a born conductor.' That elderly man was the great Hans Richter, the famous exponent of Wagnerian music, who had worked with Wagner at Bayreuth.

Bairstow's frequent appearances as an adjudicator at local music festivals often brought fear into the hearts of competitors and excitement to journalists, keen to report his judgements. His abiding concern, however, was to raise the standard of all forms of music. His *Singing Learned from Speech: A Primer for Teachers and Students* (1945) had a wide readership and an earlier book, *Counterpoint and Harmony* (1937), was reprinted three times.

It was perhaps this concern that led him to turn his back on broadcasting and recording. He was among the first to be involved in the broadcasting of Evensong, but later complained that broadcasting and recording would empty concert halls and lead to the closure of choral societies – all a reflection of the 'poisonous materialism' that he believed to be rampant. His death, in office, in 1946 signalled the end of an era in English church music.

Francis Jackson

The transition from Bairstow to Francis Jackson could not have been smoother. He, too, is a Yorkshireman, though he does not speak like one, and his style is conciliatory, rather than confrontational. He was a chorister under Bairstow, became his star organ pupil and served as his assistant for a short time before taking over from him. Moreover, he was a devotee and, later, wrote his biography *Blessed City*. He was not, however, going to be bound by his conservative taste.

Jackson's primary contribution to the music of York Minster was that of an outstanding organist – one of the foremost of his day. In demand for recitals in all parts of the world, he continued to give these long after his retirement and, now in his ninety-second year, he played the voluntary after Evensong in York Minster on Easter Day 2009. His accompaniment and embellishment of the psalms at the daily Evensong was outstanding. He was also a specialist on organ design, advising many cathedrals and parish churches when they embarked on the rebuilding of their instruments, and favoured the lighter European style, believing this to be more versatile.

When still young, he was fascinated by the music of Debussy and Ravel, and he was among the first British organists to recognize the importance of the music of Widor, Vierne, Franck and Dupré, though for performance he drew a line at Messiaen.

At the marriage of the Duke and Duchess of Kent in York Minster in 1961 he rendered a signal service to them, and to many couples everywhere after them, by substituting the Toccata from Widor's 5th Symphony for Mendelssohn's hackneyed 'Wedding March', which he believed to be sentimental and frivolous. 'Why have an unsuitable arrangement of an orchestral piece, when there is good organ music available?', he asked.

Francis Jackson was born in 1917 at Malton. One of his grandfathers was a clergyman. In 1929 he became a chorister at York and, by the time he was 16, was a good enough organist to be appointed to his home parish church, and also to assist at the Minster. The Friends of the Minster Choir had paid for him to be articled to Bairstow, but his interests were wider than those of his teacher and led him to compose a symphony, an organ concerto, chamber music, songs and incidental music for plays. At one time he had considered becoming a concert pianist and he enjoyed the kind of light music played during the 1930s by the popular bands of Henry Hall and Jack Payne.

The outbreak of war in 1939 interrupted, but did not hinder, his career. He served in the 9th Lancers throughout the conflict and it was while involved in the bitter Italian campaign in 1944 that he composed *Impromptu* for a celebration of Bairstow's seventieth birthday. In spite of the great man's antagonism to recording, he went on to record all his organ works.

He returned from the war in time to succeed Bairstow and to extend his close association with York Minster by another 36 years, enabling him to become one of its most popular and best-loved figures – and a stout defender of the Book of Common Prayer. He got on well enough with the Dean, Eric Milner-White, who was still 17 years from retirement, but, like everyone else, found him, in spite of a weekly meeting, difficult to get close to.

Jackson's own Canticles in G are very widely used, as is his Eucharist in G. Another set, Canticles in G minor, and a setting of the Benedicite have their cathedral admirers, but, although he composed over twenty anthems, only two of these, 'Blow ye trumpet in Zion' and 'People of Zion', are commonly used. There are, however, others of special interest, including 'Daniel in Babylon', which was commissioned for the consecration of Coventry Cathedral in 1962, 'Lift up your heads, great gates and sing', commissioned for a St Albans diocesan choral festival, and 'Lo, God is here', which suggests a portrait of York Minster. A good deal of his organ music is still used.

There is a tune 'East Acklam' (the village where he lives), for the hymn 'God that madest earth and heaven' composed for an old choristers' reunion. He says that if he is to be remembered by only one piece of music, he hopes it may be that tune. But it seems unlikely that the memory of his work will be so limited.

He took a Durham DMus in 1957, was President of the Royal College of organists from 1972 to 1974, and appointed CBE in 2007.

Philip Moore

The news in 1975 that Canon Ronald Jasper of Westminster Abbey had been appointed Dean of York was not universally welcomed by the Minster's congregation. The new dean was a church historian who had written the biographies of two influential bishops – Arthur Caley Headlam of Gloucester and George Bell of Chichester. But he was much more widely known as chairman of the church's Liturgical Commission and the chief architect of the *Alternative Service Book 1980*. Had they known also that, while at Westminster, he had been intensely frustrated by his inability to persuade his dean, Eric Abbott, to allow the new services to be used in the Abbey, they might have been even more apprehensive.

With good reason, for not long after his arrival Jasper changed, with the agreement of the chapter, the pattern of Sunday morning worship. As long ago as 1925 a Sung Eucharist had been started, but Choral Mattins with a substantial sermon remained, and was still regarded by many as the 'main course' on the liturgical menu. This was offensive to the modern liturgist, for whom the centrality of the Eucharist in the church's life involved deeply held convictions as well as other, pastoral considerations. Thus Jasper, undaunted by the strength of local feeling, moved the Sung Eucharist to the central hour and, inevitably and intentionally, relegated Mattins to a subordinate place. Later the nave furnishings were reordered to provide a more appropriate setting for what became an impressive and edifying act of worship, paralleled in most other cathedrals.

With the passage of the years the opposition to all this largely faded, but at the time it was deeply divisive and the cause of much unhappiness among the large number of older members of the cathedral community. Francis Jackson, jealous for the Minster's traditions, shared this sadness. But loyalty and a reconciling disposition led him to accept the new arrangements with heroic good grace, even though the final days of his long reign were clouded by them.

Philip Moore, his successor, had no such problems. For one thing, he was much younger and had grown up with the unstoppable movement to make the Eucharist central. For another, he had spent the previous nine years as organist of Guildford Cathedral – a post-war building which, in spite of its Gothic shape, was not laggard in the field of liturgical reform. He was therefore, and presumably would not have been appointed had it been otherwise, able happily to accommodate the Minster's music to the new order. And, being a composer as well as an organist, he was even able to produce new settings for the new rites.

His chief contribution to the York tradition was that of a composer, and he became one of the leading contributors to Anglican music. His output includes over 80 anthems, many settings of the psalms, a good number of sets of canticles and some organ works. All of which, astonishingly, represents only a small part of a wide-ranging repertory that extends over 400 compositions.

Much of his church music was obviously heard first in York Minster but, significantly, quite a lot was commissioned for special occasions by other cathedral organists who are not normally uncritical of the work of their colleagues. His music combines beauty, originality and accessibility, which enables cathedral and good parish church choirs to perform new music without unduly frightening the congregations.

Philip Moore was born in London in 1943 and from an early age was taught to play the piano by his father who was himself an able performer. While at Maidstone Grammar School he started to compose music and went on to the Royal College of Music to study piano, organ, composition and conducting. By this time he was competent enough to take responsibility for the music at St Gabriel's Church, Cricklewood, in North London, where he played the fine organ and trained a mixed choir.

His first cathedral appointment was in 1968 when he became assistant to Allan Wicks at Canterbury. From there he went as organist to Guildford, succeeding Barry Rose who had moved to St Paul's. Nine years there, during which his reputation as a composer grew rapidly, confirmed the view that he was destined for one of the major cathedral posts. When Francis Jackson announced his resignation from York in 1983, Moore seemed his natural successor.

Thus he began a distinguished tenure that lasted for 25 years during a critical period in the development of Anglican worship and in challenges to the life of the Church of England more generally. He arrived at York just in time to preside over the music at the enthronement of Archbishop John Habgood, was there for that of David Hope in 1995, and successfully incorporated some unusual music into the service for the enthronement in 2005 of the Ugandan-born John Sentamu. He was conductor of the York Musical Society – the oldest in the country – and in demand for organ recitals both in Britain and abroad. The choir, for the first time, undertook overseas tours.

Of his church music, three sets of canticles – *Fauxbourdon (No. 2)*, *First and Second Services* – are in frequent use, and a fourth, commissioned by David Hill for St John's College, Cambridge, in 2006, has been widely welcomed. His anthems 'All wisdom cometh from the Lord' and 'Through the day thy love has spared us' are also popular, while another, 'Two prayers of Dietrich Bonhoeffer', is specially noteworthy.

Towards the end of Moore's time at York a girls' choir was introduced and, while wholeheartedly leading this move, he made the interesting point, on his retirement in 2008, that it had required more intensive training of the boys, who no longer sang every day. Many months might pass before a particular psalm was repeated.

In 2001 John Scott Whiteley, who had been assistant organist since 1976 and become a leading recitalist, both in Britain and overseas, was appointed organist, while Philip Moore retained overall responsibility for the music. This ensured continuity and prepared the way for Moore's successor to be a specialist choir-trainer. Robert Sharpe, who is highly gifted both in this field and as an organist, came from Truro Cathedral in 2008 and the benefits of the new arrangement are already evident.

Another sign of a new dispensation at York is the introduction of a monthly Sunday evening service 'Transcendence: An Ancient and Future Mass'. A key element in this is described as 'the mixing up of the old and the new – plainsong chants over ambient beats, live video mixing using ancient iconography, beats and DJs working alongside Palestrina sung by the Minister's musicians'. There could, perhaps, be no more striking evidence of the development of church music since the days of Sir Edward Bairstow.

20

Two Post-War Giants

Benjamin Britten

Benjamin Britten, in common with Edward Elgar and Ralph Vaughan Williams, was a towering figure in twentieth-century British music and, as with them, his religious faith, which varied at different points in his life, is not easy to define. Music itself probably provided him with sufficient spiritual inspiration, nourishment and expression. After hearing a choir singing Vittoria in the semi-darkness of a monastery chapel in Spain, he said, 'It is difficult not to believe in the supernatural when in a place like this.'

He composed little strictly liturgical music, yet 34 cathedrals and other choral foundations used his anthems in 1998. Of these, five enjoyed great popularity – 'A New Year Lord', 'Hymn to the Virgin', 'O be joyful in the Lord', 'Rejoice in the Lamb' and 'Hymn to St Peter'. Altogether 45 of his works were used by these churches, 13 of them for the first time. Of his liturgical works, a *Missa Brevis* in D, composed in 1959 for the boys' voices of Westminster Cathedral, is in regular use in most cathedrals and many other churches, as are his Te Deum in C, Festival Te Deum and Te Deum in E. A Jubilate Deo was composed for St George's Chapel at the request of the Duke of Edinburgh, who hoped for a complete service, but the other canticles never materialized.

With all his music, churchgoers heard a new voice and one that took many some time to appreciate. Britten was initially inspired by the music of Henry Purcell, whose freedom in the treatment of harmony and the variety of his cadences seemed shocking in the seventeenth century and was not developed by his successors. Much less dependent than other twentieth-century composers on the music of the intervening centuries, Britten picked up Purcell's baton and carried it forward to create a great deal of distinctive, original music of his own – a process that continued until almost the end of his life. This was assisted by encounters with the music of Mahler, Shostakovich (with whom he established a close friendship) and the 12-note work of Schönberg. Different again was the influence of a chance wartime encounter in America with Colin McPhee, a Canadian-born composer and scholar, who introduced him to the oriental music of Bali and a local percussion orchestra, the gamelan. The result was music that is altogether more disturbing and challenging than that of Elgar and Vaughan Williams – reflecting the more fragmented culture of the second half of the twentieth century, as well as the conflicts in Britten's own complex personality. He seemed always to be at sixes and sevens with the world.

Beyond the boundaries of the church's worship, Britten's special, seminal, interest in opera led him to compose three 'church parables', which have some affinity with the medieval miracle plays – *Curlew River*, the story of the tragic death of a 12–year-old boy, with western and oriental music to indicate the two sides of a river; *The Burning Fiery Furnace* (taken from the book of Daniel) was first performed in Southwark Cathedral, while *The Prodigal Son* (inspired by the sight of Rembrandt's great painting in the Hermitage at St Petersburg) was first performed in Orford Church in Suffolk. Before then, Britten had produced *Noye's Fludde*, which was designed to edify and entertain children, and to be performed by them, using a variety of instruments and kitchen utensils. It incorporated three traditional hymn tunes, including, oddly as it might seem, J. B. Dykes's tune for 'Eternal Father, strong to save'.

Earlier *A Ceremony of Carols*, written for boys' voices, soon became one of his most popular choral works and *The Young Person's Guide to the Orchestra* continues to be performed worldwide. Britten had a unique ability to compose for boys' voices and had a special empathy with choristers who, in turn, generally enjoyed singing his music. The appearance in 1992 of a major biography by Humphrey Carpenter drew attention to the fact, already well known in music circles, that Britten had a long series of close friendships with attractive teenage boys. It may be that this influenced at a deep level certain of his compositions, but, while some of the relationships with boys appear to have been dangerous, there has never been any suggestion that he was a paedophile.

Standing above all Britten's many works is his *War Requiem*, now regarded not only as his masterpiece but also as one of the great choral works of the twentieth century. Commissioned for the programme surrounding the consecration in 1962 of Coventry Cathedral, rebuilt after its wartime bombing, this provided him with a special opportunity to express his own long-standing horror of war – a horror reinforced by visits to German concentration camps, where he gave recitals with Yehudi Menuhin immediately after the ending of the war. The cathedral did not wish to pay a fee for the Requiem and the first performance, given by an amateur chorus, took place in somewhat chaotic circumstances owing to the mishandling of the audience's seating arrangements. Its first London performance was given in Westminster Abbey, but the main impact came after the release of a two-disc recording when 200,000 copies were sold in five weeks. Like the resurrection of the cathedral itself, the Requiem became an icon of a world now emerging from its most destructive experience, as well as for the peace movement and left-wing intellectuals. Half a century on, it has lost none of its power.

Benjamin Britten was born in 1913 in what was then the important Suffolk fishing port of Lowestoft. His father was a dental surgeon, and his mother, an amateur singer and pianist, had a considerable influence on him. She was secretary of the local choral society, there was much music in the home and, once his musical talent was apparent, she did much to promote his career. He studied piano lessons when he was seven and, while still at a preparatory school, showed signs of a gift that would make him a top-class pianist and, if he had chosen to concentrate on the keyboard, one of international repute. When he was 14, however, the gift of *A Dictionary of Musical Terms* by John Stainer and W. A. Barratt encouraged him to explore the world of composition, for which he proved also to have an unusual talent. Later that year he was fortunate enough to meet Frank Bridge, a distinguished composer and teacher, who recognized his talent and gave him some lessons. In the following year he composed *Quatre chansons françaises* as a twenty-seventh wedding anniversary present to his parents and much later he expressed his indebtedness to Bridge ('my father in music') with *Variations on a Theme of Frank Bridge*, which was good enough to win recognition at the 1937 Salzburg Festival.

It was Bridge who encouraged him, when he was 16, to enter for a scholarship to the Royal College of Music, for which he was examined by John Ireland and Ralph Vaughan Williams. Bridge also arranged for him to be taught composition by Ireland, but this was not successful as Ireland was often too drunk to give lessons. Nonetheless Britten worked hard and won some prizes, though many of his compositions were severely criticized, possibly because he was already moving well beyond the traditional, but also because he could not get them properly performed in the college. He bore the emotional scars of this for the rest of his life.

Much more significant for the development of Britten's work were his contacts with London's musical world outside the college. Bridge took him to meet Schönberg on one of his London visits when his experiments with new ideas were beginning to arouse interest. Victor Hely-Hutchinson, a member of the BBC's music department, and himself a composer, told his colleagues, 'I do whole-heartedly subscribe to the general opinion that Mr. Britten is the most interesting new arrival since Walton, and I feel we should watch his work very carefully.' Two of his pieces were broadcast.

Also aware of his existence was John Grierson, an outstanding producer of documentary films, who was at that time working for the GPO's film unit. He engaged Britten as the unit's resident composer and music editor. This led to his first encounter with W. H. Auden who had been engaged as a film scriptwriter, and their collaboration resulted in two highly acclaimed films, *Coal Face* and *Night Mail*. He also became involved with Auden and Christopher Isherwood in the Group Theatre – a left-wing company – and he composed music for two of their finest plays. He was now aligning himself closely with the music of Schönberg, Stravinsky and Shostakovich and became highly critical of composers of the Vaughan Williams generation, declaring there to be more music on a single page of the work of the new composers than in the whole 'elegant' output of their predecessors.

It was in 1937, not long after the death of his mother, that Britten acknowledged his homosexual orientation and, having ended a liaison with Lennox Berkeley, began a close friendship with Peter Pears. In 1939 this blossomed into a full partnership that extended until Britten's death, in Pears's arms, in 1976. The partnership had a remarkably creative influence on them both. At the time of their coming together, Pears was a tenor whose voice did not suggest an important future. But Britten composed songs specifically for him, often accompanying them himself, and also outstanding operas in which he had leading roles. Thus Pears became one of the great tenors of the twentieth century and was knighted for his services to music. Pears, in turn, provided Britten with the emotional security he needed and also the encouragement and informed criticism essential to the continuous development of his music. The two men lived together and enjoyed a more intimate and harmonious relationship than that of many a heterosexual married couple, though until 1967 their union was illegal and in other circumstances might have landed either or both of them in prison. There were no problems about this in the artistic circles where they moved, but it has sometimes been suggested that Britten's lifelong sympathy with 'the outsider' may have owed something to his unconventional way of life.

Although they had not yet entered into a firm commitment to each other, they went together to North America – first to Canada, then to the United States – in April 1939. While on the transatlantic voyage Britten wrote to Aaron Copland, the American composer, and told him, 'A thousand reasons – mostly "problems" have brought me away.' It has, however, never been clear what the 'problems' were since his star was rising rapidly in the British musical firmament, and a legacy from his mother had enabled him to purchase an attractive mill house at Snape, near Aldeburgh, in which he seemed happily settled. Whatever the explanation, the outbreak of war a few months after their arrival ensured that it would not be a short visit, as their known pacifist convictions led to advice that they would not be welcomed back to the United Kingdom.

Auden and Isherwood had gone to America ahead of them and collaboration on a number of musical projects was resumed. Britten was warmly received in New York and performances of his music, some of it recently composed, were widely applauded. The next two years proved to be a creative period in his career, but by 1941 he and Pears were becoming bored. After reading in *The Listener* the text of a radio talk on George Crabbe the late eighteenth-, early nineteenth-century Suffolk poet, given by E. M. Forster, Britten felt homesick for England, the country he loved. A passage on a Swedish ship was secured in 1942 and during the slow, tedious voyage to Liverpool he composed music for Auden's poem 'A Hymn to St Cecilia' – a major choral work, demanding considerable musical resources – and also a draft of *A Ceremony of Carols*.

On their arrival in England Britten and Pears became liable for military service and both sought registration as conscientious objectors. Britten told the tribunal:

> Since I believe that there is in every man the spirit of God, I cannot destroy human life ... The whole of my life has been devoted to acts of creation (being by profession a composer) and I cannot take part in acts of destruction ... I believe sincerely that I can help my fellow human beings best by continuing the creation or propagation of music.

He agreed to join a non-combatant service, such as the Royal Army Medical Corps, but later changed his mind and appealed against the tribunal's decision. In the end he and Pears were exempted from military service on condition that they gave concerts under the auspices of the Council for the Encouragement of Music and the Arts (CEMA) – a wartime organization formed to maintain morale by making music and the other arts widely available at low cost. So they spent much of the rest of the war travelling about the country, performing with the aid of out-of-tune pianos in church halls, but also taking opportunities to appear in the Wigmore Hall and in the celebrated National Gallery lunchtime concerts.

When questioned by the tribunal about his religious beliefs, Britten said that, although he had been brought up in the Church of England, he had not attended for the past five years. Asked if he believed in the divinity of Christ, he answered 'No', but went on, 'I think his teaching is sound, and his example should be followed.' This appears to have been the extent of his religious faith for the remainder of his life. Following the composition in 1943 of an extraordinary anthem, 'Rejoice in the Lamb', based on a poem by the often mad Christopher Smart, he struck up a close friendship with Walter Hussey, the Vicar of St Matthew's, Northampton, who had commissioned the work for a church festival. Hussey, a notable patron of the arts, went on to become Dean of Chichester where he did much to re-establish a close relationship between religion and the arts, but his own faith was some way removed from orthodox Christianity.

During the closing months of Britten's life he asked Bishop Leslie Brown of St Edmundsbury and Ipswich to visit him, which he did on several occasions. Later the Bishop said, 'I think Ben wanted to have religion when he was dying, but he could never really quite come to it.' A friend explained that 'Britten wanted a spiritual sanctuary but didn't feel it was quite honourable to join the church so late and in poor condition when he had rejected it, very largely, when well and active.' Peter Pears said in a filmed interview, 'I don't think he really had any particular convictions as to what was going to happen after death, but he was certainly not afraid of dying.' Nonetheless, the Bishop, who gave the address at the funeral in 1976, celebrated the Holy Communion during one of his visits, and when the end was near said prayers for the dying.

Besides his towering achievements as a composer, and his notable work as a pianist and a conductor, Britten made three other important inter-related contributions to the development of music. The chief was his pioneering work in chamber opera – relatively small-scale works in English that did not require the massive resources of grand opera and could be performed on fairly small stages in different parts of the country. Before this, however, he had composed a grand opera, *Peter Grimes*, based on part of a poem by George Crabbe. This somewhat prim, pessimistic, savage even, portrayal of the fate of an outsider, a social reject, was first performed at Sadler's Wells Theatre in London, just after the war ended in 1945. It was not quite in tune with the celebratory atmosphere of the hour, several of the performers objected to it, and there was some hostile criticism at and after the first performance. But it took the opera world by storm and came to be seen later as a turning point in the history of European opera. With it Britten established his own distinctive 'voice'.

The Rape of Lucretia, a chamber opera, was commissioned for the re-opening of the Glyndebourne opera house in 1946 and led to the formation of the English Opera Group, of which Britten, Eric Crozier (a librettist and intimate friend) and John Piper (the painter) were artistic directors, and Tyrone Guthrie (Director of Covent Garden) and Sir Kenneth Clark (Director of the National Gallery) were among the members of a board chaired by Oliver Lyttelton (later Viscount Chandos). This was designed as a non-profit-making organization committed to annual seasons of contemporary opera in English and suitable classical works, including those of Henry Purcell.

The EOG, as it came to be known, was soon in demand for performances, not only at Glyndebourne but also in many other places in Britain and Europe, and during the next quarter of a century premiered Britten's new works – *Albert Herring* (1947), *Billy Budd* (1951), *The Turn of the*

Screw (1954), *A Midsummer Night's Dream* (1960) and, finally, *Owen Wingrave* (1970). This last, composed for a television production, and making use of both western and oriental styles of music, was based on a story by Henry James. It tells of a young man born into a military family, whose horror of war led him to reject the military career he was expected to pursue – 'crass barbarism', he called it – with fatal consequences to himself. The appeal of the story to the pacifist Britten was obvious and, although not everyone approved of the music, most of the professional critics regarded it as 'masterly'; one said, 'This is certainly the most impressive piece of TV drama I have yet seen.' *Voices for Today*, commissioned by the United Nations for its twenty-fifth anniversary in 1965, was another work on the theme of war and peace.

At the end of a European tour in 1947 Peter Pears said, 'Why don't we have a festival in Aldeburgh?' (to which he and Britten had recently returned). 'Why do we have to come abroad to perform *Albert Herring?*' They had given a recital there, in the Jubilee Hall, the previous year, and they, together with Eric Crozier, began immediately to plan what became the first Aldeburgh Festival of Music and the Arts for 1948. Besides the Jubilee Hall, which seated only 300 people, some local churches were used and, by the time of Britten's death in December 1976, it had become an important international event, attracting significant new music and many of the world's leading performers.

A specially designed concert hall, created out of a malting at Snape, was opened in 1967 but soon after the first performance of the 1969 Festival was seriously damaged by fire. The remainder of the programme, apart from a large-scale concert by the Cambridge University Musical Society, was transferred to Blythburgh Parish Church, and, as a result of prodigious effort, the hall was restored to use for the 1970 Festival. In 1979 a new building was erected alongside the concert hall to house the Britten-Pears School of Advanced Musical Studies for the training of young musicians; six years earlier the Red House at Aldeburgh, where the two men had lived since 1957, became the Britten-Pears Library.

The development of the Festival was, as might have been anticipated, not without personal as well as practical problems. Music was the whole of Britten's life and the relationship with Peter Pears central to his emotions. He was, however, afflicted with bouts of ill-health and subject to fits of anger and depression. His attitude to less avant-garde composers, no matter how distinguished, bordered on contempt. Yet he could be kind and encouraging to young musicians. Many performers and others who worked for him testified that he was wonderfully charming and had the gift of making them feel that they were the most important persons in the world. Dame Janet Baker qualified this by saying that, although he made an effort to put her at her ease in his company, he didn't quite succeed because to be with him was a bit like being with the Queen: you're never quite normal. He had a quite regal air and for many years drove about Suffolk in a Rolls Royce, later exchanged for an open-top Alvis. Yet he did not own a television set until given one for his sixtieth birthday.

The hot-house atmosphere at Aldeburgh during the annual Festivals was for some wonderfully exciting and invigorating. But, as Humphrey Carpenter's biography reveals, not for all. The Britten–Pears partnership and its entourage was likened by a number of responsible people to a Byzantine court. Peter Duncan, a librettist who was close to Britten for many years, went further in his book *Working with Britten* (1981):

> The atmosphere at Aldeburgh was reminiscent of Berchtesgaden. It was fraught with sycophancy: 'there was whispering behind shuttering', nobody knew precisely who was 'in' or who was 'out'. It was a tiny ducal court where Ben was Weimar and Goethe combined; the greatest toady became the latest chancellor. Those who had just been elevated turned to disparage colleagues who had just been abandoned.

The number abandoned was large, for Britten was ruthless in dismissing, usually without any explanation and through an intermediary, those whose performances no longer pleased him or whose faces no longer fitted. Robert Tear, the tenor, went so far as to allege: 'There was a great, huge abyss in his soul. That's my explanation of why the music becomes thinner and thinner as time passed. He got into the valley of the shadow of death and couldn't get out.'

The verdict of fellow composers was different. John Ireland, with whom Britten had had an unhappy, discouraging experience at the Royal College of Music, felt driven to concede, after listening twice to *The Turning of the Screw*, 'I am now (perhaps reluctantly) compelled to regard Britten as possessing ten times the musical talent, intuition and ability of all other British composers put together.' Michael Tippett, who for a time in the 1970s and 80s succeeded Britten as the most fashionable avant-garde composer, wrote in an obituary, 'I want to say, here and now, that Britten has been for me the most purely musical person I have ever met and have ever known.'

He was the recipient of many honorary doctorates, prizes and medals. A knighthood was declined, but in 1953 he was made a Companion of Honour, in 1965 he was admitted to the Order of Merit and shortly before his death was created, uniquely for a composer, a Life Peer. His mortal remains and those of Peter Pears, who died in 1986, lie side by side in the churchyard at Aldeburgh, and he has a memorial tablet, close to that of Henry Purcell and other great musicians, in Westminster Abbey.

Herbert Howells

Herbert Howells, while not in the same league as Britten, was one of the foremost contributors to Anglican church music during the middle of the twentieth century. His work extended far beyond this and encompassed large-scale orchestral items, chamber music and songs. But he devoted most of his time and outstanding talent to the composition of about 200 choral works, of which three-quarters were for the church. Inevitably, not all of these are of the same quality but today there is no English cathedral or large parish church where the unmistakeable sound of Howells's service settings and anthems is not heard regularly.

His music owes something to Elgar and Vaughan Williams and even more to Stanford, but from an early stage in his career he developed a distinctive voice. Kenneth Long described him as the 'Archpriest of Impressionism' – a style pioneered by Vaughan Williams, in which the composer uses harmony and harmonic devices to emphasize the colours and elements in music and thus create 'atmosphere'. Among his most ardent admirers, however – and they are many – there are some who are disappointed that much of his work, especially his service settings, has a certain 'sameness' about it, even when there was a long interval between the composition of particular items. It is also the case that only a small amount of his work is within the competence of most parish church choirs.

A man of romantic good looks, great charm and cultivated taste (in other circumstances he might well have become a fine poet), Herbert Howells was born in 1892 in Lydney, Gloucestershire, where his father was a painter and decorator and an amateur pianist. The youngest of eight children, he attended the church school and won a scholarship to the local grammar school. From an early age he was taught to play the piano by his sister. But disaster struck in 1895 when his father went bankrupt, leaving the large family in dire straits and unfortunately subject to hurtful treatment by their neighbours. Being of a particularly sensitive nature, young Herbert was deeply affected and bore the scars of it for the remainder of his life.

The local squire came to the rescue, however, and paid for him to study the piano, then the organ, with Herbert Brewer, the organist of Gloucester Cathedral. He was one of the last church musicians to be apprenticed to an organist who undertook responsibility for his training. He did not find it easy to get on with Brewer but made sufficient progress to be appointed organist of nearby Aylburton Church. A fellow pupil was Ivor Novello.

In 1910, when the Three Choirs Festival was held at Gloucester, Howells heard the first performance of Vaughan Williams's *Fantasia on a Theme by Thomas Tallis*, which made such a deep impression on him (as well as on many others who heard it) that it became in retrospect the seminal musical experience of his life. Thus inspired, he won a scholarship to the Royal College of Music in 1912 where he was fortunate enough to be taught by three great musicians – Hubert Parry, Charles Villiers Stanford and Charles Wood. Two years later his Piano Concerto No. 1 in C minor was given its premiere in the Queen's Hall, London, under the baton of Stanford who described him as 'my son in music'. A string quartet and a piano quartet soon followed.

In 1916 Howells's *Mass in the Dorian Mode* was first used in Westminster Cathedral, but soon after this he developed Graves disease and was given only six months to live. A new form of radium treatment, given twice a week in St Thomas's Hospital over the next two years, led however to a cure, and he lived until he was 91, though he was never really robust again. He was exempted on health grounds from military service in the 1914–18 war and even appointment as assistant organist of Salisbury Cathedral proved to be too taxing; he had to give this up after only six months. He was, however, well enough to use a Carnegie Trust three-year grant to assist Sir William Terry, the organist of Westminster Cathedral, in the ground-breaking task of editing Tudor church music that had recently come to light. He also composed some acclaimed chamber music and three carol anthems – 'Here is the little door', 'A spotless rose' and 'Sing lullaby' – which sounded quite different from any other carol music and remain popular today.

In 1920 Howells married Dorothy Dance and, now in need of a reliable income, went to the Royal College of Music to teach composition. This proved to be an exacting assignment and, combined with a great deal of examining and adjudicating at music festivals, left little time for his own work as a composer. Response to a commission from the Royal Philharmonic Society for a piano concerto, to be conducted by Sir Malcolm Sargent in the Queen's Hall, also turned out to be something of a disaster. A member of the audience loudly voiced his disapproval, thus creating a serious lack of confidence in the composer. This was eventually recovered, largely through the warm welcome given to a book of pieces for the clavichord, *Lambert's Clavichord*, in which the Tudor influence was evident, yet Howells had brought to them something new and distinctive.

The most traumatic and influential event in Howells's life came in 1935 when his 9-year-old son Michael died from poliomyelitis. This was a devastating blow from which he never quite recovered and thereafter most of his music bore the marks of his sorrow. It was also said to be the point at which he lost his Christian faith, and he said later, 'I am not a religious man any more than Ralph (Vaughan Williams) was.' Nonetheless the tragedy led almost immediately to the composition of *Hymnus paradisi* – a kind of requiem that is now generally considered to be his masterpiece. But he could not bear to have it performed in public and it was not until

1950 that, in response to pressure from Vaughan Williams, he felt able to conduct its premiere at the Three Choirs Festival in Gloucester, where it made a deep impression.

After Michael's death he turned, paradoxically as it may seem, to the composition, almost exclusively, of church music. The 1939–45 war years were spent mainly in Cambridge, where he was acting organist of St John's College and had sufficient leisure to compose a few orchestral pieces, but chiefly to start a long series of church services. These broke new ground and added something of considerable significance to the repertories of cathedrals and other churches with sufficiently competent choirs. *Collegium Regale*, composed for King's College, Cambridge, was the first of these and is acknowledged to be the best, followed, in quality, by the *Gloucester Service*. Several other major cathedrals then commissioned services in which Howells tried to reflect something of the atmosphere of the building in which they would first be used. His *St Paul's Service* is also widely admired and in the end he composed 20 different service settings, as well as a number of anthems. Two of these, 'Like as the hart' and 'O pray for the peace of Jerusalem', both published in 1943, have remained deservedly popular.

His output of Mass settings was relatively small but included *An English Mass*, composed for use with the Book of Common Prayer, at the request of Harold Darke, the outstanding organist of St Michael's, Cornhill, in London, and another for Coventry Cathedral, which included, unusually, responses for the recital of the Ten Commandments. A request made in 1954 by the Bach Choir for a setting of Stabat Mater did not bear fruit until 1963 and required the use of an orchestra. In the same year he was commissioned to compose a motet for the memorial service held in Washington Cathedral following the assassination of President John F. Kennedy. The result, 'Take him to thyself', incorporated some music composed at the time of Michael's death and proved to be deeply moving.

Howells was not himself an outstanding organist and he composed only a small amount of organ music, but the six voluntaries, said to be developments of his improvizations on the organ of St John's College, Cambridge, are now considered to be important, as is *Siciliano for High Ceremony*, published in 1953. All of this was composed against a background of teaching and adjudication. He was at the Royal College of Music from 1920 to 1972, Director of Music at St Paul's Girls' School from 1936 to 1962 and Professor of Music at London University from 1954 to 1964. He had honorary degrees from Oxford and Cambridge, was appointed CBE in 1953 and made a Companion of Honour in 1972. Following his death in 1983 his ashes were buried in Westminster Abbey alongside the remains of Henry Purcell, John Blow, Charles Villiers Stanford and Ralph Vaughan Williams – a clear indication of his status in English church music.

21

A Contemporary Contrast

Jonathan Harvey

Jonathan Harvey was one of Britain's leading composers during the latter part of the twentieth century and remains one of the country's chief exponents of the radical modernist style of music associated with Stockhausen, Webern and Boulez, though he is in some ways independent of them. He was the first British classical composer to explore seriously, then embrace, the new possibilities offered by electronic sound – the most important musical breakthrough of the century. By means of synthesizers, computers and other electronic equipment, listeners are treated to as wide a variety of sound as might be imagined – some beyond imagination. Tomtoms, bongo drums, chimes and bells are often used and, once, the roar of a lion. Less alarming is the ethereal sound made by oriental instruments.

The atonal character of most of Harvey's music means that much of his work is not immediately accessible to the untutored ear, and never to the intolerant. Its rewards, which are apparently considerable, go to the persevering and those with time to devote to its reception. That many do this is demonstrated by the fact that he has been commissioned by most of the major orchestras worldwide and that 150–200 performances of his work are given or broadcast every year. About 80 CD recordings are available.

Much of Harvey's work has a transcendental quality and the title of one of his books is *The Quest of the Spirit* (1999). He says that all music worth its name is transcendental and true art shapes its material in order to point beyond it. Or again, 'In a metaphysical sense music never changes; it always portrays the play of the Relative against the ground of the Absolute.'

In comparison with most of his work, Harvey's liturgical music is fairly easy, at least, not so difficult. Its composition and entry into Anglican cathedral and collegiate church worship owes almost everything to the creative partnership established between himself and Martin Neary, the organist and master of the music at Winchester Cathedral in the 1970s and 80s. This began when he was teaching at Southampton University and, at the suggestion of Neary, was commissioned to compose an anthem for the enthronement of John V. Taylor as Bishop of Winchester in 1975. Until then he had composed nothing for the church.

The resulting 'The dove descending' taxed the skill of the choir, but greatly pleased the bishop, a theologian and poet, who became an admirer. The admission of Harvey's son Dominic as a chorister encouraged parental attendance at Evensong on Sunday afternoons and over the next few years this proved to be influential. A short tonal anthem, 'I love the Lord', was offered to the choir and is now widely used by other cathedrals. But his next Winchester composition created problems. Martin Neary asked him to compose a challenging set of Evening Canticles for the 1978 Southern Cathedrals Festival. He obliged with a striking and provocative offering which the other participating choirs – Salisbury and Chichester – were initially reluctant to sing. Eventually they were cajoled into acceptance and, although one lay clerk complained that the music made him feel physically ill, the distinguished critic Nicholas Kenyon said it was 'a landmark for Anglican church music'.

A setting of the Litany requested by Bishop Taylor was less controversial. An anthem based on the 'Veni Creator' has an underlying unity provided by traditional plainchant and found more ready acceptance by all the Southern Cathedrals Festival choirs in 1984. Harvey's major work at Winchester, *Passion and Resurrection*, based on two medieval texts, had been provided for Easter 1981 and took the form of a church opera, directed by the bishop, with members of the congregation acting while the choir sang. This made a considerable impact locally and was filmed by the BBC for a television programme in which local residents were asked for their reactions to the music. In all, ten of his works were premiered at Winchester, which for him became 'a sacred place'. More commissions came from other cathedrals and when Neary moved to Westminster Abbey he secured a Missa Brevis which includes the spoken word.

Jonathan Harvey was born in Warwickshire in 1939 and went as a chorister to St Michael's College, Tenbury. Walking in the cloisters one evening he heard the organist improvising on a particular chord which gave him a Damascus Road-like musical experience. This made him determined to become a composer and led to his development as the college's most distinguished, and musically most unusual, alumnus. Tenbury was followed by Repton School and a choral scholarship to St John's College, Cambridge, under George Guest. There he won a composition prize offered by David Willcocks of King's and was rewarded by a performance of his entry in King's Chapel.

A PhD in music at Glasgow, financed by playing as a cellist in the BBC Scottish Symphony Orchestra, pointed to an academic career and it was during this time that he became interested in the music of Stockhausen. From 1964 to 1977 he was a lecturer at Southampton University with a break for a fellowship at Princeton University in the USA. A meeting with Stockhausen led to the writing of *The Music of Stockhausen* (1975), now the standard work on its subject. The posts of Reader then of Professor of Music at Sussex University claimed him until 1993, when he retired to concentrate on composition. He soon found time, however, to return to teaching as Professor of Music at Stanford University in the USA and then as a Visiting Professor at Imperial College, London.

In the early 1980s he had been invited by Pierre Boulez to work at the Institute for Research and Co-ordination of Acoustic Music in Paris, and the broad direction his own music would take was now firmly settled. Of his considerable output, which includes music for opera, orchestra, solo instruments, cantatas, as well as unaccompanied works for choirs, his contribution to church music, though important, is not large.

A number of interrelated factors inhibit its widespread use. The most important of these is that churches are essentially conservative bodies, not least in the sensitive realm of worship. Few people go to church to experience adventure or to be challenged by the innovative and the unfamiliar. It is also the case that most of Harvey's music is of such complexity that only choirs of the highest calibre can effectively perform it. Even these require a level of commitment and an extension of rehearsal time that may not always be forthcoming – as Martin Neary discovered when he wanted to introduce the Evening Canticles at Westminster Abbey. The performance on Good Friday 1998 of a new work, *Death of Light, Light of Death*, before the Isenheim Altar in Alsace was a clear indication, however, that, for a wider public, Harvey still has much to contribute to the sphere of religious experience.

John Tavener

During the entire twentieth century there was no other composer of church music quite like John Tavener, neither was there any other music that even faintly resembled his own. His espousal of the style of the Orthodox Church's music, integrated during his later period with that of the Islamic, Hindu and Sufi faiths, was an extreme reaction against the modernist, experimental music in which he had been nurtured. It is no less an extreme reaction against twentieth-century western culture as this had evolved during the previous three centuries.

He believes the Enlightenment to have been a terrible mistake and the Second Vatican Council (1962–65) the third betrayal of Christ because 'it threw out Latin and all the best music'. After the 9/11 terrorist assaults on New York and Washington in 2001 he advised politicians to 'sell cleverness and buy wonder' and on another occasion accused Wagner, Mahler and Schönberg of representing a 'downward spiral' in music. 'The language of modernism doesn't work.' The music of Beethoven does not, he asserts, express religious truth, only human truth and, while conceding that J. S. Bach may have inspired moments, these are less evident in his specifically religious music. 'Western music does not have an esoteric dimension in the way the music of the East does.'

After all this it is disarming to learn that Tavener claims divine origin for his own counter-culture music. 'The divine art is not limited if one allows the Holy Spirit to enter. When one is absolutely nothing, only then and very gently, can the Holy Spirit come in and work within you.' If this seems a large claim, its validity is readily accepted by a very large number of people who are drawn into worship by the ethereal character of Tavener's music and are both comforted and inspired by its other-worldliness. Their number was greatly enlarged when his *A Song for Athene* was performed at the end of Princess Diana's emotionally driven funeral in Westminster Abbey and broadcast worldwide in 1997. This immediately went to the top of the best-selling records chart and in the following year was performed in many English cathedrals and other choral foundations.

Since then Tavener has come under the influence of a Sufi universalist philosopher, Frithjof Schuon, who has taught him that an inner transcendence unites all religions and that 'neither religion nor music can be exclusive'. This found expression in *The Beautiful Names*, a setting of the 99 names of Allah in the Qur'an, which was first performed in Arabic by the BBC Orchestra and Chorus in Westminster Cathedral in 2007.

In the same year the linguistic skills of the singers were presented with an even greater challenge by a *Mass for the Feast of the Immaculate Conception*, which employs not only Arabic, but also Latin, Sanskrit, Aramaic, Greek, American Indian, German and Italian in order to 'express something of the divine effulgence of the feminine that the Mother of God has revealed to my soul'. The use of American Indian may owe something to the fact that he regards a series of visions that followed chatting with Apache Indians as another channel of inspiration.

Although Tavener declared in 2004, 'It strikes me now that all religions are as senile as one another', he still regards the Orthodox Church tradition as the brightest of his guiding stars and he retains a deep devotion to the Virgin Mary, to whom he feels closer than he does to Christ because, as he puts it, 'she is more mysterious, so little is known about her'. His 'Hymn to the Mother of God' (1985) is the most frequently performed of all his works in English cathedrals. Tavener's devotion to Mary leads him to lament the absence of 'the eternal feminine' in modern western culture. He was married to a Greek dancer, which lasted only 12 months, and he is now happily married with three children. But other women have been important to him and he says, 'Every woman I have ever met has actually deepened my spiritual awareness.'

John Tavener, who thinks he may well be a direct descendant of the great sixteenth-century composer of the same name, was born in North London in 1944. He had a Presbyterian upbringing, his father being organist of Hampstead Presbyterian Church. Young John went to Highgate School where, in company with John Rutter, he greatly benefited from a highly gifted music teacher – Edward Chapman. At the age of three he had begun to improvise on the piano and attempt some compositions, thus giving him 'the sense of another presence', and at school he studied piano, organ and composition. When 17 he produced a setting of the Credo, and in the following year a setting of a section of Genesis. He was now organist of St John's Presbyterian Church in Kensington and on leaving school entered the Royal Academy of Music to study piano under Solomon, and composition under Lennox Berkeley. Another teacher, David Lumsden, introduced him to contemporary music, especially the works of Messiaen and Boulez. Later he would himself become a Professor of Composition at Trinity College of Music.

His own first venture into serious composition was a dramatic rock-opera, *The Whale*, based on the story of Jonah. This caused something of a stir in musical circles and was followed by a *Celtic Requiem*. At this time his music attracted the admiration of John Lennon and some of it was recorded by the Beatles. He then embarked on a major opera, *Thérèse*, based on the story of St Thérèse of Lisieux. This had been commissioned by the Royal Opera House but it took three years of struggle to complete (1973–76) and, when finally performed at Covent Garden in 1979, received a hostile reception. By this time, however, he had moved away from the avant-garde and embraced something totally different.

This he found in the Russian Orthodox Church, which he joined in 1977, having been attracted by its theology and liturgical tradition, especially the Holy Week liturgy. Thereafter Orthodox mysticism has been the central influence on his music, and he came to believe that the Eastern tradition has retained a 'primordial essence' which the West has lost. His work *A Gentle Spirit* indicated that the new influence was taking over and he moved on to set to music some of the writings of the Fathers (theologians) of the early church of the East, especially those of St John Chrysostom.

By now Tavener's music was becoming known in a few English cathedrals. When Martin Neary moved from St Margaret's, Westminster, to Winchester in 1972 he commissioned him to compose something for the Southern Cathedrals Festival of that year. He asked for a Mass but got instead the beautiful *Little Requiem for Father Malachy Lynch*. Composer and organist got on very well and in the following year the cathedral choir, the Waynflete Singers and the Bournemouth Sinfonietta performed the much larger *Celtic Requiem* in the nave. More followed and ten of Tavener's works were premiered at Winchester, quickly spreading to other cathedrals.

In 1987 he composed a choral setting of William Blake's poem 'The Lamb' with its memorable opening line 'Little Lamb who made thee?' This was done as a third-birthday present to his nephew Simon and quickly became popular – often sung as a Christmas carol. Further exploration of Russian, and now Greek, culture followed and the millennium of the Russian Orthodox Church in 1982 was marked by *The Akathist of Thanksgiving*. Two years later, *The Protecting Veil*, performed at a BBC Prom by the London Symphony Orchestra and the cellist Steven Isserlis, created a great impression and won wider audiences. This served to renew his reputation.

Eternity's Sunrise, based on William Blake's poetry, was composed and dedicated to the memory of Princess Diana. *A New Beginning* was commissioned for the opening of the Millennium Dome in 2000. A few days later, *Fall and Resurrection* was broadcast on television and radio from St Paul's Cathedral and he was knighted in the Millennium Honours. Exploration of Islamic and Hindu music now led to its incorporation into the remarkable *The Veil of the Temple* – intended for a seven-hour all-night vigil, first performed in London's Temple Church in 2003 and scored for at least three choirs, numerous soloists and multifarious instruments positioned in all parts of the building. Shortly before the first performance of a requiem commissioned for the opening of Liverpool's Capital of Culture year Tavener was struck down by a severe heart attack and for several days his future was uncertain. He had already suffered a stroke when only 30, undergone a heart bypass operation, and continues to be afflicted by Marfan syndrome, a rare genetic disease which inhibits his power to compose. He did nonetheless write a short and very beautiful lament, 'Adieu Roger', for his younger brother in 2008.

Earlier he had been a striking figure at first performances – tall, shoulder-length blond hair, a bronzed face, and always clad in a white linen suit, a combination almost as memorable as his music.

It is not uncommon for artists of great creative genius to entertain what to many seem outlandish views on a variety of subjects, including sometimes their own music. But it is not by their views, only by their music, that they are to be evaluated. Critics of Tavener's work complain that it is repetitive and, more seriously, so backward looking and esoteric as to constitute a form of escapism. These are serious charges which contain some truth, but the ingredients of Christian worship always include music reflecting an often distant past and seeking to lift hearts and minds from the mundane to the eternal. In this sense all might be deemed 'escapism' and it is obviously highly undesirable that music of this sort should fill the menu.

But this is not the danger in a church whose worship seems all too often to be earthbound and addressed to the congregation rather than to God. Tavener's introduction of the music of the Eastern Church, and the devotion it expresses, into the life of the Anglican Church, and beyond to a wider constituency, has been a very significant achievement. He inserted some Orthodox antiphons into his Evening Canticles for King's College, Cambridge. Besides his major works, there are many minor pieces, of which 20 were sung as anthems in cathedrals and colleges during 1998. It is likely also that some of these were sung by competent choirs in parish churches. Most choirs have in fact attempted one or two of his simpler pieces and, in spite of the complexity of many of the others, have established a place of considerable importance in the life of the contemporary church.

22

Beyond Atonal Modernism

The most significant, and it seems likely to be highly significant, development in the sphere of sacred music during the closing decades of the twentieth century was the emergence of many new 'voices'. Although church attendance continued to decline in most parts of the western world and the signs of secularization in British culture cried out for recognition, there was no shortage of young and gifted composers who felt drawn to include in their wide-ranging output a number of works of a deeply spiritual character. In a few instances this was their chief motivation.

The atonal modernism pioneered by Schönberg and the Viennese school in the early years of the century had by this time enjoyed a long innings and its creativity seemed to be nearing exhaustion. The new composers had been exposed to it in most of its contemporary forms during their professional training in universities and music colleges but they were not inclined to allow their own work to be unduly influenced by a style that, in spite of its importance in the development of music, had never earned the gratitude of most music lovers. It now seemed time to move on. In a few instances there was a sharp reaction against the more radical forms of modernism, not through any desire to turn back the clock to the time of Elgar and Vaughan Williams but rather in the conviction that music should never be so esoteric that it becomes far removed from the comprehension and the spiritual needs of those who may be persuaded to listen to its performance. Dissonance was not abandoned entirely but its use became less common.

Some years before them, however, there were signs of movement in Eastern Europe where two distinguished composers began to move decisively in new directions. Little of their work is usable by the Church of England but its influence on European music generally has been considerable.

Henryk Górecki

Henryk Górecki was born in 1933 in Southern Poland where he was also exposed to Czech and German cultures as well as the all-pervading authority of the Communist regime. In his early twenties he taught in state schools but, having begun to compose, entered the High School of Music at Katowice, later to become the Academy of Music. He joined its teaching staff in 1968 and eventually became provost. During the 1950s and 60s he was much influenced by the dissonant music of Webern and Stockhausen and the style of Pierre Boulez. *Epitaph*, composed for a Warsaw Festival in 1958, brought him worldwide recognition as 'the most colourful and vibrant expression of the new Polish wave of music' and a significant development of radical modernism.

But in the mid-1970s he changed to a less complex, more traditional, romantic style in which to express his deeply held Catholic beliefs. 'Holy minimalism' is one description of it and the first sign came in 1979 with *Beatus Vir*, which was an affront to his avant-garde colleagues. This coincided more or less with his resignation from the provostship of the Academy. Throughout his time there he was in constant conflict with the Communist authorities over their interference in its affairs, and he resigned in protest against the government's refusal to allow Pope John Paul II to visit Katowice when he made his historic return to Poland. He marked this visit with an exquisite motet, 'Totus tuus Maria', which is now widely sung in English cathedrals and some parish churches.

Górecki now formed a local branch of the Catholic Intellectuals Club to oppose the Communist Party and, nationally, this played an important part in the eventual liberation of Poland from Communist rule. *Miserere* (1987) was composed for a large choir in remembrance of the police violence against the freedom-seeking Solidarity movement. More sacred music followed and he became essentially a religious composer.

Until 1992 he was a somewhat remote figure, known for his fiery temperament, but this changed with the release of a recording of his Third Symphony, *Symphony of Sorrowful Songs*, which was a sensational success and sold more than a million copies. Composed in 1977, it dwelt on motherhood and the separation caused by war, and was designed to commemorate the memory of the millions of Poles killed in the Holocaust. Surprised by its success, he commented, 'Perhaps people find something they need in this piece of music – something they were missing and I hit the right note.'

Arvo Pärt

Arvo Pärt, whose work has some affinities with that of Górecki, was born in Estonia in 1935 but emigrated in 1980 after struggles with the Communist censors who banned all 12-note modernist compositions. After some years in Vienna, where he took Austrian citizenship, he has now settled in Berlin, though he spends some time in America.

During a long period of despair, when he was unable to compose, he immersed himself in early western music – plainsong, Gregorian chant and polyphony – and when he resumed composing in 1971, his Third Symphony, which is now seen as a transitional piece, contained some early polyphony. His new style, far removed from the early dissonance, emerged clearly in *Cantus in Memoriam Benjamin Britten,* and since then he has concentrated on music for sacred texts, usually in Latin or Church Slavonic. He composed an anthem for St John's College, Oxford, in 2005, and there is a Magnificat, a Nunc Dimittis, at least two Te Deums, a *Berlin Mass* and much else.

Pärt's work is immensely popular – it has featured in over 50 films – and in some countries, including Britain, he has almost a cult following. He often employs tintinnabulation, to emulate the ringing of bells, and repetitions which can have a hypnotic effect. Durham University gave him an honorary DMus in 2005.

Judith Bingham

Judith Bingham, now one of Britain's leading composers, is not among the consciously rebellious, but her music displays a striking originality and is not like that of any of her contemporaries. Long exposure to classical polyphonic music with the BBC Singers (she is also a professional singer) led her to move from her early experimental, quixotic style to something more direct. Melody and harmony predominate and much of her orchestral work has visual and literary themes – alpine scenery, the sea, and the poetry of Shelley, together with some mythology. There is, however, controlled dissonance when the theme requires it, and she suggests that her work sometimes has 'a painful kind of beauty'. It is perhaps fair to say that, while her music is for most people immediately accessible, it is, because interesting, not undemanding.

Her considerable output of choral music displays great depth and includes a significant number of pieces composed to meet commissions from cathedrals. These are mainly anthems, but there is also a set of Evening Canticles (produced for King's College, Cambridge), a church opera (for Bury St Edmunds Cathedral) and a number of Masses.

Judith Bingham was born in Nottingham in 1952 but brought up in Mansfield, then in Sheffield. Her father, a tax inspector, was a keen amateur pianist and there was much classical music in the home. She started composing early and in her mid-teens joined the Sheffield Philharmonic Chorus in which she sang with the Hallé Orchestra and took part in John Barbirolli's last performance of *Messiah*. She always felt that composition was her vocation and began to write quite big pieces to which no one paid any attention. At the Royal Academy of Music she studied both composition and singing, but was not, it seems, the easiest of pupils, being unable to accept criticism. Nevertheless she won the Principal's Prize. Among her fellow pupils were Felicity Lott and Simon Rattle.

Soon after she left the Academy a friend suggested that she should send one of her scores to the BBC's New Music Panel, which brought her under the lasting influence of Hans Keller – a Jewish refugee from Austria, and a prominent music critic, who was a tireless advocate of Benjamin Britten and Arnold Schönberg. He took her under his wing and gave her lessons (without fee) for the next three years. During this time she received her first commission, from the King's Singers, then another, shortly before his death, from Peter Pears. More followed and in 1977 she was named BBC Young Composer of the Year.

This success was, however, followed by a period of depression which ended when she became a full-time member of the BBC Singers, then married. She spent 12 years with the Singers, taking solo parts, touring extensively and continuing to compose choral and orchestral works. The turning point in her career came in 1994 with the first performance by the BBC Philharmonic Orchestra of *Chartres*. This had been inspired by a visit to the great cathedral and completed in 1987, but not taken up by any orchestra. During the week following the acclaimed performance Bingham received four more major commissions. Her success was now assured and she became an all-round composer who, besides orchestral and much choral music, turned her hand to works for organ and other solo instruments, chamber groups, symphonic wind bands and, enthusiastically, brass bands. *Chapman's Pool*, for a piano trio, had 80 performances globally in four years and she now has an international reputation.

Her religious choral works, all of which require a high-quality choir, include 'O Magnum Mysterium' (1994), 'Ave Verum Corpus' (2002), 'O clap your hands' (2003), 'Our faith is a light' and 'Touched by heavenly fire' (both 2004) and a Christmas carol, 'God would be born in thee', commissioned by King's College, Cambridge (also in 2004). St John's College, Cambridge, Westminster Abbey and Winchester, Lichfield, Wells and Westminster Cathedrals have all commissioned her, and Bury St Edmunds marked the completion of the building of its great tower with an ambitious and highly successful church opera, *The Ivory Tree*, requiring soloists, chorus and ensemble.

Having left the BBC Singers in 1995 in order to concentrate on composing, she became their composer-in-association in 2004 and recently produced for them a substantial choral drama, *Tenebrae*. She won two British Composer Awards – one for choral, the other for liturgical, music in 2004 and became a Fellow of the Royal School of Church Music three years later.

James MacMillan

James MacMillan, the pre-eminent Scottish composer and conductor of the BBC Philharmonic Orchestra, is in many ways the most interesting of the new breed. His striking music, which most listeners find immediately accessible, includes Gregorian chant as well as the vernacular music of Scotland.

But MacMillan is also an intellectual who explores the meaning and significance of music itself and is articulate enough to reveal what he has discovered in readily understandable, sometimes forthright, language. Moreover, he is an illuminating lay theologian, whose association with the Roman Catholic Dominican Order has been influential, and who has important things to say not only about the intimate relationship between religious faith and music, but also about the fundamentals of the Christian faith. A good deal of his music has a radical political dimension that suggests a certain kinship with the liberation theologians of Latin America.

The son of a joiner father and a schoolteacher mother, he was born in 1959 in a coal-mining community in Ayrshire. As a schoolboy singer he was greatly attracted to the music of Kenneth Leighton and, by way of contrast, played the trumpet and the cornet in the village brass band. While still a boy he went on a family holiday to Edinburgh, in the course of which he was taken to Mass in the Roman Catholic cathedral. What he later described as 'the heavenly music of the choir pouring out of the sanctuary' made a deep and lasting impression. Admiration for Leighton took him to Edinburgh University to study composition and this brought an introduction to the music of the twentieth-century composers – Stravinsky, Webern, Messiaen and some modern Russian composers. During this time he also sang and played in traditional Scottish and Irish folk bands in the west of Scotland.

On completion of his BMus, he went to Durham University to complete a PhD under the supervision of John Casken, a master-composer who introduced him to the work of some Polish composers. The influence of these proved to be important. From 1986 to 1988 he lectured in music at Manchester University, then turned to full-time composing. In 1990 he attracted international acclaim when the BBC Scottish Symphony Orchestra premiered at the Proms *The Confessions of Isobel Gowdie* – a woman who had been executed for alleged witchcraft in seventeenth-century Scotland. He had been interested in politics, particularly social justice, since he was 14 and he was outraged by the story of Isobel's plight. His music – a rich fusion of the political and the spiritual – was envisaged as the requiem she never had, and, by implication, an attack on religious and political persecution.

The success of the premiere led to many commissions, including a percussion concerto *Veni, Veni, Emmanuel* – a deeply religious work which is exuberantly colourful and includes some familiar dance band harmonies. It was composed for his compatriot, the distinguished percussionist Eve-lyn Glennie, and has become the most frequently performed of all his works – over 400 worldwide. Rostropovich also commissioned a violon-cello concerto which he performed himself at its New York premiere in 1997.

MacMillan says that he nearly always has a reason for wanting to com-pose, and his theatre piece *Busqueda* (1988) is based on a series of poems by the Mothers of the Disappeared. These express the anguish of those whose sons vanished without trace in Argentina during a repressive, dic-tatorial régime in the 1970s and 80s. A *Child's Prayer* was a response to a massacre of schoolchildren in Dunblane in 1996.

But much of his church music is not so directly related to particular events. There are Tenebrae Responses, a Te Deum, a *Missa Brevis,* a can-tata *Seven Last Words* for choir and strings, *St John Passion,* commis-sioned by the London Symphony Orchestra and first performed in 2008, and much more. His largest scale work so far is *Triduum* – in three parts, expressing the sorrow and joy of Good Friday, Easter Eve and Easter Day. The *St Anne's Mass* and the *Galloway Mass* are simple enough to be taught to a congregation, and he is working with the student chamber choir of Strathclyde University on a series of motets for the Christian Year. In 2008 he received the British Composer Award for liturgical music.

All of this has been inspired by a deep Roman Catholic faith which provides a world-view informing his understanding of the meaning and purpose of music. This he sees as

> a phenomenon connected to the word of God because it invites us to touch what is deeper in our souls, and to release within us a divine force. Music opens doors to a deepening and broadening of understanding. It invites connections between organized sound and lived experience of suspected possibilities.

Stated another way, in the same important lecture given at the Centre for Christianity and Culture, at Regent's Park College, Oxford, in 2000, he said, 'I believe it (music) is God's divine spark which kindles the imagina-tion, as it has always done, and reminds us, in an increasingly dehuman-ised world, of what it means to be human.'

Music can and should therefore 'address more than just the aesthetic senses. It is the means of reaching beyond the everyday and putting the everyday in some larger perspective.' This being so, music 'is now one of the most radical counter-culture moves a composer can make'.

MacMillan is here challenging those elements in contemporary culture that he deems to be superficial and socially destructive: 'I fear for the intel-

lectual and spiritual life of a society that does not take music seriously';
again, 'Pop culture inhibits musical curiosity in the young and thus leads
to greater conformity.' He went on to blame TV and radio for 'relegating
music to being almost an afterthought and for suggesting that new popular songs lasting two to three minutes should be treated in the same way
as large-scale works lasting 20 minutes, an hour or longer'. In an article in
The Tablet he warned against the 'liberal elite's ignorance-fuelled hostility
to religion' and produced a mountain of material to support this.

But his challenge is directed equally to many, perhaps most, of his fellow composers. For if, as he believes, music can never be complete in
itself and if, as he also believes, many composers 'have tended to divorce
themselves from the possibility of music having resources and connections with life outside music', how is the exclusive abstract music of the
recent experimental modernist era and the ethereal simplicity of composers such as Tavener, Górecki and Pärt to be judged? MacMillan writes of
'the ideological differences between myself and the likes of Tavener and
also our technical and aesthetic differences in style and approach'. His
religious beliefs colour his entire approach and, while recognizing that
music has an abstract element, suggests that it 'gets into the crevices of the
human–divine experience'. 'My own music', he adds, 'simply reflects the
spiritual and even sacred, nature of music.' He believes music to be the
most spiritual of all the arts and does not hesitate to attribute true music
to divine inspiration.

In his Oxford lecture MacMillan likened the role of the composer to
that of the Virgin Mary:

> There is something in the instinct of an artist or a composer, or any
> creative person, or any Christian for that matter, which is inexorably
> drawn to the idea of Mary's 'vessel-ship' – the notion of making one-
> self as a channel for the divine will. (The lecture 'God, Theology and
> Music' constitutes a chapter in *Composing Music for Worship*, edited
> by Stephen Darlington and Alan Kreider, Canterbury Press, 2003.)

This does not, however, negate human freedom and responsibility. It
is through the interaction of all that makes us human – our intellect, our
intelligence, our emotion and our physicality, our universal experience of
joy and despair, our flesh and blood – with the breath of God which brings
forth creative fruit (for the artist new work, new art, new music). Jesus
himself was at once flesh of Mary *and* the Son of God. Mary's response at
the Annunciation was the Magnificat, which he describes as 'an inspired
and radical vision of a new life, a new revolutionary moral universe'.

Given his beliefs, it is hardly surprising that MacMillan makes a constant plea for music to be taken seriously and for adequate time to be

devoted to the hearing and the contemplating of its meaning. The self-sacrifice involved in this is a necessary element in the experience and another challenge to contemporary culture in which the sacrifice of time is not valued any more.

Judith Weir

Judith Weir is Britain's foremost woman composer today and the most popular. Her work embraces opera, orchestral, chamber, choral and solo instruments. And sometimes claiming, perhaps with tongue in cheek, that music on its own can be boring, she has worked with an Indian story-teller, a film-maker and opera librettists. Scottish and medieval sources have also provided her with material, and she is willing to compose for amateurs. Considered in the light of her considerable output, which includes large-scale works that have won international acclaim, her contribution to religious choral music is fairly modest. But it is distinctive, illuminating and needs to be further explored by serious choirs. It is too important to be overlooked.

Judith Weir was born of Scottish parents in 1954, but her early years were spent in Wembley when she attended the North London Collegiate School. Starting to compose music when in her teens, she was fortunate enough to be given a few lessons by John Tavener. This led to a degree in music at King's College, Cambridge, where she was taught composition by Robin Holloway. She was, up to a point, inspired by the modernist composers, then nearing the end of their predominance, but soon determined to move in a different direction herself. For a time she was an oboist in the National Youth Orchestra, and in 1975, when one of her pieces was played at a youth orchestra festival in Aberdeen, Aaron Copland, the renowned American composer, was among the judges. He suggested that she go to the Tanglewood Festival – a summer festival held in New England – and this proved to be a life-changing experience. Nonetheless, several years of struggle were required before she discovered her own distinctive voice.

This is best described as fairly conservative, but her music is always interesting, as well as accessible, and she has the capacity to make simple ideas seem fresh and exciting. Hence the approval of the critics and her popularity with audiences of every sort. She displays an attractive modesty, even though distinguished enough to have been appointed CBE at the early age of 41 and to have become the first composer to win the Queen's Medal for Music.

The breakthrough for her came with a highly acclaimed small-scale opera, which led to the composition of three full-length operas, one of these, *Blond Eckbert*, having been commissioned by English National Opera and premiered in 1994. Since then there has been another (2005) specially written for Channel 4 television. Simon Rattle has commissioned work for the City of Birmingham Symphony Orchestra and a song cycle, *woman.life.song*, commissioned for Jessye Norman, was first performed by her in New York's Carnegie Hall.

In 2008 a three-day festival devoted to Weir's work was held at the Barbican Centre in London. Over 50 of her compositions of every kind were performed in a dozen concerts (many of these broadcast on Radio 3), accompanied by films, talks and other educational material. Earlier in her career, she was a Fellow at Glasgow University; more recently she has been a Visiting Professor at Harvard, and is now Research Professor of Music at Cardiff University. Among her choral works 'Love bade me welcome' (1997), 'My guardian angel' (1997) and several others are attractive and useable, and doubtless there may be more for the asking. There is also a larger *Missa Del Cid* and an orchestra Sanctus.

Roxanna Panufnik

Roxanna Panufnik is the daughter of the distinguished Polish composer and conductor Sir Andrzei Panufnik, but while her music owes a lot to her Polish heritage, she belongs four-square to the evolving British tradition.

She was born in 1968, studied composition at the Royal Academy of Music, and caused a considerable stir with her first major work, the *Westminster Mass*. This was first performed in 1988 by the choir of Westminster Cathedral and was commissioned as a seventy-fifth birthday present to Cardinal Basil Hume, the much-admired Roman Catholic Archbishop of Westminster. It is indubitably a modern composition and not without dissonant harmonies, but conveys the sense of great beauty and is easy to listen to. Designed for liturgical use rather than stage performance, it is well within the capacity of a good amateur church choir.

The choice of Panufnik for this work was made by the John Studzinski Foundation for young artists, the director of which was a close personal friend of the Cardinal and a devotee of Westminster Cathedral's music. In an interview with Stephen Darlington, of Christ Church, Oxford, and Professor Christopher Rowland, also of Oxford, Roxanna explained that she had been brought up as an agnostic and did not became a practising Catholic until she was 21. She felt therefore that she had missed all the instruction about the meaning and significance of the Mass normally dispensed to children and young people, so she spent two months going through its words with a fine toothcomb, guided by a priest. She also went, on the recommendation of the Cardinal, to a retreat at Stanbrook

Abbey in Worcestershire where she established what has become a long and influential relationship with the Benedictine nuns.

Close collaboration with the cathedral choir was also important – the Cardinal wanted the Mass to be in English, a Credo was not required, and the length of the Agnus Dei had to be determined by how long a priest might be able to hold his arms aloft during its singing. James O'Donnell, the then master of music at the cathedral, now at Westminster Abbey, advised her not to make her music too complex in a rhythmic or contrapuntal way, since the acoustic of the building would reduce this to a blur. The sound of Tavener's 'Hymn to the Mother of God' performed at a Christmas celebration in the cathedral greatly affected her, but her own music is a long way removed from his.

The Mass took ten months to complete and, following its first performance, new commissions came thick and fast, though not from the churches. She has become a prolific composer, usually of quite short pieces and, while choral is her forte, she has provided music for ballet, solo instruments, including organ, chamber orchestra, film and television. Her particular gift is that of being able to take interesting and often unusual texts and set these to music in ways that illuminate their meaning and mood. Thus a song cycle based on some of Wendy Cope's poems expresses their serious yet witty content. A chamber opera, *The Mission Programme*, composed for the Polish National Opera's millennium season, had its British premiere at Covent Garden.

Her specifically religious work includes *A Kind of Otherness*, based on a poem by the eleventh-century Hermann the Lame, pleading to the Virgin for mercy. *Abraham* is a violin concerto incorporating Christian, Islamic and Jewish music, while *Love Abide,* for choir and orchestra, draws on 1 Corinthians 13 for an expression of the pain of life without love. *Stay with Me*, which conveys a strong sense of mystery, used words of the famous Italian priest Padre Pio and is for double choir and organ. *Prayer* is a setting of words by George Herbert and there is an Ave Maria and an Agnus Dei. Most of her work has been recorded on CD and during 2008–09 18 new works were premiered in nine different countries. She also began composing a plainsong Mass for the choir of the London Oratory, and there is scope for more liturgical music from a composer who is modern, without being modish.

Jonathan Dove

Jonathan Dove is firmly established as a composer of music for the stage – over 30 plays and more than a dozen operas – as well as for film, television, orchestra and chorus. His opera *Flight*, which is an airport comedy, was premiered at Glyndebourne in 1998 and has had many repeat performances there. It has also toured Europe, America and Australia. *When She Died* was commissioned as a television opera to mark the fifth anniversary of the death of Princess Diana, while *The Adventures of Pinocchio* (2007) is a children's opera commissioned by Opera North and Sadler's Wells Theatre.

Dove was artistic director of the Spitalfields Festival from 2001 to 2006 and his community cantata *On Spital Fields* involved 200 voices from that part of East London. Since 2007 he has been a patron of the London Festival of Contemporary Church Music and, among his own religious works, there is a church opera, *Tobias and the Angel*, the *Köthener Messe*, inspired by Bach and commissioned by a Berlin music academy, *Seek Him who Maketh the Seven Stars and Orion*, a Missa Brevis, and a Christmas Carol 'The Three Kings'. Many cathedrals are now using his work.

Dove was born in 1959, went to St Joseph's Academy, Blackheath, in South London and attended an Inner London Education Authority course for Young Musicians, before going to Trinity College, Cambridge. Later he took a MMus at Goldsmiths College, London, and started his career in 1987 as assistant chorus master at Glyndebourne. Since 1990 he has been music adviser to the Almeida Theatre and more recently he has composed music for plays at the National Theatre and for the Royal Shakespeare Company.

Francis Pott

Francis Pott, born in 1957, is a former chorister of New College, Oxford, who became a music scholar at Winchester College, then at Magdalen College, Cambridge, before becoming a bass lay clerk at Winchester Cathedral from 1991 to 2001. By this time he was already a professional pianist, had embarked on an academic career, teaching music at St Hilda's College, Oxford, and was soon to emerge as a composer of significance.

His massive organ symphony *Christus* (1992) was immediately recognized as a work of astonishing originality and the music critic of *The Times* described it as 'one of the most important works of our century'. In the same year a seven-movement oratorio, *A Song of the End of the World*, was premiered at the Three Choirs Festival in Worcester and at its conclusion given a five-minute standing ovation. *The Times* critic was again impressed – 'thrilling, apocalyptic and profoundly moving'. It is based on a poem written by a Polish poet, Czesław Miłosz, in Warsaw during the tragic days of 1944 and combines a plea for world peace with a quest for an answer to the problem of reconciling the fact of innocent human suffering with the loving purposes of an omnipotent God. For the poet, the crucifixion of Jesus offers the only credible answer and is repeated by cruel human beings in every age. The composer of an oratorio on this subject could hardly have chosen a more challenging task.

Another oratorio, based on the fourteenth-century English mystical treatise *The Cloud of Unknowing*, appeared to international acclaim in 2006, and his works have now been performed in 18 different countries and broadcast in many others. These include music for chamber orchestra, piano, songs, as well as more for organ, and even rag music. A large number of his choral works have religious themes, and besides a Five-Part Mass, a Te Deum and Evening Canticles, there are anthems and motets such as 'A Prayer of St Francis', 'Jesu dulcis memoria' and 'O Lord support us all the day long'.

It is not easy to place Pott's work, which has been likened, variously, to that of Fauré, Janáček, Messiaen and Tippett. Yet it is different from each of these, and can only be described as original. Since 2001 he has been Head of Music at Thames Valley University and in 2007 became its first professor of composition.

Tarik O'Regan

Tarik O'Regan, born in London in 1978, is the youngest of the new British composers. His first commission, from the choir of New College, Oxford, with James Bowman, the counter-tenor, came when he was only 19, and five years later two of his works, *Clichés* and *The Pure Good of Theory*, were premiered by the London Symphony Orchestra and the London Sinfonietta. His debut CD *Voices* (2006) had critical acclaim, including the opinion of the *Observer* that he was 'one of the most original and eloquent of young British composers'.

The CD was recorded by the choir of Clare College, Cambridge, and includes a Magnificat and a Nunc Dimittis, a Locus iste, the *Dorchester Canticles* (a *Cantate Dominus* and a *Deus Miseratus*), Three Motets from Sequence for St Wulfstan, as well as some other religious items, all in a striking, refreshing and sometimes intense style that marks him out quite distinctly from any of his contemporaries.

Partly of North African extraction, he spent his early years in Algeria, but he returned to London to attend Whitgift School and from there went to Pembroke College, Oxford. On coming down he worked for a time at J. P. Morgan Chase, the investment bank, but soon gave this up in order to undertake postgraduate work at Corpus Christi College, Cambridge, where he was designated Composer in Residence. He now divides his time between Trinity College, Cambridge, where he is Fellow Commoner in the Creative Arts, and New York. He has held fellowships at Columbia

University and Harvard, and been a research affiliate in the Yale Institute of Sacred Music.

Threshold of Night, a setting of poetry by Kathleen Raine, and designed for use in Advent, was recorded by the choir of St John's College, Cambridge, under David Hill and won the British Composer of the Year (liturgical section) award in 2007. Of it he said, 'It aims to highlight the yearning that all societies have, in their time of need, for guidance from beyond their community.' *Ecstasies Above*, a setting of a lyric poem by Edgar Alan Poe, seeks to link these with the harsh realities of life on earth.

De Sancto Ioanne Baptista (St John's College, Oxford, 2005), *Regina Coeli* (Corpus Christi College, Cambridge, 2006) and *Surrexit Christus* (New College, Oxford, 2006) all indicate that while O'Regan's music is emphatically modern, he draws from the past, as represented by the Oxbridge choral tradition. Much more will be heard from him, and with considerable profit, in the years to come.

Gabriel Jackson

Gabriel Jackson is another young composer who is not afraid to confess that he has been greatly influenced by Tudor church music. He goes further, 'I like repetition and ritualised structures', and many of his pieces reflect his interest in medieval ideas and techniques. He was in fact a chorister at Canterbury Cathedral for three years, which made an impact on him, though he now says, 'I am religious by temperament, but not by belief and several of my pieces are an attempt at a spiritual response to the great technological miracle of our times – powered flight.' He is also involved in the visual arts and some of his longer compositions are based on the work of modern artists.

He was born in Bermuda in 1962 and, on completion of his education in Canterbury, went to the Royal College of Music where he twice won the annual prize for composition. Modernist music was still in vogue, but he emerged from the college determined 'to try to write music that is clean and clear ... not about conflict and resolution and, even when animated, essentially contemplative'. This has been achieved by much use of simple melodies and chords, but there is nothing backward-looking in any of his music, which combines both dignity and power. His output of choral and instrumental music has been considerable and his fame is now worldwide, as a consequence of performances at all the major festivals, many recordings and frequent broadcasting.

Canterbury, Christ Church, Oxford, St Paul's, Wells, Truro, Guildford and Portsmouth are among the cathedrals that have commissioned and/or performed his plentiful sacred works, and at the inaugural British

Composer of the Year Award in 2003 he came first in the liturgical section. He offers a wide choice – 'I look from afar', and 'Tomorrow go ye forth', which are a pair of Advent responsories; 'Pure religion and undefiled before God' is an anthem for trebles and organ; 'Sanctorum est verum lumen' was commissioned for the 2005 Lichfield Festival. A 2008 Requiem combines a setting of the Latin Mass with funeral texts from other cultures and religious traditions.

23

Not Forgetting the Parishes

Enthusiasm for the work of the new breed of contemporary composers can all too easily lead to neglect of the fact that most of the church's music is used not in cathedrals but in parish churches, where, sadly, the desire for innovation is never considered to be urgent and, in any case, most of the new compositions require the skill of professional choirs. The best hope must be that the good use of this material by cathedrals will eventually enable its influence to seep into other, unexpected places.

In the meantime, a number of professional composers are endeavouring, with a good deal of success, to provide ordinary local congregations with music that is within their capacity to sing and which they might even come to like.

Malcolm Archer

Malcolm Archer is unique among contemporary church musicians in that he is the only organist and choir director of the first rank who is not only composing for cathedrals but also, and on a substantial scale, for parish church choirs.

His career has been distinguished. Born in Lytham, on the Lancashire coast, in 1952, he gave his first cathedral organ recital at Blackburn Cathedral when he was 14. This was at the invitation of Blackburn's dynamic organist, John Bertalot, who influenced him greatly and pointed him to the Royal College of Music, then to an organ scholarship at Jesus College, Cambridge. His musical education could hardly have been bettered – composition under Alan Ridout and Herbert Sumsion, organ under Ralph Downes, Gillian Weir, Nicolas Kynaston and, later at Hampstead Parish Church, as assistant to Martindale Sidwell.

A post as assistant organist at Norwich Cathedral (1978–83) was followed by seven years as organist and master of the choristers at Bristol Cathedral, where he also founded the City of Bristol Choir. Then came six years as a freelance organist, composer and conductor, and it was during this time that his output of choral music began to grow significantly. It now extends to over 200 items. He has given organ recitals in most European countries, as well as America and Canada, and recorded composers as diverse as J. S. Bach and Olivier Messiaen.

He returned to cathedral life in 1996 as organist and master of the choristers at Wells and in 2004 succeeded John Scott at St Paul's. But, having reached this peak of achievement, remained on the summit for only three years before being obliged to leave it for family health reasons. Nowhere, apart from Westminster Abbey, are the pressures on an organist and director of music as great as they are at St Paul's. In addition to the round of daily services, led in a vast building by an unusually large choir, the cathedral's national role attracts many special services. These include some responding to human disasters, others to joyful royal occasions; frequently, live television broadcasting is involved. The organist and director of music necessarily operates within a large and complex cathedral organization, and Archer explained, 'I felt that I was mainly an administrator, required to attend many meetings each week and, in a stressful situation, with little pastoral support for my family.'

He left in 2007 to become organist and director of chapel music at Winchester College. Following his departure from St Paul's, the offices of organist and director of music were separated and a non-organist choir director was appointed to succeed him.

Winchester College, with a choral foundation that dates back to William of Wykeham's foundation of the College in 1394, is now the sole public school with a choir, containing in this case 16 quiristers, that performs cathedral-style music in its chapel, together with a wider repertory elsewhere. Archer, who also undertakes some teaching and the training of organ and choral scholars of the future, thus has a less pressurized environment in which to develop further his work as a composer.

Although most of this work has so far been for parish churches, there is some (and likely to be more) written for cathedrals and collegiate foundations. This includes canticles, *The Four Cathedrals Service*, *Chichester* and *Wells Services*, Preces and Responses, and a Requiem with orchestral parts. Many of his anthems can be used in any church with a reasonably competent choir, and, of these, a setting of the Prayer of Richard of Chichester is specially popular. Settings of 'Rejoice the Lord is King', 'When I survey the wondrous Cross' and 'My song is love unknown' are also much used.

There are several Masses including an *English Folk Song Mass* and a *Missa Simplex* for use with Common Worship. Carols are another significant element in his output, the availability of which has been facilitated by its specialist publishers – Kevin Mayhew and the Royal School of Church Music. *All Saints to Advent*, co-edited with John Scott, and *Advent for Choirs*, co-edited with Stephen Cleobury, are both designed for parish use.

The RSCM and the Guild of Church Musicians have awarded him fellow-ships for his contribution to church music.

John Rutter

John Rutter is the best-known, and the most frequently performed of con-temporary composers of religious choral music. David Willcocks of King's College, Cambridge, who was largely responsible for the launching of his career, once described him as 'the most gifted composer that I have seen pass through the university', and said recently, 'I am a great admirer of his works, because I think that they are highly original and approachable.' NBC, the American broadcasting network, went so far as to describe him as 'the world's greatest composer and conductor of choral music'.

These views are not, however, universally shared, and among other professional musicians, including some cathedral organists, his work arouses considerable hostility. 'Unadventurous' and 'saccharine' are just two of the criticisms, and there are a few cathedrals in which his work is never heard. On the whole, however, cathedrals, as well as many par-ish churches, make considerable use of his work and, besides Christmas carols, short pieces such as 'A Gaelic blessing', 'God be in my head', 'I will sing with the Spirit' and 'The Lord bless you and keep you' are often sung. Dame Felicity Lott once confessed that she finds it almost impossible to sing the last of these, since it moves her to tears.

It is for his Christmas carols that Rutter is most widely known and, among the general public, most admired. He has composed or arranged about 30 of these and, among his own, the 'Shepherd Pipe Carol', the 'Donkey Carol', the 'Nativity Carol' and the 'Star Carol' are the most popular. Many have an orchestral accompaniment. A *Guardian* feature writer once described him as 'the musical equivalent of Dickens – synony-mous with the Christmas season', and he told an *Independent* interviewer, 'If I haven't made a Christmas musical event happen somewhere, it's not really Christmas for me.' Frequent media attention is another indication of the popularity of his music.

Among his huge amount of non-Christmas music there is a setting of the Eucharist, written for the Series 3 experimental service, which is in the traditional style and intended for use in parish churches where the choral resources are limited. This is of a much higher quality than many of the alternatives. Among his many large-scale pieces are a Requiem (1985), also for amateur choirs, a Magnificat (1990) and a *Mass of the Children* (2003). His small amount of orchestral work is rarely performed.

John Rutter, the son of a scientist, was born in London in 1945 and went to Highgate School. Among his fellow pupils was John Tavener, who became a composer of a very different stripe, and the two boys were clearly influenced by a gifted music teacher who demanded composition as well as performance. The school choir, to which Rutter belonged, was good enough to take part in a Proms performance of *Carmina Burana* in 1956 and six years later in the recording of Benjamin Britten's *War Requiem*, conducted by the composer.

For composition he was attracted to the carol form, and the 'Shepherd's Pipe Carol', which has sold more than a million copies, was completed when he was only 18. The 'Nativity Carol' was also a product of his late teens. At Clare College, Cambridge, he read music but was never attracted by the 12-note atonal style then in vogue and continued to compose carols as a subversive reaction against it. David Willcocks, to whom he went for counterpoint and harmony, was so impressed by his carols that he recommended them to the Oxford University Press for publication.

The success of the new *Carols for Choirs*, of which Willcocks was the joint editor, called for a second collection but by this time his colleague Reginald Jacques had died. Although still an undergraduate, Rutter took his place and shared in the editing of what became a five-volume series. He remained at Clare College to undertake postgraduate study and in 1975 was appointed Fellow and Director of Music of the College. He continued to compose carols, some of which were performed by the Bach Choir in its Christmas performance at the Royal Albert Hall.

A year before taking over the music at Clare, however, Rutter went to New York to conduct in the Carnegie Hall the first performance of a cantata Gloria he had been commissioned to compose. This was an immediate success and during the late 1970s it had over 100 performances. These were mainly in America where his work has always been most widely appreciated, and where he remains in constant demand for conducting and new compositions. The Carnegie Hall concert also included a performance by a young people's choir of his *Eight Childhood Lyrics*.

The success of the Gloria led to a flood of commissions, and by 1979 his income was sufficient to allow him to leave Clare in order to concentrate on composing, conducting and recording. In 1981 he founded the Cambridge Singers, a 24–strong chamber choir, to record his own and other sacred music. This led to the creation of his own label, Collegium Records, and most of his work has now been recorded. The King's Singers were attracted by his work from their beginnings. Schools make considerable use of his work and if the language of some of his carols seems somewhat twee (he writes as well as composes many of them) this is probably because they were commissioned for use by young children.

At the popular level Rutter undertakes an annual round of 'singing days' which are held in churches and school halls and open to anyone who cares to attend. On a grander scale he composed a setting of Psalm 150, which was used in the St Paul's Cathedral service marking the Golden Jubilee of the Queen's reign in 2002. In 2008 he composed for a pageant, involving a cast of 1,000, at the opening of Liverpool's year as a City of Culture.

No other composer since John Stainer (1840–1901) has raised so sharply the question of what type or quality of music is appropriate for use in Christian worship. Rutter, in common with many other composers, does not regard himself as a particularly religious man, endowed with deep theological insights, but he has always been inspired by the spirituality of sacred verses and prayers. He makes no apology for the fact that his interest is in what he calls 'accessible music' and, although he rarely writes carols now, he has pointed out that carols were the first form of vernacular choral literature in England. They were permitted in English in the fifteenth century when everything else in the liturgy was in Latin. He says that he does not compose for cathedral use.

Howard Goodall

Howard Goodall, omnipresent on television and radio, has embraced two vocations. The first is to bridge the gulf between traditional classical music and the various forms of more popular music that burst forth from the 1960s onwards. His position as composer-in-residence at radio Classic FM and his outstanding skills as a broadcaster provide him with unique opportunities in this task. The second vocation is to encourage people, especially young people, to sing, and his appointment in 2007 as the first ever National Ambassador for Singing – a four-year assignment designed to improve group singing among primary school children – takes him to schools all over the country and to festivals of singing.

He is also a prolific composer of music of every kind, and told an Oxford conference of church music composers:

> One moment I am writing the theme music of the comedy series *Red Dwarf*, the next I am writing a mass for the choir of Christ Church Cathedral, Oxford. One day I am commissioned to compose the jingle for a TV commercial campaign, the next I am rehearsing a piece of musical theatre at the Royal Opera House.

He makes these transitions without sense of disjunction or incongruity, believing that, in the mixed musical environment of the modern world, coexistence of differing styles is possible, provided that each is excellent of its kind. What is more, the cross-fertilization of styles is highly desirable.

His own music is accessible and, his critics say, undemanding. 'Melody is the key to what I do', he once said, and in this and many other ways he is close to John Rutter. Thus his setting of Psalm 23 provided the theme music for the immensely popular TV series *The Vicar of Dibley*, and at the same time is widely used, in an extended form, in the worship at parish churches and cathedrals. None of his work is apparently difficult to produce: 'My ability to write melody appears to be there all the time; it's like a constantly running tap that I choose to put the cup under or not.'

Goodall's music is not, however, to be dismissed lightly. His *In Memoriam Anne Frank* was performed at the first National Holocaust Memorial Concert in 2001 and *O Lord God of Time and Eternity* was commissioned for a service of Remembrance for those killed in the Iraq war held in St Paul's Cathedral in 2003. Ten years earlier, *Missa Aedis Christi* was commissioned by the Friends of Christ Church Cathedral, Oxford, and inspired by bells he heard in a village in the South of France. Unlike most modern settings of the Mass, it was designed to be sung in Latin, which he says is the best language for singing.

Born in 1950, Howard Goodall spent five years as a chorister in the choir of New College, Oxford, where he imbibed and came to love the music of the classical Anglican choral tradition.

At Christ Church, Oxford, he took to the organ and completed his ARCO in 1975. He has since published a collection of organ works. Besides playing the organ and taking a First, he also learned to play the electric guitar and joined a rock band on the universities circuit. This drove him to embark on a mission to deliver classical music from what he calls a 'stuffy atmosphere', so that it may be enjoyed by young people, and at the same time help the stuffy to recognize that the best of modern music deserves to be taken seriously; and that it is possible to enjoy both the old and the new. He strongly challenged Peter Maxwell Davies and Simon Rattle over their assertion that 'only classical music is serious music'. 'All good music is serious,' he retorted.

A close partnership with Stephen Darlington and the choir of Christ Church Cathedral, Oxford, has proved to be particularly productive and an anthem 'We are God's labourers' was composed by Goodall for the installation of a new dean in 2003. More recently, and on a somewhat larger scale, he composed *His Eternal Light: A Requiem* – a dance work first performed by the Rambert Dance Company in 2008 and often performed by others since then. His Magnificat and Nunc Dimittis for Marlborough College are quite traditional, except that the Gloria for the Nunc Dimittis is in a kind of gospel music style. His *Salisbury Canticles* have been recorded by the girls' choir of Salisbury Cathedral, and the choir of St David's Cathedral in Wales commissioned a *Festival Jubilate Deo*. Several Christmas carols have also been composed.

Goodall's gifts as a communicator have provided many opportunities for sharing widely his own approach to music. At the turn of the century he devoted 14 months to making a TV documentary series and writing an accompanying book on the history of western music – entitled, characteristically, *Howard Goodall's Big Bang* – and on Good Friday 2009 he presented a TV documentary on the making of Handel's *Messiah*.

Bob Chilcott

Bob Chilcott can be thought of as a successor to John Rutter, in the accessibility of his music and also in the volume of his output. At the last count, Oxford University Press had published 100 of his pieces, and there is no sign of 'composer's block'. He is also a singer and conductor with a growing international reputation.

He was born in 1955, became a chorister at King's College, Cambridge, under David Willcocks and sang the 'Pie Jesu' in the choir's renowned recording of Fauré's Requiem. Later he returned to King's as a choral scholar and spent the years 1985–97 with the popular King's Singers. Since then he has concentrated on composition and conducting. His specialism is children's and young people's choirs. He conducted a children's choir in a programme *Can You Hear Me?* in eight different countries and provided the New Orleans Children's Choir with five pieces, including a Jazz Mass, *Be Simply Little Children*. He has also published *10 Songs for Youth Choirs* and *Songs and Cries of London Town*, along with many other song books.

Besides all this, Chilcott has composed anthems and carols, two larger sacred works – *Jubilate* (first performed in New York's Carnegie Hall) and *Canticles of Light* – and, with John Rutter and Andrew Carter, *Advent Antiphons*. All of these have a certain melodic beauty and attractive harmonies; hence the many commissions from choral societies and youth choirs and their wide popularity.

The music of Taizé

The choruses and songs of the Taizé Community in Burgundy are very widely sung, though not often in the regular worship of the Church of England. They find their place in additional services in parish churches and cathedrals, sometimes on Sunday evenings, and play a big part in youth events. The secret of their success lies in their simplicity. A few lines from the Psalms or other parts of the Bible are repeated in chant or sung in canon, so that they take on the form of a mantra. The music itself is skilfully composed to mark the rhythm of the words and the aim is to lead the singer into meditation and prayer. A member of the Taizé Community explains: 'The criterion for judging sacred music is "does it express and assist its users into the way of salvation?"'

The community was formed on Easter Day 1949 by Roger Schütz and six friends in a half-ruined hilltop village in eastern France, not far from Cluny. The Rule of Taizé, drawn up three years later, was designed to be what Schütz called 'a parable of community' and involves a life commitment 'to live together in joy, simplicity and mercy', with an overarching aim of reconciliation. Initially, the members were European Protestants, but two Anglicans joined in the early 1960s, and in 1969 a young Belgian doctor became the first Roman Catholic member. Today there are about 100 brothers, of all the main churches, drawn from 25 different countries. Away from Taizé, the brothers live in small fraternities, some of which are located in the poorest areas of Latin America, Africa and Asia.

From the outset, there was the intention to attract and influence young people, that is, those between 17 and 30. In this the community has been extraordinarily successful. Over 100,000 young people go on the pilgrimage every year, and an annual European Meeting, held over several days in one of the cities, attracts huge numbers. Many of those who take part in these events form small groups in their own localities and meet regularly for worship, prayer, Bible study and social action. Once the pilgrims began to go to Taizé, the question arose as to how they might participate in the community's own regular round of worship in which prayer and meditation has a large part. Brother Robert, one of the early members, chose short passages from the Psalms, the Bible and traditional liturgical material for repeating, and Jacques Berthier was asked to compose appropriate simple music for chanting and singing.

Berthier was born in 1923 in Burgundy, where his father was organist and choirmaster at Auxerre Cathedral. He was trained at the César Franck Music School in Paris and from 1961 to 1994 was organist of the Jesuit Church of Saint-Ignace in Paris. The original invitation to compose for Taizé came in 1955 when the community, then only 20 strong, was looking for music for its own use. And it was from this starting point that, 20 years later, came the music for the pilgrims. Besides this he composed Masses and other music for the Roman Catholic Church in France, but, at his own request, none of his own music was used at his funeral in 1994.

Well before this, however, Berthier's contribution had been augmented by that of a Roman Catholic priest, Joseph Gelineau. Born in 1920 in the Loire, he entered the Jesuit order in 1941. Having studied theology in Lyons he went on to study music at the César Franck School and thereafter became a liturgist with a special expertise in liturgical chant. He was among the consultants at Vatican II who pressed, successfully, for reform of the liturgy and afterwards he wrote a widely read book, *Learning to Celebrate: The Mass and its Music*.

In spite of spending 25 years as a professor at the Institut Catholique in Paris, Gelineau always remained in close touch with parish life. Thus, in order to encourage the laity to take a fuller part in worship, he translated into modern French the Psalms of the Jerusalem Bible and composed for these a series of distinctive rhythmic repetitive chants, which require neither a choir nor even an organist. A cantor sings the verses and the congregation sings a refrain. Fairly wide use in France led to an English translation, but they did not really catch on in this country, except in the Roman Catholic Church, where they are much used, together with a similar style for responsorial psalms. Gelineau died in 2008.

24

Revolution in the Cathedral and the Rediscovery of the Counter-Tenor

Nowhere was the development of English church music during the nineteenth and twentieth centuries more clearly evident than in the quality of music offered in the cathedrals. Worshippers miraculously transported from the early part of this period to the present day would scarcely believe what they now experienced in their diocesan cathedrals. The transformation from choral music of the very lowest quality to that of a high international standard has been complete.

Previous chapters have traced this process, which occupied more than a century and was uneven in its advance, depending always on the skill and dedicated persistence of a small number of reformers, often faced with formidable obstacles and rarely with any encouragement. It was only during the second half of the twentieth century that a dramatic leap forward became possible.

The church's music could not fail to be affected by the general advance in music. The widely recognized higher standards presented cathedral choirs with a stimulating challenge which most of them were eventually able to meet. Less fortunately, the parish church choirs, with their amateur rather than professional members, were unable to reach the heights, except in some exceptional places; the rest were therefore judged unflatteringly by many music aficionados.

Decisive for the cathedral choirs was an influx of young ex-choral scholars from the leading choral foundations in Oxford and Cambridge. Highly trained by some of the most brilliant directors of music, they brought transforming skill and vigour to the tradition. The faithful bands of lay clerks they replaced had sometimes been local tradesmen, but more often were humble professional musicians who, of necessity, supplemented their meagre salaries by teaching music locally or by taking solo parts in music festivals and oratorio performances. In 1945 the lay clerks of Canterbury Cathedral received £200 per annum. In spite of reforms earlier in the century, a number of singers retained freehold offices (seen as compensation for inadequate pay) and could not therefore be compulsorily retired even when their voices had failed. The remainder stayed until well into their sixties.

The new breed were of a quite different stripe. The London choirs and those of a few major cathedrals, still had professional singers, some of whom had distinguished careers in opera or other choral work. Elsewhere the men were qualified for teaching and other professional posts that ensured a reasonable income. But, because of these responsibilities, it was no longer possible for Mattins to be sung on up to four mornings a week and Evensong had to be transferred from mid to late afternoon. Moreover (and educational demands were also influential), the continuation of choral services between Christmas and the Epiphany, and in Easter week, had to end. The overall result was that cathedral choirs began to sing much less frequently than heretofore and the deans and chapters of St Paul's and Westminster Abbey found themselves in the unaccustomed position of negotiating terms of employment and settling disputes in the presence of representatives of the Musicians' Union and Equity. Additional rehearsal time came at a price.

Other factors also conspired to change the pattern of Sunday morning worship. In most cathedrals the centrality of Choral Mattins and sermon conflicted with a new conviction that the Eucharist is at the heart of the church's life and must therefore have pride of place. A readjustment of timetables followed – and sometimes controversy. There was also anxiety lest the new emphasis might lead to a diminution of regard for Choral Mattins, which was valued not only by established churchgoers but also by those on the edges of the church's life who were not ready for the degree of commitment implicit in the Eucharist. In the 1970s Bishop Hetley Price of Ripon called them 'Duke of Wellington Christians'. That these fears were not entirely groundless was demonstrated by the advertised services at the 42 cathedrals for the Fourth Sunday of Easter 2009: at 16 cathedrals, Choral Mattins was held, usually before but sometimes after a Sung Eucharist; at 15, Mattins was said; at 11, it was not mentioned.

Change was also taking place in the organ lofts. The Oxbridge choral foundations produced outstanding ex-organ scholars who looked on the cathedrals as spheres appropriate to the development of their careers. There had been a few of these prior to 1939 but most aspiring organists had been articled to established cathedral organists who augmented their often meagre salaries this way. This system worked well enough for a century or more and bred many outstanding musicians. All were competent professionals who often worked faithfully for many years in one cathedral, with scant encouragement and little reward apart from satisfaction in work well done and, for a few, promotion to the loft of a major cathedral.

Lack of funds, or more probably commitment, meant that most of these men worked single-handed, with assistance only from the best of their pupils. They were essentially organists rather than choir trainers, with limited opportunities or even desire for conducting during the services.

Their successors tended to be more adventurous, with full-, or at least part-time, assistants who usually accompanied the services while the newly styled directors of music conducted below. Although there is now a serious shortage of organists in the parishes, cathedral posts still attract strong competition, though it has become less common for brilliant young organists to devote their entire careers to this work even in the most prestigious of appointments. In 2009 Chichester and Guildford cathedrals acquired talented women organists and directors.

Choristers were not immune from these changes, most especially in those cathedrals fortunate enough to have boarding choir schools. In these the change was, however, social, rather than musical. Rising educational standards, as well as parental aspiration, turned many of them into desirable preparatory schools, made even more attractive by the fact that choristers were admitted at greatly reduced fees. Thus the schools came to be populated by the children of ambitious middle-class parents, rather than those of a humbler background. Cathedrals without choir schools continued to recruit from local independent schools and, in less privileged areas, from whatever schools encouraged their pupils to sing. Everywhere, standards were raised by the new attention to music in all schools and the new emphasis on choir direction. During the 1990s girls' choirs were introduced, sometimes controversially, by most cathedrals and quietly established themselves as an integral part of their choral foundations.

The cost of all these developments was not inconsiderable. A report of an Archbishops' Commission on Cathedrals, *Heritage and Renewal*, published in 1994, revealed that the cathedrals together were then spending £4.6 million annually on their music. This represented, on average, 12 per cent of their total expenditure, less for the smaller parish church type of cathedral, more for major cathedrals with choir schools. By the end of the century some of these were spending over £500,000 annually, and in London very much more than this.

Many cathedrals have to manage with much less, and this is always true in the case of those that were formed from former parish churches to serve the new dioceses created during the late nineteenth and early twentieth centuries. These are required to manage on quite meagre resources and it can be argued that the decision to model their life on that of the ancient cathedrals was a mistake. A different pattern might have been more valuable as well as more easily attainable. Nonetheless the comparatively recent foundations produce a good deal of fine music, even if on a lesser scale than that of their more venerable parents.

Blackburn is an interesting example of this. When the diocese was carved out of the densely populated Manchester in 1926, the Victorian parish church of the cotton town became its cathedral but with little additional income to sustain, much less develop, this new role. Today it has an impressively vibrant life, and music probably as good as any in the North of England. The 18 men of the choir are entirely voluntary. They rehearse on Friday evenings and sing at the two principal Sunday services. The choristers are drawn from several local schools, rehearse on Tuesday and Friday evenings and Saturday mornings, sing with the men on Sundays and by themselves at Evensong on Wednesday. Therein lies a crucial distinction: cathedral choirs of this sort are unable to perform at daily services – historically a basic duty – though they are in the stalls for major observances such as Holy Week and Ascension Day, and for important special services.

Nonetheless, Blackburn, continuing a long Northern tradition of choral music, is the centre of a remarkable expression of musical creativity that extends well beyond its own boundaries. The cathedral itself has a girls' choir that takes part in the regular services, a girls' chamber choir that sings more adventurous music, a choir for children between the ages of 7 and 11, another for 4- to 7-year-olds, and yet another for young men and women of 14 to 21 that usually sings one of the Sunday morning services. The Renaissance Singers perform major choral works. In an average week almost 200 people are involved in music-making, and there are many additional performances by other choral societies and orchestra. The cathedral's musicians have unusually strong links with parish church choirs and the schools of the region. A quarterly glossy magazine, *Music and More*, with 30 or more pages of news, opinion and coloured illustrations, is of the highest standard of journalism. The demands made of the professional organist and director of music and his assistant are obviously different from those made of their colleagues in the older foundations, but their contribution to the church's music is no less important.

Since its foundation in 1956 the Friends of Cathedral Music has given invaluable assistance to many cathedrals and other choral foundations, amounting by 2008 to £1.6 million. Supported by generous enthusiasts, it has endowed many choristerships and also aims to increase public knowledge and appreciation of the unique English choral tradition. But this alone cannot solve what is becoming a serious problem, and a few cathedrals have launched successful fundraising campaigns to augment, sometimes by £2–3 million, the capital reserves that yield a regular income for music. A reduction in the size of choirs is no longer unthinkable.

Curiously, as it might at first seem, the general decline in church attendance, which became more steep from the 1960s onwards, was accompanied by a sharp rise in the number of organizations, many of them secular, desiring to mark some aspect of their corporate life with a service in their local cathedral. Deans and chapters welcomed this and sought to be creative in the designing of special services to meet their needs. Organists and choir directors were naturally involved, too, but it was not always possible to secure the attendance of the full choir. Instead, competent women singers began to be recruited to join as many lay clerks as might be available and together these produced fine music. In some cathedrals chamber choirs were formed and these proved to be a valuable resource for all sorts of services. Precentors are busy meeting liturgical and musical demands.

The 1960s also saw the beginning of a remarkable increase in tourism that soon brought to most cathedrals an unprecedented flow of pilgrims and visitors. Again, this was welcomed as an opportunity for Christian witness and as a source of new funds. Educational and refreshment facilities were provided. Yet cathedral choirs are invariably away for several weeks of the summer when the number of visitors is at its peak. Those who had heard of the fame of the English cathedral choral tradition, and may even have heard recordings of the choirs, were naturally disappointed to be offered only 'said Evensong'.

At this point a number of the best parish church choirs, and some other choral groups, came to the rescue by taking on responsibility for the services for a few days or even a whole week – and usually at their own expense. It was not to be expected that many of these would attain the standard of the absent choir, but they nearly always proved to be acceptable. This was valuable for the cathedrals, and also for the visiting choirs who turned it into an enjoyable working holiday enabling their skills to be honed, especially if one of the cathedral's own musicians was involved. Rarely was it possible, however, to cover the entire period and, perhaps surprisingly, the advent of girls' choirs has not enabled gaps to be filled, either in the summer or at other times of the year.

The Rediscovery of the counter-tenor

Within the general renewal process of years following the Second World War, there was a particular development which enriched not only the music of cathedrals but also that of the wider community. This was the revival of the counter-tenor voice, which had been commonplace in the fifteenth and sixteenth centuries but not been heard in England for more than 200 years, except in cathedrals where it was associated with the altos.

There was nothing specially noteworthy about the musical career of Alfred Deller until 1946. Born in Margate in 1912, he had been a treble in two parish choirs and when his voice broke continued to sing in a high register. He also taught himself more about singing and music generally, and in 1940 secured a place, as an alto, in the choir of Canterbury Cathedral. Himself a conscientious objector to military service, he survived the wartime bombings of Canterbury and, although born with unusual musical gifts which he cultivated to the full, nothing more than a lifetime of service as a lay clerk seemed to lie before him.

One day in 1946, however, Michael Tippett, the composer, and a BBC producer attended Evensong to hear him sing and were struck by the beauty of his voice. Tippett was at the time active in the revival of the music of Henry Purcell, for much of which a counter-tenor voice is required. He saw Deller immediately after Evensong and recruited him to sing in a performance of Purcell's *Come Ye Sons of Art*, which was broadcast later that year in the opening programme of BBC radio's new Third Programme. Tippett invented the term 'counter-tenor' to distinguish the voice from that of the alto.

The broadcast made a considerable impact in musical circles. Nothing quite like Deller's voice had been heard before in the concert world. He moved to London in 1947 to become a lay clerk at St Paul's, thus enabling him to accept a rapidly growing number of invitations to perform and record. Bernard Rose said he was so talented that he never needed to rehearse. In 1948 he founded the Deller Consort to give what were described as 'authentic performances' of some choral works, especially the folk songs of Tallis, Dowland, Purcell and Bach.

These attracted much attention and led to a revival of interest in Elizabethan music. Benjamin Britten recognized the potential in Deller's voice for the part of Oberon in the opera version of *A Midsummer Night's Dream* he was then composing. Deller took the part, to great acclaim, in the first performances at the Aldeburgh Festival, and it was said to have been the first time the counter-tenor voice had been used in English opera in the twentieth century. But, although he had great charisma and presence on a concert platform, he was no actor and did not appear again in opera. Instead, he developed an international career with his consort and as a solo performer. He was appointed CBE and died in 1970.

Today all cathedral choirs include counter-tenors of varying degrees of skill, and the 1960s saw the emergence of another with a voice of singular beauty. James Bowman was born in Oxford in 1941. He was a chorister in Ely Cathedral and attended the King's School there before going as an academical clerk (choral scholar) to New College, Oxford. There his talent was carefully nurtured by David Lumsden, and, while still an undergraduate, was auditioned by Britten, in the crush bar at Covent Garden, for the role of Oberon in *A Midsummer Night's Dream*. This he subsequently performed with great success at Covent Garden and Glyndebourne. In Oxford he often managed to sing at Evensong both in his own college chapel and in Christ Church, with just sufficient space in the times to make this possible.

Bowman was a lay vicar of Westminster Abbey from 1969 to 1974, leaving to concentrate on a career which has taken him to all the world's great opera houses and made him, like Deller, an international star. Yet he has retained his love of church music and, whenever possible, sings in the choir of the Chapel Royal – something of which Henry Purcell, who was organist of the Chapel Royal from 1682 to 1695, would surely have approved. Besides being appointed CBE in 1997, he has been awarded a medal by the city of Paris for his contribution to music in the French capital.

25

The Twentieth-Century Renewal of Hymnody

Hymns Ancient and Modern Revised, which appeared in 1950, was purged of the many Victorian hymns that had gone largely unused. But it remained a highly conservative contributor to worship. The overwhelming majority of the hymns still came from the nineteenth century and the new, twentieth-century items were of a similar style. Five years later, however, things began to change. In October 1955 a broadcast from Martock Parish Church in Somerset included a hymn tune, '*Chesterton*', of a quite different idiom. Its composer, Geoffrey Beaumont, a priest of the Community of the Resurrection, was at the time Vicar of St George's Church, and Warden of the Trinity College Cambridge Mission in Camberwell, South London. He made no claim to great talent as a composer, but he was a good pianist who, as part of his ministry in a desperately difficult South Bank parish, often played in a local pub. He also had a certain flair for composing light music in the style of the 1930s.

This became apparent to a wider audience in 1956 when, in response to a commission from the Rector of Stepney, he produced a setting of the Eucharist in this idiom. Broadcast later in the year from St Augustine's, Highgate, it made a considerable impact. No one pretended it was fine music and, although it seemed 'modern' to the church, it was dated and bore little resemblance to the emerging 'pop' music of the time. But it was something quite new and lively, and when accompanied by guitar, saxophone and drums had a dramatic effect on the worship. Many of the more forward-looking parishes embraced it enthusiastically. There were also a few new hymn tunes to go with it, of which a swinging version of 'Now thank we all our God' became specially popular.

Next came Malcolm Williamson with his *Procession of Palms*, which was initially well received, and he also composed some hymn tunes. He was a serious musician who came to London from Australia in the 1950s, converted to Roman Catholicism, made a living for a time as an organist and nightclub pianist, and embraced 12-note serialism as a composer. In 1972 he became a highly controversial Master of the Queen's Music. He composed a great deal of choral music, including the *Mass of Christ the King*, commissioned for the Three Choirs Festival in 1977, but virtually all his work is now ignored.

Patrick Appleford, an amateur, was Youth and Education Secretary of the Society for the Propagation of the Gospel when he composed *Mass of Five Melodies*, which was welcomed by many parishes and is still used. He subsequently became Dean of Lusaka in Zambia and a few of his hymns are in the new hymnals – the best and most popular being 'Lord Jesus Christ, you have come to us', for which he also composed the tune. He was one of the leading lights in the formation of the 20th Century Church Light Music Group – an informal group of authors and composers, clerical and lay, that came into being in the early 1960s with the declared aim of 'producing and promoting the use of new lyrics and new music in the worship and teaching of the church'. They saw this as an essential part of mission. While this may now seem an innocent enough aim, it was not then so seen by many in the church.

Appleford confronted head on the frequently asked question, 'Will it last?' and declared, 'Would that we could rid ourselves of this irrelevant question, and ask instead "Does it help with the task in hand?"' He added, 'We are not in the least worried if the music used now is not used by our successors.' New words and music were also written for use in schools and the group made an important contribution to renewal.

Emerging at about the same time, though not a member of the group, Sydney Carter quickly became known throughout the English-speaking world with his 'Lord of the dance'. Its remarkable success was owed to two interrelated elements: the words are optimistic and the tune, adapted from an air of the American Shaker movement, is lively, catchy and memorable. The fact that its underlying theology is a long way removed from Christian orthodoxy has never precluded its use, often when not really appropriate, at weddings, baptisms, funerals and on a multitude of other occasions. It was not, however, the work of an amateur musician. Carter, a delightful man, gentle, humble and a pacifist who had served in a Friends' Ambulance Unit during the war, was already established as a leading writer and singer of folk songs in pubs and clubs. He provided material for his more famous friends, Michael Flanders and Donald Swann, and was good enough to sing with Judy Collins, Pete Seeger and Ewan MacColl.

Some of Carter's other compositions, though not strictly hymns, were readily incorporated into new hymn books and widely used. Of these the most popular, particularly with young people, was 'No use knocking on the window' – a satire on the 'No room at the inn' theme which suggests that if Jesus were to return to earth today he would get a no less dusty response –

No, we haven't got a manger,
No, we haven't got a stable
We are Christian men and women
Always willing, never able.

And, in a similar vein, a modern expression of the parable of the sheep and the goats:

I was hungry and thirsty, were you there,
were you there?
I was hungry and thirsty, were you there?
And the creed and the colour and the name won't matter,
were you there?

The succeeding verses relate to the cold and naked, those in need of shelter and of healing. Both songs reflected the strong 1960s belief, fortunately still not completely dispelled, that Christians should be deeply involved in social issues, particularly the quest for social justice.

Fred Kaan joined in with his 'Sing we a song of high revolt'. Inspired by the Magnificat, the final verses are a call to the barricades:

By him the poor are lifted up:
he satisfies with bread and cup
    the hungry men of many lands;
    the rich are left with empty hands.

He calls us to revolt and fight
with him for what is just and right,
    to sing and live Magnificat
    in crowded street and council flat.

Fred Kaan, a minister of the Dutch Reformed Church, spent several years on the staff of the World Council of Churches before moving to England to serve in the United Reformed Church. He became one of the most successful hymn writers of the second half of the twentieth century and wrote several more on sacred and political subjects, including one for United Nations Sunday and another for Harvest Festival that emphasizes the plight of the hungry.

Hymns of this sort became plentiful and Richard G. Jones, a Methodist, caused a stir with one in praise of God the creator which begins:

God of concrete, God of Steel,
God of piston and of wheel,

God of pylon, God of steam,
God of girder and of beam,
God of atom, God of mine,
All the world of power is thine.

Before long the stream of new hymn writing had become a torrent, incorporating every conceivable (and some inconceivable) subject and, inevitably, of very varying quality. Enterprising publishers produced collections, and in 1969 even the proprietors of *Hymns Ancient and Modern* were moved to publish *100 Hymns for Today*. Their choice was not, however, confined to hymns of recent vintage. Opportunity was taken to include 'The Lord's my Shepherd' to the tune 'Crimond', and Percy Dearmer's 'Jesus, good above all other'. In some instances older and popular hymns had become available through expiry of copyright, but Sydney Carter, Patrick Appleford, Fred Kaan and many others were included. It was immediately successful and, although Archbishop Michael Ramsey mischievously suggested that it was a good source book for students of the ancient heresies of the church (which could apply equally to any hymn book), a second volume appeared in 1980. Three years later the volumes were incorporated, as supplements, into *Hymns Ancient and Modern New Standard*.

During this creative period the need for more and better eucharistic hymns had become urgent. *The English Hymnal* was always strong in this area and the 1950 revision of *Hymns Ancient and Modern New Standard* made wider provision for the increasing number of churches where the Eucharist had become the chief act of Sunday worship. It was not until 1986, however, that the editors of *The English Hymnal* felt the need to publish a new edition that would take account of the changed situation. They eliminated about 250 hymns from the original collection of 656 and regretted that it had been necessary to retain others solely on the grounds of their popularity. About 100 hymns were introduced but no more than half of these had been written since 1950.

Sydney Carter's 'Lord of the dance' was included, as was Patrick Appleford's 'Lord Jesus Christ, you have come to us' and Fred Pratt Green's Advent hymn 'Long ago, prophets knew Christ would come, born a Jew', with its less than penitential refrain, 'Ring bells, ring, ring, ring!' But, these apart, the traditional style of hymnody was retained. The chairman of the editors, G. B. Timms (a notable liturgical scholar), was the chief contributor of new material with 14 hymns, most of these designed to fill gaps in the provision for particular saints' days and festivals. All are good enough of their kind, but few have become popular, possibly because their subjects do not require frequent use.

A short section, 'Church and People', was unadventurous, the nearest it got to social reform being a fine hymn by R. T. Brooks, a United Reformed Church minister, 'O Christ the Lord, O Christ the King', which includes a verse

Lord, vindicate against men's greed
The weak, whose tears thy justice plead:
Thy pity, Lord on men who lie
Broken by war and tyranny;
Show them the cross which thou didst bear,
Give them the power that conquered there.

The author still felt the need to use non-modern language and the editors, a distinguished group of church musicians, were nothing if not candid in their explanation of the basis of their choices:

> The post-war surge of hymn-writing has not been ignored, but we regard much of it as poor in quality and ephemeral in expression. In particular, while the social gospel is an important element in Christian teaching, its translation into verse can be so contemporary that it quickly becomes dated ... We have not overlooked the social duty of Christians, but we believe its application to immediate needs can often be better expressed in sermon and prayers than in hymnody.

They recognized, however, the importance of the works of Timothy Dudley-Smith and by including six of his hymns, introduced him for the first time to mainstream Anglican worship. Much more would be heard of him.

He was at the time of the publication of *The New English Hymnal* Bishop of Thetford in the Diocese of Norwich. Born in 1926 and educated at Tonbridge School, Pembroke College and Ridley Hall, Cambridge, he was firmly attached to the Church of England's Evangelical wing. After pastoral experience in south east London he became Editorial Secretary of the Evangelical Alliance (later he would become its President), then spent 14 years with the Church Pastoral-Aid Society, first as Assistant Secretary, then as Secretary. In 1973 Bishop Maurice Wood, an evangelical Bishop of Norwich, appointed him Archdeacon of Norwich and eight years later he became Suffragan Bishop of Thetford.

Dudley-Smith, whose evangelical faith is of the intelligent, inclusive sort, has the rare combination of theological depth and the gifts of a poet. He started by writing poetry and it was only when his friends began to put his poems to music that his potential as a hymn writer emerged. Thus his now well-known hymn 'Tell out my soul, the greatness of the Lord' (based on the Magnificat but more elegantly than Fred Kaan's 'council flat' version), began life as a poem inspired by a first encounter with the

New English Bible. Linked to 'Woodlands', a perfect tune for its purpose, this was taken into *The New English Hymnal*, along with 'Faithful vigil ended', based on the Nunc Dimittis, 'O Christ the same through all our story's pages', set to the 'Londonderry Air', and three others.

Initially, his writing of poems, then of hymns, was limited by the time available while on holiday – perhaps six items a year – but as his work became widely known the demand for more became irresistible. Some went into two evangelical-inspired collections, *Anglican Hymn Book* (1965) and *Psalm Praise*. Four single-author collections were, after wide circulation separately, incorporated into one volume, *A House of Praise 1961–2001*, others have appeared since then, and now over 300 of Dudley-Smith's hymns are to be found in about 250 hymnals throughout the English-speaking world.

Their style is uncompromisingly traditional. Not all are equally successful but the best – a large number – express the Christian faith in new and refreshing ways. Himself no musician, Dudley-Smith insists that hymns must be singable and, therefore, linked to memorable tunes. This has contributed significantly to their popularity and his important contribution to hymnody has been recognized by appointment as OBE, the honorary vice-presidency of the Hymn Society of Great Britain and Ireland and a fellowship of the Hymn Society of the United States and Canada – two long-established organizations which exist to promote the singing and study of hymns.

While the editors of the established hymn books were debating the merits of the new material and selecting few items for inclusion in their revised editions, the torrent of new hymns, fed by songs and choruses, became a mighty flood. The Anglican contribution to this was barely noticeable when compared with the unceasing flow of items emanating from a revived Evangelical movement and its charismatic wing. Enterprising publishers moved in to produce collections of new hymns and songs which soon grew into sizeable hymn books, incorporating both old and new. Chief among these was Kevin Mayhew, an East Anglian publisher of considerable flair, who was also a significant handler of new Roman Catholic liturgical material and now trades in an international market.

Among a multitude of new writers three more emerged as outstanding, though the style and content of each is different.

John Bell, born in 1949, is a Church of Scotland minister, composer and music director of the Iona Community, which publishes much of his writing. He is a former student activist and was elected Rector of Glasgow University while still a student. After two church youth posts, he became involved full-time in music and worship matters with the Wild Goose Resource Group. He has been honoured by an RSCM fellowship and a Glasgow honorary doctorate.

His hymn texts, many written in collaboration with Graham Maule, plug many gaps in traditional hymnody, and some were written for specific occasions: 'There is a place for little children' was a response to the Dunblane massacre. He frequently makes use of folk music from Scotland and the Celtic traditions, and he has also collected songs from the world church.

Collections of these, often short pieces, are described as 'wee songs for worship' and can be sung easily in harmony by parish choirs and congregations. His own compositions, simple and effective in their use of folk tradition, have often won acceptance from church musicians who do not always embrace the worship-song style. They are to be found in many of the new hymn books.

The more traditional Michael Forster was born in 1946 and served as a Baptist minister for some years before transferring his allegiance to the United Reformed Church. He is now working in Leicestershire as a community health chaplain, specializing in mental health. Like many successful hymn writers, going back as far as Charles Wesley, his output is enormous and at the beginning of 2009 there were about 600 hymns and lyrics bearing his name, as well as some Christian and secular musicals and a Christian pantomime. He had also written more than 50 books – mainly of teaching material – and appeared on Radio 4 as a satirist.

Such an output is bound to raise questions about quality, and there is an unevenness, but Forster shares with Timothy Dudley-Smith the combined gifts of the theologian and the poet. The result is often both illuminating and challenging. The light of the gospel and the liberating power of the gospel are frequent themes, and a particularly striking hymn on freedom includes these verses:

Cry 'Freedom!' for the victims
of the earthquake and the rain:
where wealthy folk find shelter
and the poor must bear the pain;
where weapons claim resources
while the famine strikes again.

Cry 'Freedom!' in the church when
honest doubts are met with fear:
when vacuum-packed theology
makes questions disappear:
when journeys end before they start
and mystery is clear!

Each of five verses has a refrain, 'Cry "Freedom!" Cry "Freedom!" in God's name.'

Forster has displayed his versatility by writing a hymn for every Sunday in the calendar of *Common Worship*, and his provision for the festivals is particularly useful: those on the Blessed Virgin Mary being outstanding.

Forty of his hymns, together with 21 children's songs and 6 liturgical items were published in 2000 in *Complete Anglican Hymns Old and New*, of which he was the theological editor.

Designed for use by churches of every sort and described as 'traditional and radical', the choice of material – 978 items in all – is comprehensive. No traditional hymn of any importance has been omitted and there are probably sufficient songs and choruses to satisfy all but the most charismatic of congregations. The large children's section contains many astonishing items, the quality of which can be judged only by those involved in education, and most of which are totally unsuitable for use by adults. Settings for the Eucharist include *A New People's Mass* by Dom Gregory Murray, a *Missa Simplex* by Malcolm Archer and a Kyrie by Colin Mawby – all composed for congregations, rather than choirs alone.

The editors felt free to make minor changes to a number of traditional texts, pointing out that there are ample precedents for this. On the whole this was carried out sensitively and helpfully, and in some instances living writers made their own alterations, but it is not necessary to be ultra-conservative to wish that classics such as the 'Veni Creator' and George Herbert's 'King of Glory, King of peace' had not been tampered with. In spite of five helpful indexes, busy clergy and choir directors have some justification for their complaint that size makes it unmanageable.

Graham Kendrick, who contributed 37 hymns, songs and choruses to the same volume, is the leading exponent in Britain of the music of the charismatic renewal. His chorus 'Shine, Jesus, shine', published in 1992, and often sung by congregations with uplifted arms, epitomizes the charismatic approach and, while greatly loved in this quarter, is loathed not only by dyed-in-the-wool traditionalists but by many others who regard it as a betrayal of the standards essential to dignified, intelligent worship.

Kendrick, the son of a Baptist minister, was born in 1950. An early attempt to introduce him to the piano failed as he disliked formal teaching and did not wish to be constrained by the notes of the pieces set before him. On leaving school he trained as a teacher and when he was about 21 had a spiritual experience known in charismatic circles as baptism in the Holy Spirit, which often leads to 'speaking in tongues' and other spontaneous outbursts in worship. While at college he taught himself to play the guitar and, instead of moving into school teaching, joined a band that performed religious songs in Christian coffee bars. In 1976 his musical talent was recognized by appointment as Director of the British Youth for Christ Choir and about this time he took to the road with Oliver Calver, who had just emerged from a Bible college, and they performed for young people in many different parts of the country.

For several years Kendrick's work went unpublished, but eventually wide demand took him into print and stimulated a remarkable creativity. His output has been phenomenal and he is now published worldwide in many different languages. Some 25–30 albums of his recorded music have also been marketed and a professionally run organization promotes his work and arranges his appearances at festivals and other venues – again worldwide.

His contribution is to be seen, however, as part of a wider concern for the church's worship which he regards as an integral part of its mission. It is, he argues, necessary to operate within the culture outside the church, using its eclectic styles of music and unsophisticated language in order, as he puts it, 'to engage in spiritual warfare against Satan who is ever seeking to control the world'. He also believes it to be necessary to prepare Christians to meet persecution and disaster. The presentation and staging of worship is important and where Kendrick's writ runs, the platform has replaced the pulpit and the microphone become the primary channel of communication. Lighting, multi-media techniques and a variety of musical instruments all have a part to play in the drawing of congregations into wholehearted, sometimes frenzied, worship. Trained worship leaders, who may or may not be ordained, are seen as essential.

Hymns Ancient and Modern marked the dawn of a new millennium with another revision, *Common Praise,* launched at about the same time as Common Worship and the fruit of liaison with the Liturgical Commission. The work of a distinguished editorial committee, headed by Henry Chadwick, the new volume consolidated a good many (but by no means all) of the new hymns that had previously appeared in two supplements. It also added many more, and 43 authors whose main work was after about 1960 contributed to the 628 items. The fact that the book is only two-thirds the size of *Complete Anglican Hymns Old and New* meant that its editors had to apply different criteria to their choices and users will not always agree with their decisions. Apart from 'Shine, Jesus, shine', there are few concessions to charismatics.

Overall, *Common Praise* (published by Canterbury Press) is now the most comprehensive and serviceable hymn book for mainstream churches.

Unfortunately the flood of new hymns has not been paralleled by a deluge of first-class new tunes though a few, notably Cyril Taylor's 'Abbot's Leigh', Maurice Bevan's 'Corvedale' and Ken Naylor's 'Coe Fen', have reinvigorated some older hymns. The wisest of the new writers have therefore linked their work to long-established, well-known tunes, thus ensuring more ready acceptance. Others have bravely opted for new music and in too many cases are going unsung. Except in Evangelical circles, hymns are still not regarded as sufficiently important an ingredient in worship to require the teaching of congregations to sing them. Until this is changed the worship of most Anglican churches will remain impoverished.

26

Coda – Three Challenges

The report of the last Archbishops' Commission on Church Music (*In Tune with Heaven*, 1992) made 56 recommendations designed to aid the protection and development of this most important element in the church's life. Many of these recommendations still await implementation, so it is not for me to add more, even if I were qualified to do so. In the course of writing this book, however, I have become acutely aware of three particular challenges that now confront those responsible for the ordering of the church's worship.

The first concerns the parishes. I have of necessity devoted a great deal of space to the making of music in cathedrals, colleges and other privileged places. Some of the great musicians of my period – men of genius – have enriched the worship led by the best choirs. No one doubts that the standard of these choirs has never been higher.

They are one of the wonders of the world of music.

Yet there are probably no more than 100 of them, and most worship is offered in just over 16,000 parish and district churches where the situation is very different. It is not to be expected, of course, that even the most enthusiastic bands of amateur musicians will consistently achieve cathedral standards, though the organists and choirs of some of the larger parish churches are often very fine. It is also arguable that the nineteenth-century decision to emulate the cathedral style in parish churches was a serious mistake, since it inhibited the growth of appropriate variety as well as the fullest congregational involvement. Surpliced choirs are not essential.

This raises the fundamental issue of the relationship between music and liturgy, and the fact that music is always the handmaid of well-ordered and sensitively performed worship. Here it is unfortunately necessary to record that in far too many local churches the standard of worship is very much lower than it ought to be. A diocesan missioner recently reported that, having visited some hundreds of parishes in his diocese, there were only three that he would himself wish to attend unless required by duty to do so.

The consequences of low standards could not be more serious. God is not glorified when that which is offered to him is less than the best attainable, congregations are unedified and casual attenders are repelled. The church's witness is thereby weakened. It can only be a matter for wonder that those responsible for the leadership of the church do not have sleepless nights over this problem, and that in the daylight hours they are not working ceaselessly to set matters right. What could be more important to the Christian cause?

Fortunately, there is no shortage of ideas, expertise and experience for dealing with this challenge. The Archbishops' Commission identified the need and indicated how it might be met. The Royal School of Church Music has the necessary skills and a vast experience of parish worship of every kind. In every diocese there are talented priests and musicians who have much to share in this field. The urgent need now is for the existing resources to be strengthened and so deployed that no parish is without the advice needed for the renewal of its worship. None of this will make a scrap of difference without a deep conviction in every place that standards need to be raised and that the slap-dash is simply not acceptable.

Returning to the cathedrals, there is every reason to believe that, provided the present supply of highly trained, committed singers, organists and directors is maintained, their glorious tradition will continue unhampered. But this is obviously a critical proviso. At the 2009 annual conference of the Choir Schools Association the chairman announced that in the 37 UK choir schools the total of boy choristers had during the previous year risen by nearly 5 per cent to a total of 737; the number of girl choristers by 3.5 per cent to 209; the number of auditions by 14 per cent to 477.

That was good news, but it is necessary to remember that the cost of boarding education in all independent schools has risen astronomically and that responsibility for paying half or more of a chorister's fees may cost a dean and chapter up to £200,000 a year. Only a buoyant cathedral income can cope with this, and in difficult times only a strong commitment to the choir will overcome the temptation to make economies of a destructive kind.

The supply of lay clerks is now much less plentiful than it was in the recent past. This is due partly to the collapse of the many good parish choirs that, together with the Oxbridge colleges, once provided a good recruiting ground. A more serious problem, however, is related to the fact that salaries (perhaps £7,000 per annum in major cathedrals, a good deal less elsewhere) are inadequate for their support. The attractive environment of most cathedral cities results in well above average house prices, and unless cathedrals are able to provide accommodation in their closes, which most are not, the problems facing a lay clerk, even with an additional salary, are not difficult to imagine. In varying degrees, the same problems face organists and choir directors.

Money is the challenge here and, as always, the scale of priorities determines the response. Much more will be needed by every cathedral if the current standard of music is to be maintained. Some Friends organizations, recognizing that a well-conserved and beautifully furnished building is of limited value without the best of worship offered within its walls, have changed or bent their constitutions to permit the allocation of funds to music. A few cathedrals have had successful appeals to augment the capital in their, usually small, music funds. Where there is conviction the required money can always be raised, but not without imagination, hard work and sacrifice. Therein lies the challenge.

Lest, however, I leave readers with the impression that all in the realm of church music is either gloomy or threatened, it is good to be able to conclude with a quite different, encouraging challenge. This has arisen from the fairly recent emergence of a new generation of highly gifted composers, a significant number of them women, who are not only transforming choral music generally, but also offering the church new types of music that are both uplifting and useable.

For much of the second half of the twentieth century most of the innovative music was not suitable for the worship of even the most adventurous cathedrals and parish churches. This has changed, and it is now possible to believe that we have entered what may come to be seen as a new golden age for the composition of church music. Yet this needs to be performed if the church's worship is to be enhanced, and if the writing of more is to be encouraged. Since composers have to live, additional money will be needed, though the cost of new commissions is nearly always extraordinarily low.

Much more important is a readiness to risk the introduction of music that may not always appeal immediately to the majority of those who attend cathedrals and parish churches. (Henry Purcell's music was given a rough reception when first performed in the seventeenth century.) Christ Church, Oxford, and King's College, Cambridge, who may be less constrained by considerations of this sort, are setting an example for others to follow, and the BBC Singers, under David Hill, are displaying to much wider audiences the new choral treasures available to all.

During the last two centuries much has changed in the realm of church music and there is no reason to suppose that this will not continue to be so, since human life never stands still. But the objective remains the same. Music is an instrument that enables Christians to worship God in the beauty of holiness and in tuneful accord, so that ultimately the whole earth may stand in awe of him.

Further Reading

Over the years a great deal has been written about church music, but not so much recently. This volume is designed to bring the story up to date, but, although nothing of significance has been omitted, it is by no means comprehensive in its dealing with either the past or the present.

Those who wish to learn more must turn first to Kenneth R. Long's classic study, *The Music of the English Church* (Hodder and Stoughton, 1972). This is indispensable.

Also important, as a supplement to it, is the American Nicholas Temperley's *The Music of the English Parish Church* (Cambridge University Press, 1979).

Looking wider to the musical context in which church music was developed during the twentieth century, an essential book is *The Rest is Noise* by Alex Ross, music critic of the *New Yorker* (Harper Perennial, 2009). This is as delightful as it is illuminating.

All the important composers of the nineteenth and twentieth centuries have their biographies, most of them available second-hand, and these provide valuable insights without overmuch use of music's technical language.

Erik Routley, a Congregational minister, was in his time (the late 1960s) a prolific and hugely well-informed writer on the subject. His *The Musical Wesleys*, *Twentieth Century Church Music* and *The English Carol* were all published by Herbert Jenkins and, again, are out of print, yet should not be too difficult to track down second-hand.

More recently, *The English Chorister* by Alan Mould (Hambledon Continuum, 2007) is likely to remain the standard work on its subject for many more years. It tells a fascinating story with scholarship and an eye for the amusing

Hymn lovers can do no better than turn to Ian Bradley's *The Penguin Book of Hymns* (Penguin Books, 1990) and especially *Abide With Me: The World of Victorian Hymns* (SCM Press, 1997) – erudite and enthusiastic.

Composing Music for Worship, edited by Stephen Darlington and Alan Kreider (Canterbury Press, 2003), is a small volume of essays by a number of contemporary composers, including James MacMillan, Howard Goodall and Roxanna Panufnik, and of considerable interest.

In Tune with Heaven (Church House Publishing and Hodder and Stoughton, 1992) is an important report of an Archbishops' Commission on Church Music which leaves no stone unturned in its examination of the present situation in the Church of England. Little has changed since it reported, in spite of a host of valuable recommendations.

Those who wish to keep up to date should subscribe to *Church Music Quarterly,* the magazine of the Royal School of Church Music (19 The Close, Salisbury, SP1 2EB)

Index of Musical Items

Note: This index includes the titles of major and minor works, short pieces such as anthems but not of unnamed service settings or individual hymns unless of particular significance.

General Index